Glorious Crocheted Sweaters

Published in paperback 1990 by Sterling Publishing Company, Inc.
387 Park Avenue South, New York, N.Y. 10016

© 1989 Altamont Press.

Photos and Instructions © Ariadne/Eska Tijdscriften,
Utrecht, Holland.
English Translation by Networks, Inc.
English Translation © 1988 Altamont Press.

A Sterling/Lark Book
Produced by Altamont Press, Inc.
50 College Street, Asheville, NC   28801

ISBN 0-8069-6991-1

Printed and bound in Hong Kong

Glorious Crocheted Sweaters

Edited by Nola Theiss

A Sterling/**Lark** Book

 Sterling Publishing Co., Inc.   New York

Expert Assistants and Advisors:
    Diane Murphy, Janet Stollnitz, Patricia Syslo,
    Kay Wisniewski, Terry Zalenski
Editor: Dawn Cusick
Art Director: Rob Pulleyn
Production: Dawn Cusick
Typesetting: Diana Deakin
Drawings:
    Thom Boswell, John Koosner, Sarah Warren

Table of Contents

Introduction 6
Stitches and Techniques 7
Helpful Notes 13

Chapter One: Simple Stitches Simple Stripes

Tweed Coat 17
Crayon Striped Pullover 19
Velvety Striped Pullover 21
Woman's Polo Pullover 22
Child's Pullover 22
Child's Polo Pullover 23
Bag 23
White Cardigan 26
Tweed Boucle Jacket 29
Child's Checkered Pullover 31
Nursery Rhyme Pullover 32
Yellow Filet Top 34

Chapter Two: Color

Jacquard Jacket 35
Child's Arrowhead Boatneck 38
Arrowhead Boatneck 39
Jacquard Pullover 43
Child's Jacquard Cardigan 44
Child's Plaid Cardigan 45
Artwork Jacquard Jacket 48
Desert Jacket 51
V-Neck Plaid Cardigan 52
Highland Tartan Cardigan 53
Child's Pastel Boatneck 56
Child's Pastel Ribneck 58
Pastel Tweed Jacket 59
Mohair Cardigan 62
Mohair Diagonal Pullover 64
Child's Geometric Pullover 65
Child's Red Pullover 68
Folklore Cardigan 69
Autumn Jacquard Cardigan 72
Shawl Collar Pullover 79

Chapter Three: Relief Stitches

Cotton Pullover 81
Batwing Pullover 82
Coral Pullover 84
Teen Pullover 86
Mohair Jacket 89
Lattice Pullover 91
Bobble Cardigan 94
Aran-Style Cable Cardigan 96
Boatneck Pullovers 101
Basketweave Pullover 103
Cable Cardigan 105
Zig-Zag Pullover 107
Child's Striped Pullover 108
Relief Stitch Pullover 111

Chapter Four: Pattern Stitches

Child's Lilac Polo Top 114
Child's Yellow Polo Pullover 114
Child's Green Polo Pullover 115
Woman's Top 119
White Boatneck Pullover 120
Gold Lace Pullover 121
Linen Pullover 124
White Jacket 125
Black Jacket 125
Pullover 128
Zig-Zag Pullover 130
Zig-Zag Cardigan 132
Gold Pullover 136
Teal Batwing Pullover 136
Toddler's Flower Bud Pullover 140
Toddler's Baby Cable Pullover 141
Cardigan and Top 143

Introduction

As a craft, crochet has developed quite differently in North America and Europe.

Crochet is a typically American craft, perhaps best exemplified by the afghan. Crocheted afghans are in countless homes combining warmth and texture and a colorful handmade touch to any room. Even the sets of television shows, trying to create a home-like atmosphere, frequently have a crocheted afghan folded neatly over the back of a couch or chair. Afghans can be carefully planned and executed; or, as is more often the case, they can be made in a spontaneous burst of creativity using leftover pieces of scrap yarn with the pattern created as the project progresses.

In a sense, crochet is the craft most closely akin to the family traditions of patchwork quilts and early knitting. It is a skill taught by a relative or friend or by the next-door neighbor to a child who is fascinated by the flash of a crochet hook at work. A crocheter determined to learn new stitches usually learns them from another crocheter or by examining samples of work she admires.

Lacking a written literature, crochet in America has relied on folk tradition for subsistence — handed down, literally, from one generation to the next. American crocheters, like early quilters, enjoy the challenge of making something whole from leftover scraps, often producing unique color combinations. The items American crocheters produce are usually quite functional — such as an afghan or baby blanket — and are often presented as gifts to celebrate important occasions.

European crochet is quite different. Because knitting is so popular in Europe, crocheters usually lack the helpful next-door neighbor for instruction, relying instead on written directions. Most crocheters in Europe are also fervent knitters, so it's not unusual for them to use knitted borders and edgings in their crochet work. European knitters have long taken pride in the fashionable garments they produce, and are willing to invest in quality materials. European crocheters, eager to create their own fashionable garments with their craft, have designed new crochet stitches that, when combined with quality yarns and patterns, make truly glorious sweaters.

If you, too, feel limited in crocheting only afghans and baby blankets or don't feel particularly experienced in crocheting fashionable garments, **Glorious Crocheted Sweaters** will be a revelation. Like most crochet projects, these garments can be made quickly and do not require extensive knowledge. We have included a bibliography of some helpful instruction books and we also recommend you seek out an experienced crocheter if you need help with some of the stitches.

All of the patterns are labelled with their level of difficulty. Projects marked with a single star are recommended for the novice; projects with two stars for the intermediate crocheter who is eager to try something new; and projects with three stars for the advanced crocheter ready for a challenge.

We have also divided the patterns into four chapters. The novice crocheter would probably do well to start with the first chapter, SIMPLE STITCHES, SIMPLE STRIPES, and will be amazed at how fashionable crocheted sweaters can be. The second chapter, COLOR, is very colorful indeed. Beautiful jacquard patterns, bold geometrics and plaids, and unusual techniques of crocheting around contrasting strands of yarn make this a fascinating chapter. The third chapter, RELIEF STITCHES, highlights texture. By working around the post of the stitches in previous rows, all sorts of ridges, basketweaves, cables and lattices are achieved. This chapter is the most three-dimensional and most akin to knitting. The fourth chapter, PATTERN STITCHES, contains a vast array of stitches, most of which are not difficult, but give a unique look to the garments. Work your way through the book from beginning to end or choose garments by level of difficulty from all four chapters. For a quick reference we have included a brief description of the most commonly used stitches.

As an added note, we have been referring to the crocheter as female, although we realize that crochet, along with other crafts, can be enjoyed by anyone, regardless of gender. We hope our readers will be inspired to embark on a voyage of glorious crocheting.

Nola Theiss

Stitches and Techniques

Making a Slip Knot

When following the instructions, it is very important to read carefully and to pay attention to the position of the hook at all times. Make a sample gauge to learn the stitch and check measurements and tension (more about this later). Often you will be called upon to place the hook at the back or front of the work; but remember, unless specified, always insert the hook in the front of the stitch under both loops and work from right to left. Frequently, it will be necessary to skip stitches and then come back to them. Position of the hook is very important in this case because you must know whether to work in front or in back of the stitches worked after the skipped stitches. Use the photos as a guide.

Asterisks

The asterisk, *, is used in crochet as a repeat sign. All instructions included between two asterisks are to be repeated the total number of times indicated.

Yarn over (yo)

Technically a yarn over is not really a stitch in itself, but no crochet stitch is possible without it. Wrap the yarn around the hook from back to front to form a loop. Depending on the stitch, more yarn overs are formed and drawn through loops. In essence, this is crochet — a very simple process that no machine can duplicate.

Chain Stitch (ch)

Starting the chain (ch), make a slip knot; insert the hook from right to left through the loop. With the hook in front of the yarn, wrap the yarn around the hook from back to front. With the hook pointing down, draw a new loop through the loop on the hook. One chain stitch has been completed.

Slip Stitch (sl st)

Insert hook into chain or stitch; wrap the yarn over the hook from back to front; draw a loop through both the chain or stitch and the loop on the hook. One slip stitch has been completed.

Single Crochet (sc)

Insert hook into the 2nd chain from the hook. Wrap the yarn around the hook from back to front. Draw the yarn through the chain making 2 loops on the hook. Wrap the yarn around the hook from back to front and draw the yarn through the 2 loops on the hook. One single crochet stitch has been completed. Continue by inserting the hook in the next chain. After the last stitch, chain 2 and turn; insert the hook into the first stitch to begin the next row.

Shrimp Stitch

This stitch is used frequently as a finishing edge on necklines and other borders. It is worked like single crochet, but worked in the opposite direction that is, left to right, instead of right to left. Keep the right side of the work facing you as you work. If shrimp stitch is worked correctly, it will feel as if you are working backwards. If it feels like you are doing single crochet, you have probably turned the work and you *are* doing single crochet.

Half-Double Crochet (hdc)

Wrap the yarn around the hook from back to front; insert the hook into the 3rd chain from the hook; wrap the yarn over the hook and draw the yarn through the chain making 3 loops on the hook. Wrap the yarn around the hook from back to front and draw through the 3 loops on the hook. One half-double crochet stitch has been completed. Continue by wrapping the yarn around the hook and inserting the hook in the next chain. After the last stitch, chain 2 and turn; wrap the yarn over the hook; insert the hook in the first stitch to begin the next row.

Double Crochet (dc)

Wrap the yarn around the hook from back to front; insert the hook into the 4th chain from the hook; wrap the yarn over the hook and draw the yarn through the chain making 3 loops on the hook. Wrap the yarn over the hook and draw it through 2 loops; wrap the yarn over the hook again and draw the yarn through the last two loops completing the stitch. Continue by repeating the sequence in each chain stitch. After the last stitch, chain 3 and turn; insert the hook in the 2nd stitch to begin the next row.

Treble Crochet (tr)

Wrap the yarn around the hook from back to front twice and insert the hook in the 5th chain from the hook. Wrap the yarn over the hook and draw a loop through the chain making 4 loops on the hook. Wrap the yarn over the hook and draw the yarn through 2 loops; wrap the yarn over the hook and draw the yarn through 2 more loops; wrap the yarn over the hook again and draw through the yarn through last 2 loops completing the stitch. Continue by repeating the sequence in each chain. After the last stitch, chain 4 and turn; insert the hook into the 2nd stitch to begin the next row.

Afghan Stitch

Using an afghan crochet hook, make a chain equal to the desired number of stitches plus 2.

Row 1: Insert the hook into the 2nd chain from the hook, wrap the yarn over the hook and draw through a loop through the chain. Continue by wrapping the yarn over the hook pulling a loop through each chain in the row. Do not turn the work — always work with the right side facing you.

Row 2: The next row is worked by wrapping the yarn over the hook and pulling a loop through the first loop on the hook. Wrap the yarn over the needle and draw a loop through the next 2 loops on the hook. Repeat until there is one loop left on the hook. The remaining loop forms the first st of the next row.

Row 3: Skip the first vertical loop in the row below and insert the hook from right to left through the 2nd vertical loop. Wrap the yarn over the needle and draw the loop through making 2 loops on the hook. Continue across the row. Note: insert the hook through the center of the last loop leaving 2 strands of yarn at the edge.

Row 4: Same as row 2.

Repeat rows 3 and 4 until desired length is reached.

Filet Stitch

There are many versions of the filet stitch, but this is the most common. To make beautiful motifs, fill in the desired squares with 1 st.

Row 1: *1 Dc, ch 1*, rep * to * across.

Row 2 and all foll rows: Ch 4 to turn (beg of first square). Always work 1 dc in dc of previous row, ch above ch of previous row.

Relief Stitches

All relief stitches are the same: basically one inserts the hook around the post, that is the length of the stitch found in a previous row, and work whichever stitch one desires. The texture depends on the stitch, which previous row is worked, and whether the stitch is worked on the back or front of the work makes the texture. We've listed a few variations to give you the general idea.

Front Relief Sc

Worked in sc by working around the post of the st below. For front relief sts, insert hook from right to left around the post of the indicated st at front of work. Yo, and draw through loop, yo and draw through both loops.

Back Relief Sc

Worked in sc by working around the post of the st below. For back relief sts, insert hook from right to left around the post of the indicated st at back of work. Yo, and draw through loop, yo and draw through both loops.

Front Relief Dc

Worked in dc by working around the post of the st of the previous row. Yo over hook, insert hook from right to left around the post of the indicated st at front of work. Yo, and draw through loop, yo and continue as you would a dc.

11

Back Relief Dc

Worked in dc by working around the post of the st of the previous row. Yo over hook, insert hook from right to left around the post of the indicated st at back of work. Yo, and draw through loop, yo and continue as you would a dc.

Border Stitches

Most American crocheters are not accustomed to the term border stitch. The first and last stitches, usually the chain at the beg of the row and the last st of the row, are considered as border stitches by Europeans because they are worked into the seams and are not part of the pattern. They are worked in the same color as adjoining stitches in most cases. On jacquard patterns, they are usually not included on the chart. When border stitches are used, some explanation will be given in the pattern. Often when joining seams, one sews or crochets between the border stitch and the adjoining stitch.

Many of the patterns use a knitted ribbing rather than a crochet edging. We have included a description of all the stitches used here, as well as some alternatives. Again, a glance at other crochet reference books will provide you with even more ideas. Feel free to substitute your own preferred edgings. Knitted ribbings are more elastic, but don't let a knitted edge stop you from making a design; crochet your edgings instead.

1/1 ribbing:
Row 1: *K1, p1*. Rep * to * across.
Row 2 and all foll rows: Work sts as established in previous row, by knitting the stitches which were purled in the previous row and look flat on the 2nd row, and purling the stitches which were knitted in the previous row and have a loop next to the needle.
2/2 ribbing:
Row 1: *K2, p2*. Rep * to * across.
Row 2 and all foll rows: Work sts as established in previous row.
Crochet Ribbing - Post stitch ribbing (single crochet).
Worked on an even number of stitches. The idea is always to work a back relief post st in a front relief post stitch of the previous row so alternate ridges are formed on the back and front of work.
Row 1: 1 Sc in each ch.
Row 2: Ch 1 (= 1 border st) *1 front relief sc, 1 back relief sc*, 1 sc in last space (= 1 border st).
Row 3: Ch 1, *1 back relief sc, 1 front relief sc*, 1 sc in last space.
Repeat Rows 2 and 3.
Post Stitch Ribbing (double crochet).
Same as single crochet post st with longer posts.
Row 1: 1 Dc in each st.
Row 2: Ch 2 (= 1 border st) *1 front relief dc, 1 back relief dc*, rep * to * across row, end with 1 front relief dc, 1 hdc (= 1 border st).
Row 3: Ch 2, *1 back relief dc, 1 front relief dc*, rep * to * across row, end with 1 back relief dc, 1 hdc.
Always rep rows 2 and 3.
Crochet Ribbing - Ridge stitch ribbing
Note: Ridges are formed horizontally, and when turned sideways form ribbing. Chain desired depth of ribbing. When used as ribbing on a garment, the ridge stitch is usually crocheted separately to the desired length and then attached to the garment.
Row 1: Skip 1 ch, *1 sc in each ch*, ch 1, turn.
Row 2: *1 sc in back loop of each st*, ch 1 turn.
Repeat Row 2 for the pattern.

Helpful Notes

Notes on Establishing Gauge

The correct gauge is important for the proper size of a garment. If you are used to making afghans only, it may not have mattered if the finished piece was a few inches bigger or smaller than you planned. Those inches can be critical on a garment, so be careful. Each pattern has a specific gauge — the number of stitches and rows that equal a 4 in. (10 cm) square. It is important to crochet a sample square using the yarn and hook size specified before starting the garment. If your square measures less than 4 in. (10 cm) try a larger hook size. If your square measures larger than 4 in. (10 cm) try a smaller hook size. Be sure to measure your swatch on a flat surface and avoid stretching it.

Increasing

To make a single increase, work 2 stitches in one stitch. To make a double increase, work 3 stitches in one stitch. You may want to work in the back loop for one increase and the front loop for the next. To add more stitches at the end of a row, make an additional chain stitch for each additional stitch needed plus the required number of turning chain stitches. On the next row, crochet a pattern stitch in each added chain. Some of the patterns give specific directions for increasing in that pattern stitch. We recommend you follow them or experiment with your own method. The goal is to make as smooth an edge as possible and to get the correct number of stitches.

Decreasing

To decrease a single stitch, insert the hook in a stitch, draw through a loop, insert the hook into the next stitch, draw through a loop. Wrap the yarn over the hook; draw through the yarn through all 3 loops.

To decrease 2 stitches in single or half double crochet, insert the hook in a stitch, draw through a loop, skip the next stitch, insert the hook in the following stitch, draw through up a loop. Wrap the yarn over the hook; draw through the yarn through all 3 loops — this is called slip stitching across stitches and is the most common way to decrease at the beginning of a row. To decrease at the end of a row, work across until you have the specified number of sts unworked at the end of row. Turn and continue as directed across the next row. Be sure to work the correct number of turning chains to beg the following row. To avoid a staircase effect at the edge, you may wish to leave 1 less st unworked than specified, then slip st across the first st of the foll row to give a slanted edge.

Reversing Shapings

Although both sides of a neckline are generally shaped the same, keep in mind that they're in mirror image of each other. Usually, the directions will be very specific for the right side of the neckline and then say to reverse shapings for the left side. This simply means that the shapings that were worked at the beginning of the row will now be worked at the end of the row and vice versa. If you slip stitched across 6 sts at the beginning of a row on the right edge before, now work to the last 6 sts of the row and leave them unworked and so on. Increases will also be worked on the opposite edge on the second half.

On a cardigan, directions will only be given for one half of the front and you will reverse the instructions so that the two fronts will correspond in shaping. Keep the completed half nearby so that you do not forget which half you are working on.

Jacquard charts or pattern stitch motifs also may reverse pattern placement from one side of the front to the other or from the back to the front.

The directions may tell you to work the chart beginning at the left edge for the back and to begin the chart from the right edge on the front so that the motifs will match at the side seams. Always try to visualize the finished garment as you work and the logic of the design will guide you.

Yarns and substitutions

When possible, the names of specific yarns have been included in the directions for the garment. For the best results, please use those yarns. Always choose a comparable yarn when making a substitution. When it was not possible to name a specific yarn, a description of the type, weight, and yardage has been given to help you choose an appropriate yarn.

Making Buttonholes

Horizontal buttonholes:

Single crochet: at desired location for buttonhole, crochet chain stitches equal to length needed for buttonhole. Skip the corresponding number of stitches in the previous row; continue with single crochet. On following row, work the same number of stitches across the chained sts.

Knitted buttonholes:

On the right side of the work row, bind off the desired number of stitches. Work to the end of the row. On the wrong side of the work row, work to where you have bound off stitches. Cast onto the right hand needle the number of stitches that were bound off. Continue working to end of row.

Finishing Techniques

Blocking and pressing:

Check the yarn label before proceeding. Always heed the recommendation of the yarn manufacturer. Most crocheted garments need very little blocking. If it is necessary to block, block the individual sections of the garment separately. Using the correct measurements, draw an outline of the finished section on heavy paper. Place the paper on a flat surface padded with several soft towels. Using rustproof pins, pin the crocheted piece to the paper. Carefully work the piece to the correct size and shape. Cover the piece with a very damp cloth. Following the yarn manufacturer's recommendations you may either use the steam method or simply weight down the piece. **Steam method —** keep the weight of the iron above the work and gently steam the piece. Remove the damp cloth and leave the piece in position to dry thoroughly. **Weight method —** place additional towels on top of the very damp cloth and then place a wooden board on top of the towels. Leave all in place until the piece is completely dry.

Joining Methods

The pieces of a garment may be joined together using several methods.

Backstitch: Pin the right sides of the pieces together. Use a yarn or tapestry needle and the yarn used in crocheting the pieces. Work from right to left, using small, even stitches, inserting the needle back through the pieces at the point where it emerged on the previous stitch, bringing the needle through to the front slightly to the left of where it went into the fabric.

Slip stitch: Pin the right sides of the pieces together. Using a crochet hook and yarn, insert the hook through both pieces of the garment and draw through a loop through the fabric and the loop on the hook. Repeat until the seam is completed.

Invisible weaving (vertical): Lay the edges to be joined next to one another, right side up. Using a yarn needle and yarn, insert the needle up through the lower half of the end stitch on one piece, draw the yarn through. From the front insert the needle through the upper half of the edge stitch on the other piece, draw the yarn through. Continue inserting the needle through alternate sides.

Invisible weaving (horizontal): This is used on the final row-edges. Lay the edges to be joined next to one another. Using a yarn needle and yarn, insert the needle between the front and the back loops of the edges.

Crochet seams: Hold two pieces with right sides together unless specified otherwise. Insert hook through both thicknesses and draw up loop. Insert hook in next stitch and draw up loop, yo and draw through both loops. Continue along seam.

Tips on Using Two or More Colors

Single crochet: using the first color, work to the last stitch in one color. Insert the hook in the next stitch, wrap the yarn over the hook and draw through a loop. Drop the first color to the wrong side of the work and with the second color, wrap the yarn over the hook and draw through a loop. It is important to always change to a different color in the same manner.

Half double crochet: yarn colors in half double crochet are changed in the same manner as single crochet. Always work the last wrap over the hook with the new color so that the stitch before the new color is completed with the new color.

Double colorwork: the new color is also used to complete the previous stitch before starting the stitch with the changed color. The color not being used is carried across the top of the previous row and the new row is worked over it making the fabric reversible. Do not draw through the new colored yarn too tightly when using it again or it will distort your work.

Blocks of color: When using two colors alternately across a row, they can be carried along the wrong side of work when not in use as described above. If you are using large blocks or isolated motifs, separate balls or bobbins are needed for each section. The bobbins or balls of yarn hang at the back of the work and the colors are changed by dropping the first color to the back and using the second color to

wrap the yarn over the hook to complete a stitch and start the new stitch with the 2nd color. Either weave the ends in or work over the ends when you change to a new color.

Changing yarns: The directions given above apply to changing yarns as well as changing the colors of threads.

Hooks

Crochet hooks are made of plastic, coated aluminum, steel and wood in a range of sizes. The three sizing systems are the U.S. system, the British system, and the metric system. Since all of these patterns were originally worked with metric size hooks, we are including an interchange chart for metric-U.S.-U.K. size hooks. If possible, we tested the yarn on a U.S. sized hook; thus you may sometimes find that there is a slight discrepancy between the chart interchanges and the ones given in the instructions, or that another chart in another book is slightly different. In any case, you should use the chart as a guide only and always check your gauge and change hooks accordingly.

Metric	U.S.	U.K.
2.5	B/1	12
3	C/2	11
3.25	D/3	10
3.5	E/4	9
4	F/5	8
4.5	G/6	7
5	H/8	6
5.5	I/9	5
6	J/10	4
7	K/10.25	2

Steel hooks are generally used with lightweight yarns and threads and for finer, lacy work. Aluminum and plastic hooks are used with most popular weight yarns. Wood hooks are usually found only in the larger and longer lengths. A special hook called an afghan hook is made of aluminum and has a straight shaft with a knob or cap at one end and a hook at the other. They are sized like the aluminum and plastic hooks.

Bibliography

Complete Guide to Needlework.
   The Reader's Digest Association,
   Inc., Pleasantville, New York, 1979.

Goldberg, Rhoda Oscher.
The New Crochet Dictionary.
   Crown Publishers, Inc., New York,
   1986.

Harding, Sally.
Crochet Style.
   Ballantine Books. New York, 1987.

   Modern Guide to Crocheting.
   Mon Tricot. Paris, France, 1981.

The Pattern Library.
Crochet.
   Ballantine Books, New York, 1981.

Righetti, Mary.
Crocheting in Plain English.
   St. Martin's Press, New York, 1988.

Schapper, Linda P.
**Complete Book of Crochet-Stitch
Designs.**
   Sterling Publishing Co., Inc., New
   York, 1985.
Complete Book of Border Design.
   Sterling Publishing Co., Inc., New
   York, 1987.

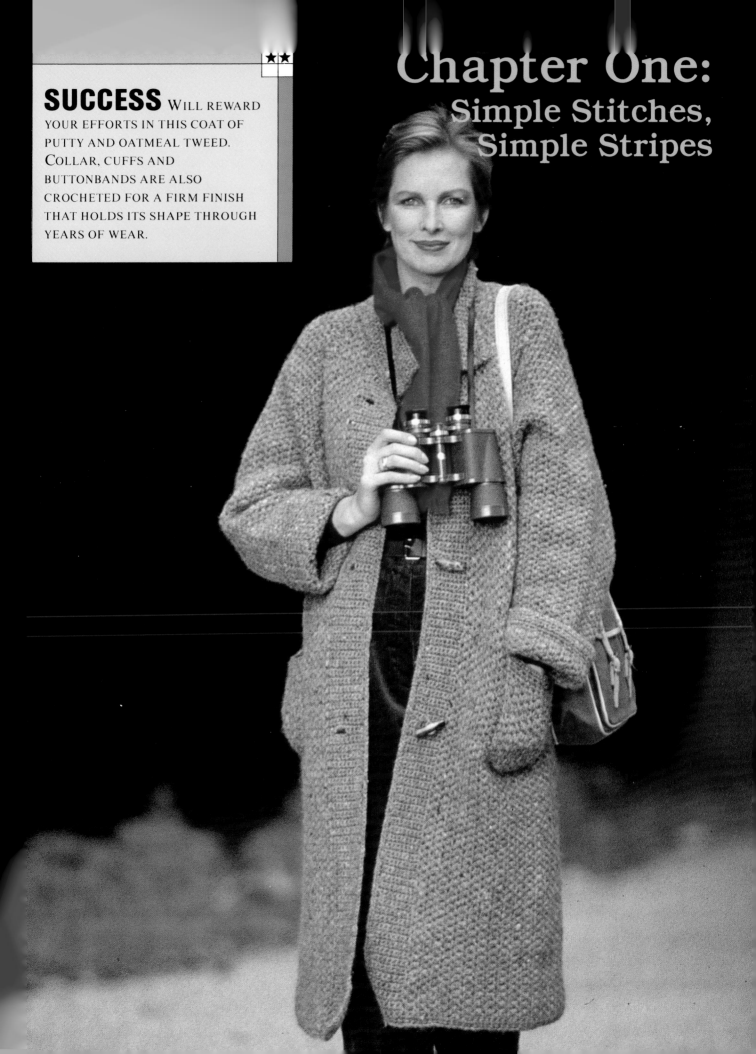

★★

SUCCESS WILL REWARD YOUR EFFORTS IN THIS COAT OF PUTTY AND OATMEAL TWEED. COLLAR, CUFFS AND BUTTONBANDS ARE ALSO CROCHETED FOR A FIRM FINISH THAT HOLDS ITS SHAPE THROUGH YEARS OF WEAR.

TWEED COAT

SIZE

Women's size Large, bust 36-38 in. (91.5 - 97 cm). Finished bust measurement: 51¼ in. (130.5 cm), length: 41½ in. (105 cm), sleeve seam: 17½ in. (45 cm).

MATERIALS

35 skeins bulky weight yarn (approx. 75 yds per 50 g skein) color gray. Crochet hooks U.S. sizes H/8 and K/10.5 (U.K. sizes 6 and 2) (Metric sizes 5 and 7) or size needed to obtain gauge. 3 buttons. **To save time, take time to check gauge!**

GAUGE

9 sc and 11 rows = 4 in. (10 cm).

STITCHES

Chain stitch (ch), single crochet (sc), double crochet (dc), slip stitch (sl st)
Pattern stitch: Row 1: Sc across.
Row 2: 1 sc in the sc in the row below, *1 sc in the foll sc, 1 sc in the sc in the row below *, rep * to * across.
Row 3: 1 sc, *1 sc in the sc in the row below, 1 sc*, rep * to * across. Rep rows 2 to 3.

BODY

With the larger hook, ch 125 + ch 2 (counts as first sc). Work in pat st.
Row 1: Work first sc in the 4th ch from the hook, sc across = 125 sc.
Row 2: 6 sc = left border, 113 sts of pat st, 2nd row of pat st, 6 sc = right border.
Row 3: 6 sc, 113 sts of pat st, 3rd row of pat st, 6 sc = right border. Continue as established for 27½ in.

(70 cm). **At the same time**, make 3 buttonholes on right border, beg when piece measures 21½ in. (55 cm), then spacing 2 more buttonholes about 6 in. (15 cm) apart. At right border, work 3 sc, ch 3, skip 3, continue across border. On foll row, work 3 sc in ch-3 sp. Mark center 55 sts. Work across first 33 sts as established, turn, leaving last 2 sts before marker unworked. *Sl st over first st, work to end of row. Turn, work 1 row even.* Work * to * 17 times more. With right side facing, sl st over first 7 sts, work across, turn. Sl st over first st, work to last st or row, turn, leaving last st unworked. *Sl st over first st, work to end of row, turn. Work across to last st, turn, leaving last st unworked*, work * to * twice. Fasten off. Join yarn to first marker and *sl st over first st, work to end of row*, rep * to * 40 times total. Work 1 row across rem 15 sts, then fasten off. Join yarn 2 sts from 2nd marker for left front. Work to end of row, turn. Work to last st, turn, leaving last st unworked. Continue by rev shapings of right front.

SLEEVES

With larger hook, ch 27 + ch 2. Work 3¼ in. (8 cm) in sc, then continue in pat st. Inc 1 st at each edge of every 4th row 10 times = 47 sts. When piece measures 19 in. (49 cm) from beg, shape raglans. *Sl st over first st, work to last st, leave last st unworked*, rep * to * 40 times. Work across 7 sts. Fasten off.

POCKET

With larger hook, ch 15 + ch 2 to turn. Work first sc in 4th ch from hook. Work pat st over 15 sts for 5½ in. (14 cm). End with 1¼ in. (3 cm) of sc. Fasten off.

FINISHING

Block pieces to indicated measurements. Sew raglan seams. Fold sleeve borders to inside and sl st in place. Sew sleeve seams. With smaller hook, work 1 row of sc around neck, continue in sc for 6¼ in. (16 cm). Fasten off. Fold collar in half to inside and sew to first row of collar. Work 1 row of sc along collar ends, front edges and lower edge of body as foll: with smaller size hook, beg at top of collar end, work 1 sc in each sc, 3 sc in corner, work 1 sc in each row along front, then 3 sc in corner. Change to larger size hook and work in sc in each st and 3 sc in corner, along lower edge. Change to smaller size hook, work 3 sc in corner, work in sc along front edge, work 3 sc in corner, work 1 sc in each sc along collar end. Fasten off. Sew the pockets to each front placed 16½ in. (42 cm) from lower edge and 6 in. (15 cm) from front edges. Sew on buttons.

PIECES

SLEEVE

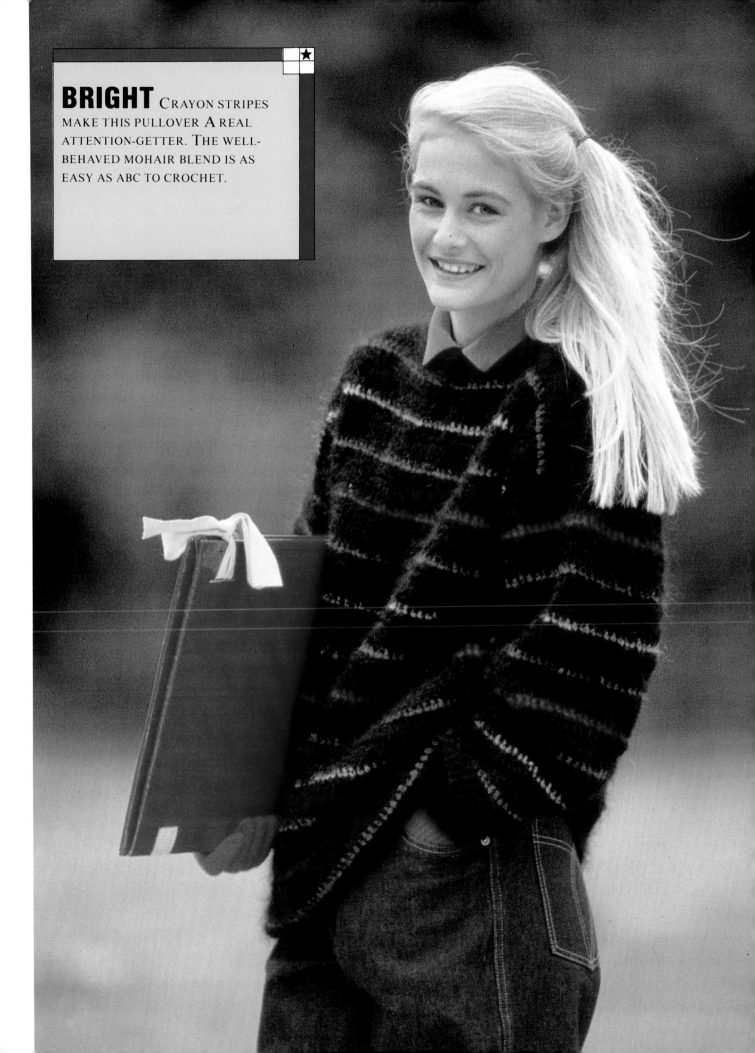

BRIGHT CRAYON STRIPES MAKE THIS PULLOVER **A** REAL ATTENTION-GETTER. THE WELL-BEHAVED MOHAIR BLEND IS AS EASY AS ABC TO CROCHET.

CRAYON STRIPED PULLOVER

SIZE

Women's Medium (Large, X Large), bust 33-35 (36-38, 39-42) in. - 84-89 (91.5-97, 99-107) cm. Finished bust measurement: 40 (45, 48) in. - 102 (114, 122) cm., length 28¼ in. (72 cm), sleeve seam 18¾ in. (48 cm).

MATERIALS

10 (11, 12) skeins "Scheepjeswol Selena" (65% kid mohair, 29% wool, 6% nylon — approx. 111 yds per 50 g skein) color black, 1 skein each color red, gold, blue, green.
Crochet hook U.S. size I/9 (U.K. size 5) (Metric size 5.5) or size needed to obtain gauge. Knitting needles U.S. size 7 (U.K. size 7) (Metric size 4.5).
To save time, take time to check gauge!

GAUGE

12 dc and 8½ rows = 4 in. (10 cm)

STITCHES

Single crochet (sc), double crochet (dc), chain stitch (ch), slip stitch (sl st)
1/1 ribbing: Row 1: *K1, p1*, rep * to * across.
Row 2: Work sts as they appear.

Stripe pattern: *3 rows of dc in black, 1 row of sc in green, 3 rows of dc in black, 1 row of sc in red, 3 rows of dc in black, 1 row of sc in blue, 3 rows of dc in black, 1 row of sc in gold.* Rep these 16 rows for stripe pattern. Beg each row of dc with ch 3 as the first st. Beg each row of sc with ch 1 for the first st.

BACK

With knitting needles and black, cast on 84 (90, 96) sts and work 2¾ in. (7 cm) in 1/1 ribbing. Bind off loosely.
With crochet hook and black, crochet 62 (68, 74) dc along bound off row of ribbing. Continue by foll stripe pattern until piece measures 28¼ in. (72 cm) from beg. Ending with 1 row of sc in green and 3 rows of dc in black. Fasten off.

FRONT

Work same as back.

SLEEVES

With knitting needles and black, cast on 44 sts and work 2¾ in. (7 cm) in 1/1 ribbing. Bind off loosely.
With crochet hook and black, crochet 44 dc along bound off row of ribbing. Continue in stripe pattern, beg with 3 rows of dc in black and 1 row of sc in blue. At each edge of every row of sc, inc 1 st 8 times. You now have 60 sts. End with 1 row of sc in red and 3 rows of dc in black. When sleeves measure 21½ in. (48 cm), fasten off.

FINISHING

Sew shoulder seams over 5½ (6¼, 6½) in. - 14 (16, 17) cm. Sew sleeves to armholes, matching center of sleeve with shoulder seams. Sew side and sleeve seams.

FRONT-BACK

![FRONT-BACK diagram with measurements: top 5½-6¼-6½ (14-16-17), 9-10-11 (23-25-27), 5½-6¼-6½ (14-16-17); height 25½ (65); ribbing 2¾ (7); bottom 20-22½-24 (51-57-61)]

SLEEVE

![SLEEVE diagram with measurements: top 19¾ (50); height 5½ (14); ribbing 2¾ (7); bottom 11 (28), 13¾ (35)]

VELVETY STRIPED PULLOVER

SIZE

Women's Small, Medium (Large, X Large), bust 30-35 (36-42) in. - 76-89 (91.5-107) cm. Finished bust measurement: 39½ (47) in. - 100 (120) cm, length 28¼ in. (72 cm), sleeve seam 18¾ in. (48 cm).

MATERIALS

2 (3) skeins worsted weight, mohair-blend yarn (approx. 190 yds per 50 g skein) color dark gray-blue, 2 skeins each color purple, dark blue, and light gray-blue.
Crochet hook U.S. size F/5 (U.K. size 8) (Metric size 4) or size needed to obtain gauge. Knitting needles U.S. size 4 (U.K. size 9) (Metric size 3.5).
To save time, take time to check gauge!

GAUGE

14 dc and 6 rows = 4 in. (10 cm)

STITCHES

Chain (ch), single crochet (sc), double crochet (dc), slip stitch (sl st)
Stripe pattern: Work in dc as foll:
Row 1: dark gray-blue.
Row 2: light gray-blue.
Row 3: dark gray-blue.
Rows 4 to 6: purple.
Row 7: dark gray-blue.
Row 8: light gray-blue.
Row 9: dark gray-blue.
Rows 10 to 12: dark-blue.
Rep these 12 rows for the stripe pattern. Beg each row with ch 3 which counts as the first dc. Let the unused strands hang at the edges and carry them along the sides to be used in pattern repeat. Note: Some colors will hang at both edges.
1/1 ribbing: *K1, p1*, rep * to * across.

BACK

With knitting needles and dark gray-blue, cast on 70 (84) sts and work 2¾ in. (7 cm) in 1/1 ribbing. Bind off loosely.
With crochet hook and dark gray-blue, work 1 sc in each bound off st. Then work in dc, working 12 rows of stripe pattern 3 times total, end with first 3 rows. Fasten off.

FRONT

Work same as back.

SLEEVES

With knitting needles and dark gray-blue, cast on 40 sts and work 2¾ in. (7 cm) in 1/1 ribbing. Bind off loosely.
With crochet hook and dark gray blue, work 54 sc along bound off row of ribbing, working 2 sc in 14 sts evenly spaced across row. Work in dc, 12 rows of stripe pattern twice total. **At the same time,** inc 1 dc at each edge of every 3rd row 8 times = 70 dc. (Work 2 dcs in each edge dc.) End with 1 row of dark gray-blue. Fasten off.

FINISHING

Block pieces to indicated measurements. Sew shoulder seams over 5½ (6½) in. - 14 (17) cm. With dark gray-blue, work 1 row of sc around neck. Fasten off. Sew sleeves to armholes, matching center of sleeve with shoulder seams. Sew side and sleeve seams.

SLEEVE

![SLEEVE diagram with measurements: top 19¾ (50); height 16 (41); ribbing 2¾ (7); bottom 14½ (37)]

FRONT-BACK

![FRONT-BACK diagram with measurements: top 5½-6½ (14-17), 8½ (22), 5½-6½ (14-17); height 25½ (65); ribbing 2¾ (7); bottom 19¾-23½ (50-60)]

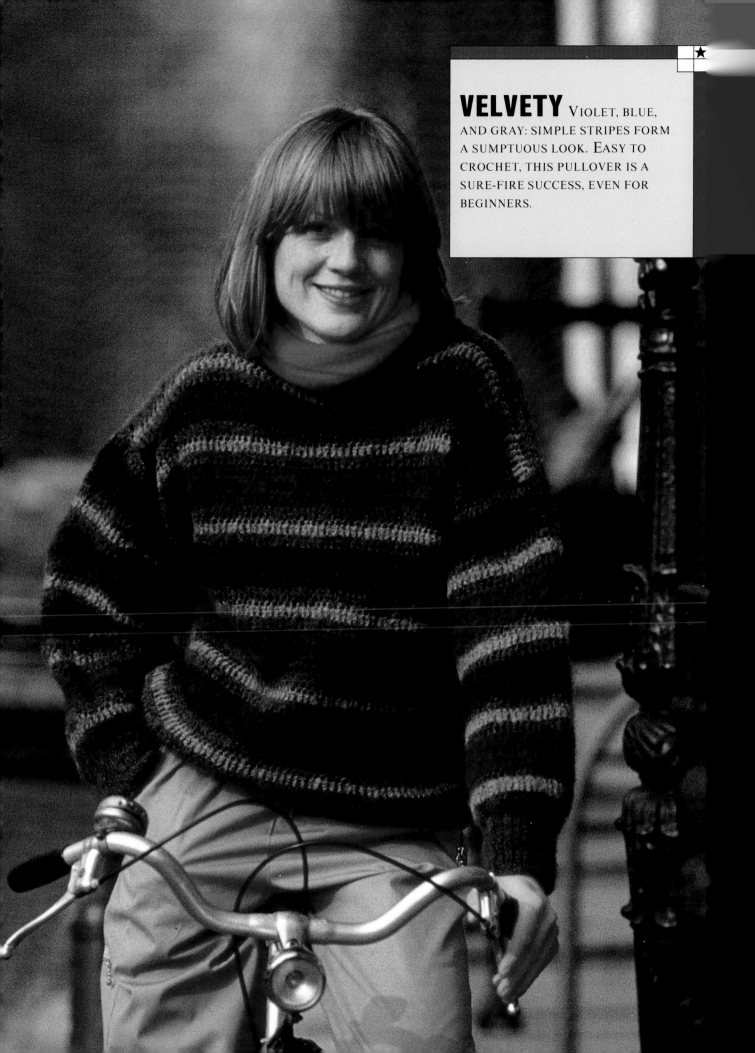

VELVETY VIOLET, BLUE, AND GRAY: SIMPLE STRIPES FORM A SUMPTUOUS LOOK. EASY TO CROCHET, THIS PULLOVER IS A SURE-FIRE SUCCESS, EVEN FOR BEGINNERS.

★★
★
★

MARITIME STRIPES HIT THE BEACHES IN A BIG WAY WITH THIS POLO-COLLARED PULLOVER. MINIATURE VERSIONS COME IN BOATNECK AND POLO STYLES. A MATCHING BEACH BAG IS THE PERFECT ACCESSORY FOR WATERSIDE EXCURSIONS.

WOMAN'S POLO PULLOVER

SIZE
Woman's Small (Medium, Large), bust 33-35, (36-38, 39-42) in. - 84-89 (91.5-97, 99-107) cm. Finished bust measurements: 37½ (40, 41½) in. - 96 (101, 106) cm, length: 23¼ (23½, 24) in. - 59 (60, 61) cm, sleeve seam: 11¾ in. (30 cm).

MATERIALS
4 (5, 6) skeins "Scheepjeswol Mayflower Helarsgarn" (100% cotton - approx. 88 yds per 50 g skein) each color pink, purple and gold, 2 skeins color white. Crochet hook U.S. size F/5 (U.K. size 8) (Metric size 4) or size needed to obtain gauge. Knitting needles U.S. size 6 (U.K. size 8) (Metric size 4). 3 buttons. **To save time, take time to check gauge!**

GAUGE
16 sc and 19 rows = 4 in. (10 cm).

STITCHES
Chain (ch), single crochet (sc), slip stitch (sl st).
Stripe pattern: Sc as foll: *2½ in. (6 cm) purple, 2½ in. (6 cm) gold, 2½ in. (6 cm) pink*, rep * to *. When changing colors, work the last loop of the last st with the color of the next st.

Ch 1 at the beg of each row (= 1 border st).
1/1 ribbing: Row 1: *K1, p1*. Rep * to * across.
Row 2 and all foll rows: Work sts as established in previous row.

BACK
With knitting needles and white, cast on 77 (81, 85) sts and work 2¾ in. (7 cm) 1/1 ribbing. With purple, knit 1 row on right side of work. Bind off loosely. With crochet hook, work 1 sc in every st of bound off row of ribbing. Work in stripe pat until piece measures 22½ (22¾, 23¼) in. - 57 (58, 59) cm from beg. Mark the center 19 (23, 27) sts. Work each shoulder separately. Beg at right edge of right side of work row, work to last 2 sts before marker, turn, leaving 2 sts unworked. Sl st over 2 sts, ch 1, then work to end of row = 25 sc. Work until piece measures 23¼ (23½, 24) in. - 59 (60, 61) cm from beg, fasten off. Beg 2 sts from 2nd marker, work to end of row = 25 sc. Turn, ch 1, and work to 2 sts from end of row. Work until same measurement as first shoulder. Fasten off.

FRONT
Work same as back until piece measures 14½ in. (37 cm) from beg. Divide work as foll: with right side facing, work 41 (43, 45) sc and work for 6 in. (15 cm), then shape neck. Work to last 8 (10, 12) sts, ch 1, turn, leaving these sts unworked. *Work next row. On foll row, work to last 2 sts

before end of row at neck edge, ch 1, turn, leave last 2 sts unworked.* Rep * to * 4 times total = 25 sc. Work until piece measures 23¼ (23½, 24) in. - 59 (60, 61) cm from beg, fasten off.

Work 2nd part the same for 6 in. (15 cm), then shape neck. At neck edge, sl st over the first 3 (5, 7) sts. Then at neck edge of every 2nd row, sl 2 sts 4 times = 25 sc. Work until piece measures 23¼ (23½, 24) in. - 59 (60, 61) cm from beg, fasten off.

SLEEVES

With knitting needles and white, cast on 48 (51, 54) sts and work 2½ in. (6 cm) in 1/1 ribbing. With pink, knit 1 row on right side of work. Bind off loosely. With crochet hook, work 1 sc in each bound off st. Continue in striped pat, beg with pink. Inc 1 st at each edge of every 2nd row 11 times. (For each inc, work 2 sc in each edge st.) You now have 70 (73, 76) sc. When sleeve measures 11¾ in. (30 cm) from beg, fasten off.

FINISHING

Block pieces to indicated measurements. With knitting needles and white, pick up and knit 30 sts along right side of front opening and work in 1/1 ribbing. **At the same time**, when border measures 1/2 in. (1.5 cm), make 3 buttonholes as foll: work 3 sts, bind off 2 sts, work 9 sts, bind off 2 sts, work 9 sts, bind off 2 sts, work 3 sts. On the foll row, cast on 2 sts over bound off sts. Bind off when border measures 1¼ in. (3 cm). Sew shoulder seams. With knitting needles and white, pick up and knit 75 (85, 95) sts around neck, beg and end 1/2 in. (1.5 cm) from front edges. Work 3¼ in. (8 cm) of 1/1 ribbing. Bind off. Sew sleeves to side seams, matching center of sleeve with shoulder seam. Sew side and sleeve seams. Sew on buttons.

CHILD'S PULLOVER

SIZE

Child's size 4 (6, 8) years, chest 23 (25, 27) in. - 58.5 (63.5, 69) cm. Finished chest measurements: 27½ (29, 30½) in. - 70 (74, 78) cm, length: 15¼ (17, 18½) in. - 39 (43, 47) cm, sleeve seam: 5 (6, 6½) in. - 13 (15, 17) cm.

MATERIALS

2 (2, 3) skeins "Scheepjeswol Mayflower Helarsgarn" (100% cotton - approx. 88 yds per 50 g skein) each color gold, green and pink, 1 skein color white.
Crochet hook U.S. size F / 5 (U.K. size 8) (Metric size 4) or size needed to obtain gauge. Knitting needles U.S. size 6 (U.K. size 8) (Metric size 4). 6 buttons. **To save time, take time to check gauge!**

GAUGE

16 sc and 19 rows = 4 in. (10 cm).

STITCHES

**Chain (ch),
single crochet (sc),
slip stitch (sl st).**
Stripe pattern: Sc as foll: *1¾ (2, 2¼) in. - 4.5 (5, 5.5) cm pink, 1¾ (2, 2¼) in. -4.5 (5, 5.5) cm gold, 1¾ (2, 2¼) in. - 4.5 (5, 5.5) cm green*, rep * to *. Ch 1 to turn at beg of each row. When changing colors, work the last loop of the last st with the color of the next st.
1/1 ribbing: Row 1: *K1, p1*. Rep * to * across.
Row 2 and all foll rows: Work sts as established in previous row.

BACK

With knitting needles and white, cast on 56 (59, 62) sts and work 1¾ (2, 2¼) in. - 4.5 (5, 5.5) cm in 1/1 ribbing. Knit 1 row on right side of work in pink, bind off. With crochet hook, work 1 sc in each st of bound off row of ribbing. Continue in stripe pat until piece measures 8½ (9½, 10¼) in. - 22 (24, 26) cm from beg. Sl st over 5 sts, ch 1, work to last 5 sts, turn, leaving last 5 sts unworked = 46 (49, 52) sc. Continue until piece measures 14 (15¾, 17¼) in. - 36 (40, 44) cm from beg. Fasten off. With knitting needles and white, knit 1 row on right side of work, inc 8 sts evenly spaced across row. Work 1¼ in. (3 cm) in 1/1 ribbing. Bind off center 20 (23, 26) sts. Working each half separately, work 1¼ in. (3 cm) more in 1/1 ribbing. Bind off.

FRONT

Work same as back until upper ribbing measures 1/2 in. (1.5 cm), then shape buttonholes as foll: *work 3 sts, bind off 2 sts*, work * to * 3 times total, then work to last 15 sts: *bind off 2 sts, work 3 sts*, work * to * 3 times total. On foll row, cast on 2 sts over bound off sts. When border measures 1¼ in. (3 cm), bind off all sts.

SLEEVES

With knitting needles and white, cast on 38 (40, 42) sts and work 1 (1¼, 1¾) in. - 2.5 (3, 3.5) cm in 1/1 ribbing. Knit 1 row in gold on right side of work. Bind off. With crochet hook, work 1 sc in each st of bound off row of ribbing, then work in stripe pat, beg with gold stripe. Inc 1 sc at each edge every 1/2 in. (1.5 cm) 5 (7, 9) times. (Work 2 sc in each edge st.) You now have 48 (54, 60) sc. When sleeve measures 6¼ (7¼, 7¾) in. - 16 (18, 20) cm, fasten off.

FINISHING

Block pieces to indicated measurements. Lap the front border over the top 1¼ in. (3 cm) of upper ribbing of back and baste in place. Sew sleeves to armholes, matching center of sleeve with shoulder seams. Sew side and sleeve seams. Remove basting and sew on buttons.

SLEEVE

FRONT-BACK

SLEEVE

FRONT

BACK

CHILD'S POLO PULLOVER

SIZE

Child's size 4 (6, 8) years, chest 23 (25, 27) in. - 58.5 (63.5, 69) cm. Finished chest measurements: 27½ (29, 30½) in. - 70 (74, 78) cm, length: 15¼ (17, 18½) in. - 39 (43, 47) cm, sleeve seam: 5 (6, 6½) in. - 13 (15, 17) cm.

MATERIALS

2 (2, 3) skeins "Scheepjeswol Mayflower Helarsgarn" (100% cotton - approx. 88 yds per 50 g skein) each color green, red and purple, 1 skein color white.
Crochet hook U.S. size F/5 (U.K. size 8) (Metric size 4) or size needed to obtain gauge. Knitting needles U.S. size 6 (U.K. size 8) (Metric size 4). 3 buttons. **To save time, take time to check gauge!**

GAUGE

16 sc and 19 rows = 4 in. (10 cm).

STITCHES

Chain (ch),
single crochet (sc),
slip stitch (sl st).
Stripe pattern: Sc as foll: *1¾ in. (4 cm) green, 1¾ in. (4 cm) red, 1¾ in. (4 cm) purple*, rep * to *. Beg each row with ch 1. When changing colors, work the last loop of the last st with the color of the next st.
1/1 ribbing: Row 1: *K1, p1*. Rep * to * across.
Row 2 and all foll rows: Work sts as established in previous row.

BACK

With knitting needles and white, cast on 56 (59, 62) sts and work 2 in. (5 cm) in 1/1 ribbing. Knit 1 row in green on right side of work. Bind off loosely. With crochet hook and green, work 1 sc in each st of bound off row. Work in stripe pat until piece measures 8½ (9½, 10¼) in. - 22 (24, 26) cm from beg. Sl st over first 5 sts, ch 1, work to last 5 sts of row, turn, leaving last 5 sts unworked. Work rem 46 (49, 52) sc until piece measures 15 (17, 18½) in. - 39 (43, 47) cm from beg, fasten off.

FRONT

Work same as back until piece measures 9½ (10½, 11¾) in. - 24 (27, 30) cm from beg, divide work as foll: right side facing, work 21 (22, 24) sc. Work even for 4 in. (10 cm). Then work to 3 (3, 4) sts before neck edge, turn. Sl st over 2 (3, 3) sts, ch 1, work to end of row, turn. Work to 1 (0, 0) st before end of row, turn. When piece measures 15 (17, 18½) in. - 39 (43, 47) cm from beg, fasten off. Work 2nd part for 4 in. (10 cm), then, right side facing, sl st over 3 (3, 4) sts at neck edge, ch 1, work to end of row, work to last 7 (8, 8) sts. Work until piece measures 15 (17, 18½) in. - 39 (43, 47) cm from beg, fasten off.

SLEEVES

With knitting needles and white, cast on 38 (40, 42) sts and work 1¼ in. (3 cm) in 1/1 ribbing. Knit 1 row in red on the right side of work. Bind off loosely. With crochet hook, work 1 sc in each st of bound off row of ribbing, then work in stripe pat, beg with red. At each edge every 1/2 in. (1.5 cm), inc 1 st 5 (7, 9) times = 48 (54, 60) sc. When piece measures 6¼ (7¼, 7¾) in. - 16 (18, 20) cm from beg, fasten off.

FINISHING

Block pieces to indicated measurements. Sew shoulder seams. With knitting needles and white, pick up and knit 22 sts along left edge of front opening and work 1 in. (2.5 cm) of 1/1 ribbing. **At the same time,** when border measures 1/3 in. (1 cm), make 3 button-holes as foll: work 2 sts, bind off 2 sts, work 6 sts, bind off 2 sts, work 6 sts, bind off 2 sts, work 2 sts. On the foll row, cast on 2 sts over bound off sts. Bind off in ribbing. With knitting needles and white, pick up and knit 51 (61, 71) sts around neck, beg and end 1/2 in. (1.5 cm) from each edge of front opening. Work 2½ in. (6 cm) in 1/1 ribbing. Bind off loosely. Sew sleeves to armholes, matching center of sleeve with shoulder seams and sewing top 1¼ in. (3 cm) of sleeve to armhole edge. Sew side and sleeve seams. Sew on buttons.

BAG

MATERIALS

3 skeins of "Scheepjeswol Mayflower Cotton 8" (100% cotton - approx. 180 yds per 50 g skein) color gold.
Crochet hook U.S. size C/2 (U.K. size 11) (Metric size 3).

GAUGE

10 squares and 10 rows = 4 in. (10 cm).

STITCHES

Chain (ch),
slip stitch (sl st),
double crochet (dc).
Filet st: *Ch 2, skip 2, 1 dc*, rep * to * across.

BAG

Ch 180 and join with sl st in round. **Round 1:** Ch 5, 1 dc in the 3rd ch from hook, *ch 2, skip 2 ch, 1 dc in the foll ch*, rep * to *, end with ch 2, skip 2 ch, 1 sl st in the 3rd ch from the beg. **Round 2:** Ch 5, *1 dc in the dc in the row below, ch 2, skip 2*, rep * to *, end with 1 sl st in the 3rd ch from the hook. Always rep the 2nd round until piece measures 25½ in. (65 cm). Fasten off.

FINISHING

Ch cord 59 in. (150 cm) long and thread through squares at each edge. Knot ends tog.

Filet stitch bags can be made in different sizes and shapes and are perfect for beachwear. When worked in fancy yarns and lined, they also make attractive evening bags.

FRONT-BACK

3¾ - 3¾ - 3½ (8-8-8,5) 5-6-6¼ (13-15-16) 3¼ - 3¾ - 3½ (8-8-8,5)

6½ - 7½ - 8¼ (17-19-21)

6½ - 7½ - 8¼ (17-19-21)

8½ - 9¼ - 10¼ (22-24-26)

13¾ - 14½ - 15¼ (35-37-39)

2 (5)

SLEEVE

11¾ - 13 - 14½ (30-33,5-37)

5 - 6 - 6¾ (13-15-17)

1¼ (3)

9½ - 9¾ - 10¼ (24-25-26)

POLISHED WHITE CARDIGAN IS A WARDROBE ESSENTIAL. COTTON BOUCLE YARN ADDS A TEXTURAL TWIST TO THIS UNCLUTTERED CLASSIC.

★★ ☐☐

WHITE CARDIGAN

SIZE

Woman's Small (Medium, Large), bust 30-32 (33-35, 36-38) in. - 76-81.5 (84-89, 91.5-97) cm. Finished bust measurements: 39½ (43, 47½) in. - 101 (110, 121) cm, length: 22¾ (23¼, 23½) in. - 58 (59, 60) cm, sleeve seam: 17¾ in. (45 cm).

MATERIALS

11 (12, 13) skeins sport weight boucle yarn (approx. 143 yds per 50 g skein) color white. Crochet hook U.S. size F/5 (U.K. size 8) (Metric size 4) or size needed to obtain gauge. Knitting needles U.S. size 3 (U.K. size 10) (Metric size 3). 7 buttons. Stitch holders. **To save time, take time to check gauge!**

GAUGE

10 motifs (20 sts) and 17 rows = 4 in. (10 cm).

STITCHES

**Chain (ch),
single crochet (sc),
half double crochet (hdc),
slip stitch (sl st)
Pattern st:** Worked on a foundation row of sc.
Row 1: Ch 2 to turn (= 1 border st), *in 1 sc: 1 hdc, 1 sc; skip 1 sc*, rep * to *, end with 1 hdc in the last st (= 1 border st).
Row 2: Ch 2 to turn, * in the sc of the previous row: work 1 hdc, 1 sc; skip 1 st*, rep * to *, end with 1 hdc around the turning ch of the previous row. Repeat rows 1 and 2.
1/1 ribbing: Row 1: *K1, p1*. Rep * to * across.
Row 2 and all foll rows: Work sts as established in previous row.

BACK

With knitting needles, cast on 102 (112, 122) sts and work 2 in. (5 cm) in 1/1 ribbing. Bind off. With crochet hook, work 1 sc in each st across bound off row = 102 (112, 122) sc. Continue in pat st across = 50 (55, 60) motifs with 1 border st at each edge. When piece measures 11¾ in. (30 cm) above ribbing, shape armholes. Sl st over 2 motifs, work to last 2 motifs and turn, leave last 2 motifs unworked. Work 1 row even, then sl st over first 1 (2, 2) motifs, work to last 1 (2, 2) motifs, leave last 1 (2, 2) motifs unworked. Work 1 row even. *Sl st over first motif, then work to last motif on row, turn, leaving last motif unworked. Work 1 row even.* Work * to * twice total = 40 (43, 48) motifs. Work even until armhole measures 8 (8¼, 8½) in. - 20 (21, 22) cm. Mark the center 10 (11, 12) motifs. Sl st over first 4 (4, 5) motifs, work to first marker, turn. Work to end of row. Sl st over first 4 (4, 5) motifs, work to 3 motifs before first marker, leave last 3 motifs unworked, turn. Work to end of row. Sl st over first 4 (5, 5) motifs. Fasten off. Join yarn to 2nd marker and work 2nd half to correspond.

RIGHT FRONT

With knitting needles, cast on 58 (62, 68) sts and work in 1/1 ribbing. When border measures 1/3 in. (1 cm), make 1 buttonhole. Bind off the 5th and 6th sts from the right edge. On foll row, cast on 2 sts over bound off sts. Continue in 1/1 ribbing until piece measures 2 in. (5 cm) from beg. Make a 2nd buttonhole above previous one. Work 1 row even, then place 9 sts at right edge on holder. Work 49 (53, 59) sc over the rem sts = 24 (26, 29) motifs. When piece measures 11¾ in. (30 cm) above ribbing, shape armhole. Work to last 2 motifs and turn, leave last 2 motifs unworked. Work 1 row even, turn, work to last 1 (2, 2) motifs, turn, leave last 1 (2, 2) motifs unworked. Work 1 row even. Turn. *Work to last motif on row, turn, leaving last motif unworked. Work 1 row even.* Work * to * twice total = 19 (20, 23) motifs. Work even until armhole measures 6 (6¼, 6¼) in. - 15 (16, 16) cm, shape neck. Sl st over first 2 (2, 3) motifs, work to end of row. Turn, work to end of row. Sl st over first 2 motifs. Work to end of row, turn. Now at right edge of every 2nd row, sl st over first motif 3 times. **At the same time,** when piece measures 8 (8¼, 8½) in. -20 (21, 22) cm, shape shoulder. With right side facing, work to last 4 (4, 5) motifs, turn, leave last 4 (4, 5) motifs unworked. Sl st over first 4 (4, 5) motifs, work to end of row, turn. Work to last 4 (5, 5) motifs. Fasten off.

LEFT FRONT

Work same as right front, rev shapings and omitting buttonholes.

SLEEVE

With knitting needles, cast on 44 (46, 48) sts and work 2 in. (5 cm) in 1/1 ribbing. Bind off. With crochet hook, work sc across, working 2 sc in 8 (10, 12) sts evenly spaced across = 52 (56, 60) sts. Work in pat st = 25 (27, 29) motifs + 1 border st at each edge. Inc 1 st at each edge of every 4th row 13 times. Work inc sts in pat st as you inc = 38 (40, 42) motifs. When piece measures 15¾ in. (40 cm), shape cap. Sl st across first 2(3, 3) motifs, work to last 2 (3, 3) motifs of row, turn, leave last 2 (3, 3) motifs unworked. Sl st across first 2 motifs, work to last 2 motifs of row, turn, leave last 2 motifs unworked. *Sl st first motif of row, work to last motif, turn, leaving last motif unworked*. Rep * to * 14 times. Sl st over first 2 (2, 3) motifs, work to last 2 (2, 3) motifs, turn, leave last 2 (2, 3) motifs unworked. Sl st over first 3 motifs, work to last 3 motifs, turn. Work across rem 8 motifs. Fasten off.

FINISHING

Block pieces to indicated measurements. With knitting needles, pick up 9 sts from holder at left edge. Inc 1 st at center edge and work in 1/1 ribbing. Work until ribbing, slightly stretched, reaches to neck. Dec 1 st at center edge and place sts on holder. Work right front border the same, making 4 buttonholes as previous ones spaced about 3½ in. (9 cm) apart along front edge, allowing for the 7th buttonhole on neck edge. Bind off. Sew shoulder seams. With crochet hook, work 1 row of sc along neck edge, fasten off. Then with knitting needles, pick up 9 sts from holder, 2 sts from each sc, 9 sts from 2nd holder = 105 (109, 111) sts. Work 1¼ in. (3 cm) of 1/1 ribbing, making last buttonhole above previous ones when border measures ½ in. (1.5 cm). Sew sleeves to armholes, matching center of sleeve with shoulder seams. Sew side and sleeve seams. Sew borders to fronts. Reinforce buttonholes. Sew on buttons.

1/2 BACK

8-8½-9 (20-21-22)

8-8½-9½ (20-21-24)

12-12-12 (30-30-30)

9¾-10½-11¾ (25-27-30)

1/2 FRONT

8-8½-9 (20-21-22)

7½-9-9½ (19-22-24)

12-12-12 (30-30-30)

9-10¼-11½ (23-26-29)

1/2 SLEEVE

7½-8-8½ (19-20-21)

14-14-14 (35-36-35)

5-5½-6 (13-14-15)

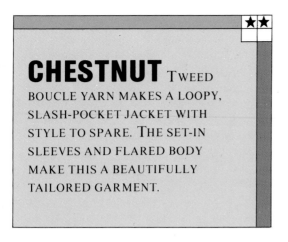

★★

CHESTNUT TWEED

BOUCLE YARN MAKES A LOOPY, SLASH-POCKET JACKET WITH STYLE TO SPARE. THE SET-IN SLEEVES AND FLARED BODY MAKE THIS A BEAUTIFULLY TAILORED GARMENT.

TWEED BOUCLE JACKET

SIZE

Woman's Medium (Large, X Large), bust 33-35 (36-38, 39-42) in. - 84-89 (91.5-97, 99-107) cm + 2 in. (5 cm) front border overlap. Finished bust measurements: 39¾ (41¼, 43¾) in. - 101 (106, 111) cm. length: 28 (28¼, 28¾) in. - 71 (72, 73) cm, sleeve seam: 18½ in. (47 cm).

MATERIALS

27 (29, 31) skeins bulky boucle yarn (approx. 40 yds per 50 g skein) color brown tweed.
Crochet hook U.S. size J / 10 (U.K. size 4) (Metric size 6) or size needed to obtain gauge. 3 buttons.
To save time, take time to check gauge!

GAUGE

8.5 hdc and 7 rows = 4 in. (10 cm).

STITCHES

**Chain (ch),
slip stitch (sl st),
single crochet (sc),
half double crochet (hdc).**

BACK

Ch 50 (52, 54) + ch 1. Work 1 sc in the 2nd ch from hook, then work in sc across. Continue in hdc, beg each row with ch 2. Work even for 4 in. (10 cm). *Sl st over first st, hdc to last st, turn, leaving last st unworked. Work 3 rows even.* Work * to * 4 times = 42 (44, 46) hdc. When piece measures 19 in. (48 cm), shape armholes. Sl st over first 2 (2, 3) sts, work to last 2 (2, 3) sts, turn, leave last 2 (2, 3) sts unworked. Sl st over first 2 sts, work to last 2 sts, turn, leave last 2 sts unworked = 34 (35, 36) hdc. Work until armhole measures 8¼ (8½, 9) in. - 21 (22, 23) cm. Mark center 10 (11, 12). Sl st over first 5 sts, work to first marker, turn. Sl st over first 2 sts.

Work to end of row. Turn. Sl st over first 5 sts. Fasten off. Work 2nd half to correspond.

RIGHT FRONT

Ch 28 (30, 32) + ch 1, and work 1 row of sc. Continue in hdc. Work even for 4 in. (10 cm). *Then with right side facing, work to last st, turn, leaving last st unworked. Work 2 rows even.* Work * to * 4 times = 20 (22, 24) hdc. **At the same time**, when piece measures 6½ in. (17 cm) from beg, shape pocket. With right side facing, work 13 hdc at right edge, then work rem sts for 6¼ in. (16 cm). Leave these stitches unworked. Now work 13 sts at right edge for 6¼ in. (16 cm). Rejoin all sts and work across. **At the same time**, make 1 buttonhole at right edge when piece measures 8 in. (20 cm) as foll: work 3 sts, skip 2 sts and ch 2 over skipped sts. Space 2 other buttonholes 6 in. (15 cm) apart. On foll row work 2 sts in ch-2 sp.
When piece measures 19 in. (48 cm), shape armhole and shawl collar. At right edge, inc 1 hdc, work to last 2 (2, 3) sts, turn, leave last 2 (2, 3) sts unworked. Sl st over first 2 sts, work to end of row, turn, leave last 2 sts unworked. **At the same time**, at right edge every 2 in. (5 cm), inc 1 st 3 more times. Work until armhole measures 8¼ (8½, 9) in. - 21 (22, 23) cm. With right side facing, work to last 4 (4, 5) sts, turn, leave

last 4 (4, 5) sts unworked. Sl st over first 5 sts, work to end of row. Continue on rem sts, working the 6 sts at shoulder edge in sc on right side of work rows. Work the same sts in hdc on wrong side of work rows. (This will make the shoulder edge shorter than the neck edge.) When the shoulder edge of collar measures 3¼ in. (8 cm) from shoulder, fasten off.

LEFT FRONT

Work same as right front, rev shapings and omitting buttonholes.

SLEEVES

Ch 35 (36, 37) + ch 1, and work 1 row of sc. Continue in hdc, beg each row with ch 2 until sleeve measures 18½ in. (7 cm) from beg, then shape cap. Sl st over 3 sts, work to last 3 sts, turn, leave last 3 sts unworked. Sl st over 2 sts, work to last 2 sts, turn, leave last 2 sts unworked. *Sl st over first st, work to last st, turn, leaving last st unworked.* Rep * to * 7 (8, 9) times. Sl st over 3 (2, 2) sts, work to last 3 (2, 2) sts, turn, leave last 3 (2, 2) sts unworked. Work over rem 5 (6, 5) sts. Fasten off.

POCKET BORDER AND LININGS

Along center edge of pockets, work 3 rows of sc. Fasten off. Join edge to lower edge of pocket opening and ch 8. Work in hdc. After 1½ in. (4 cm), sl st over first st of every row. When piece measures 4 in. (10 cm), fasten off. Sew pocket linings and border ends in place.

FINISHING

Block pieces to indicated measurements. Sew shoulder seams. Set in sleeves. Sew side and sleeve seams. Sew back seam of collar and sew to back neck. Reinforce buttonholes. Buttons: make a chain long enough to go around each button and sl st to join in ring. Work 8 sc in this ring, insert button and work in rounds of sc until piece covers the button. Break yarn and thread through sts to gather. Sew to front.

When sewing pocket linings to inside of fronts, take care to sew through back loops of stitches only so that the outline of the pocket doesn't show on the right side of your work.

RIGHT FRONT

BACK

SLEEVE

SCORE BIG POINTS BY MAKING THIS CHILD'S PULLOVER WITH CHECKERED STITCH IN HIS TEAM COLORS.

CHILD'S CHECKERED PULLOVER

SIZE

Child's size 4 (6, 8, 10) years, chest 23 (25, 27, 28½) in. - 58.5 (63.5, 69, 72.5) cm. Finished chest measurements: 27½ (29½, 31½, 33½) in. - 70 (75, 80, 85) cm, length 15¾ (17, 18¼, 19) in. - 41 (44, 48, 50) cm, sleeve seam 13½ (13¾, 15, 16¼) in. - 27 (30, 33, 36) cm.

MATERIALS

5 (5, 6, 7) skeins worsted weight yarn (50 g skein) color dark blue, 3 (4, 5, 6) skeins color red.
Crochet hook U.S. size E/4 (U.K. size 9) (Metric size 3.5) or size needed to obtain gauge. Knitting needles U.S. size 4 (U.K. size 9) (Metric size 3.5).
To save time, take time to check gauge!

GAUGE

16 sc and 15½ rows = 4 in. (10 cm).

STITCHES

**Chain (ch),
single crochet (sc),
half double crochet (hdc),
slip stitch (sl st).**
Block st: Rows 1-4: Ch 1 to turn (does not count as first st), *4 sc in red, 4 sc in dark blue*. Rep * to * across row. Use a separate ball of yarn for each section of color. When changing colors, always work the last loop of 1 st with the color of the next st. Do not carry unused yarn across wrong side of work. Work 4 rows in established colors.
Rows 5-8: Ch 1 to turn, *4 sc in dark blue, 4 sc in red*. Rep * to * across row. Alternate colors by working opposite color of previous row for 4 rows. Always rep these 8 rows.
1/1 ribbing: Row 1: *K 1, p1*. Rep * to * across.
Row 2 and all foll rows: Work sts as established in previous row.

BACK

With knitting needles and dark blue, cast on 56 (60, 64, 68) sts and work 2¾ in. (7 cm) 1/1 ribbing. Bind off.
With crochet hook, work 1 sc in each st of bound off row of ribbing, then work in block st: You will have 14 (15, 16, 17) block motifs. Work until piece measures 9¾ (10¾, 11¾, 12) in. - 25 (27.5, 30, 31) cm from beg. Sl st over 2 block motifs at right edge, work to last 2 blocks, turn and continue in block motif on the rem 10 (11, 12, 13) block motifs = 40 (44, 48, 52) sc. Work in sc until piece measures 6 (6¼, 6½, 7) in. - 15 (16, 17, 18) cm from beg of armhole. With the color of the next st, mark center 16 (16, 18, 18) sc. Then shape shoulder: sl st over 4 (5, 5, 6) sc, then work 8 (9, 10, 11) sc in block st. Ch 1 and turn. Work 4 (5, 5, 5) sc. Fasten off. Join yarn to 2nd armhole edge and work by rev shapings. Fasten off.

FRONT

Beg front same as back, but beg block motif with dark blue so that the block motif will continue when side seams are joined. Work same as back until armhole measures 4¾ (5, 5, 5½) in. - 12 (13, 13, 14) cm. Then shape neck: mark the center 8 (8, 10, 12) sc. Work sc at right edge as foll: work to 2 sc from marker. Turn, sl st over first st, work in block st to end of row. With right side facing, work to 1 sc from end of row. Ch 1, turn. Work sc to end of row. When armhole measures 6 (6¼, 6½, 7) in. - 15 (16, 17, 18) cm, work shoulder shapings same as back. Work 2nd half by rev shapings.

SLEEVES

With knitting needles and dark blue, cast on 40 (42, 46, 48) and work 1½ (1½, 2, 2) in. - 4 (4, 5, 5) cm in 1/1 ribbing. With crochet hook, work in 1 sc in each st of bound off row, then continue in block st, centering the pat as foll: 0 (1, 2, 3) sc in dark blue, 3 (4, 4, 4) sc in red, then work *4 sc in dark blue, 4 sc in red*, rep * to * across, end with 4 sc in dark blue, 3 (4, 4, 4) sc in red, 0 (1, 2, 3) sc in dark blue. Inc 1 sc at each edge of every 6th (6th, 8th, 8th) row 4 times. (For each inc, work 2 sc in each sc at edge.) You now have 48 (50, 54, 56) sc. When piece measures 10½ (11¾, 13, 14¼) in. - 27 (30, 33, 36) cm from beg, work 2 in. (5 cm) even, then fasten off.

FINISHING

Sew shoulder seams for 3/4 in. (2 cm) from armhole edges. Sew sleeves to armholes, matching center of sleeve with shoulder seams and sewing top 2 in. (5 cm) of sleeve seam to armhole edges of body. Sew side and sleeve seams. With knitting needles and dark blue, pick up and knit 21 (21, 23, 23) sts along back neck and work 2¾ in. (7 cm) in 1/1 ribbing. Bind off. With knitting needles and dark blue, pick up and knit 27 (27, 29, 31) sts along front neck and work 2¾ in. (7 cm) in 1/1 ribbing. Bind off. Fold neckband in half to inside and sl st in place. With crochet hook and dark blue, work 2 rows of sc along each back shoulder edge. On the front shoulder edge, make 4 buttonholes evenly spaced across row. For each buttonhole, ch 2 and skip 2 sts. Sew on buttons.

9¾ - 10¾ - 11¾ - 12¾
(25 - 27,5 - 30 - 32,5)

6¼ - 6½ - 6¾ - 7
(15 - 16 - 17 - 18)

7 - 8 - 9 - 9¼
(18 - 20,5 - 23 - 24)

2¾
(7)

13¾ - 14¾ - 15¾ - 16¾
(35 - 37,5 - 40 - 42,5)

FRONT-BACK

11¾ - 12¼ - 13¼ - 13¾
(30 - 31 - 33,5 - 35)

9 - 10¼ - 11 - 12¼
(23 - 26 - 28 - 31)

1½ - 1¾ - 2 - 2
(4 - 4 - 5 - 5)

9¾ - 10¼ - 11¼ - 11¾
(25 - 26 - 28,5 - 30)

SLEEVE

STEAL THE SHOW AT THE NEXT BABY SHOWER WITH THIS NURSERY RHYME SWEATER. THE SHEEP MOTIF IS SIMPLE TO MAKE.

NURSERY RHYME PULLOVER

SIZE

Child's size: 6 (9, 12, 18) months. Finished chest measurements: 21¼ (22, 22¾, 23½) in - 54 (56, 58, 60) cm, length 10¼ (10½, 11, 11½) in. - 26 (27, 28, 29) cm, sleeve seam 7 (7½, 8, 8¼) in. - 18 (19, 20, 21) cm.

MATERIALS

2 (2, 3, 3) skeins baby weight yarn (approx. 183 yds per 50 g skein) color light green, 2 skeins color light blue, 1 skein color white, small amount of light gray for eyes. Crochet hook U.S. size B/1 (U.K. size 12) (Metric size 2.5) or size needed to obtain gauge. Knitting needles U.S. size 1 (U.K. size 12) (Metric size 2.5). 6 buttons. **To save time, take time to check gauge!**

GAUGE

19 sc and 23½ rows = 4 in. (10 cm).

STITCHES

**Chain (ch),
single crochet (sc),
half double crochet (hdc),
slip stitch (sl st).**
Bobble: All in the same st: yo, insert hook and draw up loop 7 times, yo draw through all loops on hook.

SHEEP APPLIQUE

Ch 5, 1 sc in the 4th and 5th ch from hook = 1 foot, ch 12, 1 sc in the 4th and 5th ch from hook = 2nd foot.
Row 1: Ch 3, 1 bobble in the foot, *Ch 1, skip 1 ch, 1 bobble*, rep * to * 4 times, end with 1 dc. (The 5th bobble will come on top of the 2nd foot.)
Row 2: Ch 3, 1 bobble between the first ch and the bobble, *ch 1, 1 bobble between 2 bobbles of the previous row*, rep * to * 4 times, end with ch 1, 1 bobble between the last bobble and the dc, ch 1, 1 dc = 6 bobbles.
Row 3: Work same as the 2nd row, making 7 bobbles.
Row 4: Ch 3, 1 bobble between the first and the 2nd bobbles, *ch 1, 1 bobble between the next 2 bobbles*, work * to * 5 times = 6 bobbles. For the head, work 1 row of sc along the edge of the 4th, 3rd,and the 2nd rows,

turn. Ch 4, then insert hook in the first st and work 1 sc, then 1 dc in the foll sc, 1 hdc, 1 sc, then ch 7, 1 sc in the 3rd ch from the hook, 1 hdc, 2 dc, 1 sc = ear, 1 sc in each of the last 2 sc. **Row 5:** Ch 1, 5 bobbles worked between the 6 bobbles, working 1 dc between the bobbles instead of a ch 1 between the bobbles: 1 sc in the last dc of the border st of the 4th row, ch 7, 1 sc in the 7th ch from the hook, 3 sc. Break yarn and draw end through between the last bobble and the border st of the 4th row and sew to last 3 sc from the border st. Sew ears to body so they flap toward the front. Sheep may face left or right. Place ear on right side of work. Embroider an eye in gray. **1/1 ribbing: Row 1:** *K1, p1*. Rep * to * across. **Row 2 and all foll rows:** Work sts as established in previous row. **NOTE:** Worked entirely in sc. Beg each row with ch 2.

BACK

With crochet hook and green, ch 51 (53, 55, 57) + ch 2. **Row 1:** 1 sc in the 4th ch from the hook = 49 (51, 53, 55) sc + 1 border st at each edge = 51 (53, 55, 57) sts. Work even until piece measures 4¾ (5, 5¼, 5½) in. - 12.5 (13, 13.5, 14) cm. Continue in blue until piece measures 9 (9¼, 9¾, 10¼) in. - 23 (24, 25, 26) cm from beg. Fasten off.

FRONT

Work same as back until piece measures 8¼ (8½, 9, 9¼) in. - 21 (22, 23, 24) cm. Mark center 9 (9, 11, 11) sts. Work to first marker, sl over first st on foll row. Sl st over 1 st at neck edge, wrong side facing 3 times total. When piece measures 9½ (9¾, 10¼, 10½) in. - 24 (25, 26, 27) cm, fasten off. Join yarn to 2nd marker and work to correspond to first half, rev shapings.

SLEEVES

With crochet hook and green (green, blue, green), ch 28 (30, 32, 34) + 2 ch to turn. **Row 1:** Work 1 sc in the 4th ch from the hook, 26 (28, 30, 32) sc + 1 border st at each edge = 28 (30, 32, 34) sts. Continue in sc. At each edge of every 4th row, work 2 sc in each st 6 times. **At the same time,** change colors as foll: 2(4,

0, 1) row in green, *4 rows in blue, 4 rows in green*, work * to * 4 (4, 5, 5) times, then work 1 (2, 0, 1) row in blue. When sleeve measures 6 (6¼, 6½, 7) in. - 15 (16, 17, 18) cm, fasten off 40 (42, 44, 46) sc.

FINISHING

Block pieces to indicated measurements. Make 3 sheep and sew to fronts. Along the lower edge of sleeves, with knitting needles and green, pick up and knit 28 (30, 32, 34) sts and work 1¼ in. (3 cm) in 1/1 ribbing. Bind off. Along lower edge of front and back, pick up and knit 46 (50, 52, 54) sts and work 1¼ in. (3 cm) in 1/1 ribbing. Bind off. With crochet hook along the upper edge of back, work 1 row of sc in green. Along front neck edge, work 1 row of sc in blue. Along the front shoulders and neck, work 1 row of sc in green, making 3 buttonholes evenly spaced on each shoulder. For each buttonhole, ch 2 and skip 2 sc of previous row. Lap the front shoulders over the back and baste in place. Sew the sleeves to side seams, matching center of sleeve with shoulder seam. Sew the side and sleeve seams. Sew on buttons.

SLEEVE

8¼ - 8½ - 9 - 9¼
(21 - 22 - 23 - 24)

6 - 6¼ - 6½ - 7
(16 - 16 - 17 - 18)

5¾ - 6¼ - 6½ - 7
(14,5 - 15,6 - 17 - 18)

10½ - 11 - 11½ - 11¾
(27 - 28 - 29 - 30)

8 - 9¼ - 9¾ - 10¼
(23 - 24 - 25 - 26)

BACK

3¾ - 4 - 4 - 4¼   3½ - 3½ - 3½ - 3½   3¾ - 4 - 4 - 4¼
(9,5 - 10 - 10 - 10,5) (8 - 8 - 9 - 9) (9,5 - 10 - 10 - 10,5)

1¼
(3)

8¼ - 8½ - 9 - 9¼
(21 - 22 - 23 - 24)

10½ - 11 - 11½ - 11¾
(27 - 28 - 29 - 30)

FRONT

AUGUST AFTERNOONS
CALL FOR SUN-DRENCHED COTTONS. FILET CROCHET IS EASY TO MAKE, EVEN EASIER TO WEAR.

YELLOW FILET TOP

SIZE

Women's Small (Medium), bust 30-32 (33-35) in. - 76-81.5 (84-89) cm. Finished bust measurements: 39½ (42½) in. - 100 (110) cm, length 24½ in. (62 cm).

MATERIALS

8 (9) skeins "Neveda Valentine" (50% cotton, 50% acrylic - approx. 126 yds per 50 g skein) color yellow.
Crochet hook U.S. size F/5 (U.K. size 8) (Metric size 4) or size needed to obtain gauge. Knitting needles U.S. size 3 (U.K. size 10) (Metric size 3). **To save time, take time to check gauge!**

GAUGE

10 squares and 10 rows = 4 in. (10 cm).

STITCHES

Chain (ch), single crochet (sc), double crochet (dc), slip stitch (sl st) Filet stitch: Row 1: *1 Dc, ch 1*, rep * to * across. **Row 2 and all foll rows:**

Ch 4 to turn (beg of first square). Always work 1 dc in dc of previous row, ch above ch of previous row.
1/1 ribbing: Row 1: *K1, p1*. Rep * to * across. **Row 2 and all foll rows:** Work sts as established in previous row.

BACK

With knitting needles, cast on 76 (80) sts and work 2¾ in. (7 cm) in 1/1 ribbing. Bind off. With crochet hook, work sc in each bound off st across row, then work in filet st = 50 (55) squares. Work in filet st for 21½ in. (55 cm). Fasten off.

FRONT

Work same as back.

SLEEVES

Ch 81. Ch 4 to turn. Work in filet st, working first dc in 7th ch from hook = 40 squares. Work in filet st for 6 in. (15 cm). Fasten off.

FINISHING

Block pieces to indicated measurements. Sew shoulder seams, leaving center 9¾ in. (25 cm) open for neck. Sew the sleeves to side seams, matching center of sleeve with shoulder seams. Sew side and sleeve seams.

5 - 5¾   9¾   5 - 5¾
(12½)   (25)   (12½)

FRONT-BACK

21½
(55)

19¾ - 21¼
(50 (55))

2
(5)

6
(15)

15¾
(40)

SLEEVE

FESTIVE COLORS
CELEBRATE THE SUNSET IN
THIS SHOWOFF JACKET, AN
EXTRAVAGANT DISPLAY OF
JACQUARD CROCHET. LONG AND
LOOSE, IT'S STYLED FOR TOWN OR
TRAVEL.

JACQUARD JACKET

SIZE

Woman's Small (Medium, Large), bust 30-32 (33-35, 36-38) in. - 76-81.5 (84-89, 91.5-97) cm. Finished bust measurements: 42 (45, 47) in. - 106 (112, 118) cm, length: 27½ in. (70 cm), sleeve seam: 17 in. (43 cm).

MATERIALS

3 (4, 5) skeins kid mohair blend (approx. 135 yds per 50 gr skein) color dark green, 3 (3, 4) skeins color lilac, 2 (2, 3) skeins color dark rose, 2 skeins color light green, 1 skein each color purple, light rose and white. 8 buttons. Crochet hook U.S. size C/2 (U.K. size 11) (Metric size 3) or size needed to obtain gauge. Knitting needles U.S. size 6 (U.K. size 8) (Metric size 4). 8 buttons. **To save time, take time to check gauge!**

GAUGE

18 dc and 9 rows = 4 in. (10 cm).

STITCHES

**Chain (ch),
double crochet (dc),
slip stitch (sl st).
Bobble:** Work 5 dc in 1 st, keeping the last loop of each dc on hook, then draw the last loop through the first dc, yo and draw through the 2 loops.
Jacquard dc: Work in dc foll chart. Beg each row ch 3 which counts as first dc = border st. When changing colors, always work the last loop of 1 st with the color of the next st. Carry the yarn not in use loosely across wrong side of work, catching the yarn under the strand as you work in the new color.

Stockinette stitch: Knit 1 row on right side of work rows, purl 1 row on wrong side of work rows.
1/1 ribbing: Row 1: *K1, p1*. Rep * to * across.
Row 2 and all foll rows: Work sts as established in previous row.

BODY

With crochet hook and dark green, ch 187 (197, 207) + ch 3 (counts as first st). Work in dc foll jacquard chart. Center point A (B, A). Work the first dc in the 5th ch from hook. Work 36 rows of chart. [Piece will measure 15¾ in. (40 cm) from beg.]
Shape right front: Work 46 (48, 50) dc continuing in jacquard st. Shape raglans as foll: *work to last 2 sts, leave last 2 sts unworked, turn. Sl st over the first st of row*. Work * to * 3 times. Work the last dec on the 42nd row. Fasten off. Work the center 95 (101, 107) sts in jacquard st, working raglan dec at each edge of every row as foll: *sl st over 2 sts, work to last 2 sts, leave last 2 sts unworked, turn. Sl st over first st, work to last st, leave last st unworked, turn*, work * to * 3 times total. Fasten off after the 42nd row.
Work the last 46 (48, 50) sts as on right front, rev raglan shapings. Fasten off.

SLEEVES

With dark green, ch 43 (47, 51) + ch 3 (counts as first st). Work in dc by foll chart, centering point A of chart. At each edge of every 2nd row inc 1 dc 16 times. (For inc, work 2 dc in each edge st.) You now have 75 (79, 83) dc. Work 36 rows. [Piece will measure 15¾ in. (40 cm) from beg.] Shape raglans: At each edge of every row, dec as on back. After the last dec, fasten off.

YOKE

Sew raglan seams taking in 1 dc at each raglan edge. Work across in dc. You now have 255 (273, 291) dc + 1 border st at each edge. Continue by foll chart. Dec as foll:
Row 1: Dec 6 sts evenly spaced across row = 249 (267, 285) dc + 1 border st at each edge. **Row 2:** Work without dec. **Row 3:** Dec 18 (19, 20) sts by foll chart = 231 (248, 265) dc + 1 border st at each edge. **Rows 4 and 5:** Work without dec. **Row 6:** Dec 18 (19, 20) sts by foll chart = 213 (229, 245) dc + 1 border st at each edge. **Rows 7 and 8:** Work without dec. **Row 9:** Dec 36 (38, 40) sts by foll chart = 177 (191, 205) dc + 1 border st at each edge. **Row 10:** Work without dec. **Row 11:** Dec 36 (38, 40) sts by foll chart = 141 (153, 165) dc + 1 border st at each edge. **Row 12:** Work without dec. **Row 13:** Dec 36 (38, 40) dc by foll chart = 105 (115, 125) dc + 1 border st at each edge. **Rows 14 and 15:** Work without dec. **Row 16:** Dec 36 (38, 40) sts by foll chart = 69 (77, 85) sts + 1 border st at each edge. Fasten off.

FINISHING

With knitting needles and dark green, pick up and knit 70 (70, 86) sts around neck and work 1¼ in. (3 cm) of 1/1 ribbing. Bind off loosely. With knitting needles and dark green, pick up and knit 43 (47, 51) sts from lower edge of sleeves and work 1¼ in. (3 cm) of 1/1 ribbing. Bind off loosely. Sew side seams. With knitting needles and dark green, pick up and knit 187 (197, 207) sts along lower edge of body and work 2½ in. (6 cm) of 1/1 ribbing. Bind off loosely. With knitting needles and dark green, pick up and knit 130 sts along left front edge and work 1½ in. (3.5 cm) of 1/1 ribbing. Bind off loosely. Work same border on right front, but when border measures 1/2 in. (1.5 cm), make buttonholes as foll: beg at neck edge, work 2 sts, k2 tog, yo, *work 15 sts, k2 tog, yo*, work * to * 7 times, work 7 sts. Sew front border seams. Sew on buttons.

KEY TO CHART

- |•| = dark green
- |o| = light green
- ⌣ = dark pink
- ⊞ = light pink
- ◣ = purple
- ◢ = lilac
- |·| = white
- ◪ = bobble with purple
- ⊞ = bobble with light green

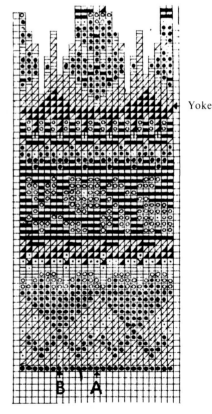

Yoke

When a square no longer is indicated on yoke, it indicates 1 decrease.

PIECES

SLEEVE

★★

SENSATIONAL

SPORTY BOATNECK TEAM
EMPLOYS ARROWHEAD STITCHES.
THESE SWEATERS ARE ALWAYS
READY FOR THE ACTIVE LIFE.

ARROWHEAD BOATNECK

SIZE

Woman's Small (Medium, Large), bust 30-32 (33-35, 36-38) in. - 76-81.5 (84-89, 91.5-97) cm. Finished bust measurements: 41½ (45¾ 47½) in. - 106 (114, 121) cm, length: 23½ in. (60 cm), sleeve seam: 17¼ in. (44 cm).

MATERIALS

6 (7, 7) skeins "Scheepjeswol Voluma" (85% acrylic, 15% kid mohair - approx. 209 yds per 50 g skein) color dark blue, 2 skeins color blue and 1 skein color light blue.
Crochet hook U.S. size E/4 (U.K. size 9) (Metric size 3.5) or size needed to obtain gauge. Knitting needles U.S. size 3 (U.K. size 10) (Metric size 3).
To save time, take time to check gauge!

GAUGE

19 hdc and 14 rows = 4 in. (10 cm).

STITCHES

**Chain (ch),
single crochet (sc),
half double crochet (hdc),
slip stitch (sl st).**

Jacquard hdc: Work in hdc by foll chart. Beg each row with ch 2 (counts as first hdc). When changing colors, work the last st in 1 color with the color of next st. Carry the yarn not in use loosely across wrong side of work, catching the yarn under the strand as you work in the new color.
1/1 ribbing: Row 1: *K1, p1*. Rep * to * across.
Row 2 and all foll rows: Work sts as established in previous row.

BACK

With crochet hook and dark blue, ch 103 (110, 117) + ch 2 (counts as first hdc). **Row 1:** wrong side of work: 1 hdc in the 4th ch from the hook, 1 hdc in each ch = 103 (110, 117) hdc. **Row 2:** right side of work: *2 hdc in light blue, 1 hdc in dark blue*, rep * to *. Continue in jacquard hdc foll chart, working between points B and D. Then work dot pattern by rep rows between D and E for 34 rows, beg and end with 1 row of light blue dots, then work from point E to point H. Piece will measure 21½ in. (55 cm) with 77 rows. Fasten off.

FRONT

Work same as back.

SLEEVES

With dark blue, ch 56 (60, 64) + ch 2 (counts as first hdc). Work jacquard hdc by centering the chart and work from point A to point D. Work 30 rows of dot pattern (point D to E). The piece will measure about 11¾ in. (30 cm). Then work 12 rows from point E to point F, end with 1 row of light blue dots. **At the same time,** inc 1 st at each edge of every 4th row 13 times (work 2 hdc in each edge st) = 82 (86, 90) hdc. Piece will measure about 15¼ in. (39 cm) from beg. Fasten off.

FINISHING

Block pieces to indicated measurements. Sew shoulder seams, leaving center 9 (9¼, 9¾) in. - 23 (24, 25) cm open for neck. Work 1 row of sc in dark blue around neck. Fasten off. With knitting needles and dark blue, pick up and knit 46 (48, 50) sts along lower edge of each sleeve and work 2 in. (5 cm) in 1/1 ribbing. Bind off loosely. With knitting needles and dark blue, pick up and knit 96 (100, 104) sts along lower edge of back and work 2 in. (5 cm) in 1/1 ribbing. Bind off loosely. Knit same ribbing along lower edge of front. Sew sleeves to side seams, matching center of sleeve with shoulder seam. Sew side and sleeve seams.

CHILD'S ARROWHEAD BOATNECK

SIZE

Child's size 4 (6, 8, 10) years, chest 23 (25, 27, 28½) in. - 58.5 (63.5, 69, 72.5) cm. Finished chest measurements: 24½ (27, 30½, 33) in. - 62 (69, 77, 84) cm, length: 14 (15¼, 16½, 17¼) in. - 36 (39, 42, 44) cm, sleeve seam: 10½ (11¾, 13, 14) in. - 27 (30, 33, 36) cm.

MATERIALS

3 (4, 4, 5) skeins "Scheepjeswol Voluma" (85% acrylic, 15% kid mohair - approx. 209 yds per 50 g skein) color dark blue, 2 skeins color blue and 1 skein color light blue.
Crochet hook U.S. size E/4 (U.K. size 9) (Metric size 3.5) or size needed to obtain gauge. Knitting needles U.S. size 3 (U.K. size 10) (Metric size 3).
To save time, take time to check gauge!

GAUGE

19 hdc and 14 rows = 4 in. (10 cm).

STITCHES

**Chain (ch),
single crochet (sc),
half double crochet (hdc),
slip stitch (sl st).**

Jacquard hdc: Work in hdc by foll chart. Beg each row with ch 2 (counts as first hdc). When changing colors, work the last stitch of the last stitch of 1 color with the color of next stitch. Carry the yarn not in use loosely across wrong side of work, catching the yarn under the strand as you work in the new color.
1/1 ribbing: Row 1: *K1, p1*. Rep * to * across.
Row 2 and all foll rows: Work sts as established in previous row.

BACK

With crochet hook and dark blue, ch 61 (68, 75, 82) + ch 2 (counts as first hdc). **Row 1:** Beg at point B (wrong side of work): 1 hdc in the 4th ch from hook, 1 hdc in each ch = 61 (68, 75, 82) hdc. **Row 2:** right side of work: work jacquard hdc by foll chart from point A to D, then work in dot pattern working from D to E [working stripe pattern foll chart 14 (18, 22, 26) rows, beg and end with 1 stripe of light blue]. Then work point E to G. You now have 45 (49, 53, 57) rows total and piece measures about 12½ (13¾, 15, 16) in. - 32 (35, 38, 40.5) cm. Fasten off.

FRONT

Work same as back.

5-5½-6-6¼
(13-14-15-16)

12¼-13½-15¼-16½
(31-34,5-38,5-42)
12¼-13¾-15¼-16½
(32-35-38-40,5)

FRONT-BACK

10¼-11¼-12-13¾
(26-28,5-30,5-32,5)

8-8¼-8½-9
(20-21-22-23)

9-9¼-9-9¾
(23-24-25)

21½
(55)

20¾-22½-23¾
(53-57-60,5)

SLEEVE

16½-17¼-18
(42-44-46)

15¼
(39)

11¼-12-12¾
(28,5-30,5-32,5)

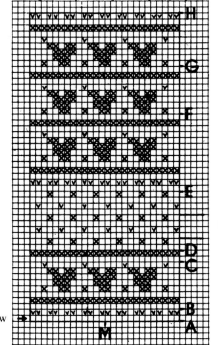

first row

repeat

SLEEVES

With crochet hook and dark blue, ch 40 (42, 44, 46) + ch 2 (counts as first hdc). Work jacquard hdc by centering chart. Work from point C to point D, then work 18 (22, 26, 30) rows of dot pattern D to E until piece is about 5½ (6½, 8, 9) in. - 14 (17, 20, 23) cm from beg, then work point E to F, ending with dark blue row. **At the same time,** inc 1 st at each edge of every 4th row 0 (1, 2, 3) times, inc 1 st at each edge of every 5th row 6 times. (For each inc, work 2 hdc in each edge st.) You now have 52 (56, 60, 64) hdc and piece will measure about 9 (9¾, 11½, 12½) in. - 23 (26, 29, 32) cm from beg. Fasten off.

FINISHING

Block pieces to indicated measurements. Sew shoulder seams, leaving center 5 (5½, 6, 6¼) in. - 13 (14, 15, 16) cm open for neck. With crochet hook and dark blue, work 1 row of sc around neck. Fasten off. With knitting needles and dark blue, pick up and knit 32 (32, 34, 36) sts along lower edge of sleeve. Work 1½ in. (4 cm) in 1/1 ribbing. Bind off loosely. With knitting needles and dark blue, pick up and knit 58 (60, 62, 64) sts along lower edge of back. Work 1½ in. (4 cm) in 1/1 ribbing. Bind off loosely. Knit same ribbing on front. Sew sleeves to armholes, matching center of sleeve with shoulder seams. Sew side and sleeve seams.

JACQUARD PULLOVER

SIZE

Woman's Medium/Large, bust 33-38 in. (84-97 cm). Finished bust measurement: 46½ in. (118 cm), length 24 in. (61 cm), sleeve seam 17¾ in. (45 cm).

MATERIALS

5 skeins mohair yarn (approx. 135 yds per 50 g skein) color black, 3 skeins color light yellow and 2 skeins color light pink.
Crochet hook U.S. size H/8 (U.K. size 6) (Metric size 3.5). Knitting needles U.S. size 10 (U.K. size 4) (Metric size 6) or size needed to obtain gauge.
To save time, take time to check gauge!

GAUGE

11 hdc and 10 rows = 4 in. (10 cm).

STITCHES

Chain (ch), single crochet (sc), half double crochet (hdc), slip stitch (sl st).
Jacquard hdc: Work in hdc by foll chart using single strand of yarn. The border sts are not shown on chart. Work border sts in the same color as the adjacent yarn. Beg each row with ch 2 which counts as the first hdc. When chancing colors, work the last loop of the last st with the color of the next st. Hold the unused yarn against wrong side of work. When inserting hook, work around the unused yarn so that the new sts hold it against the work.
1/1 ribbing: Use double strand of yarn for knitting borders. **Row 1:** *K1, p1*. Rep * to * across.
Row 2 and all foll rows: Work sts as established in previous row.

BACK

With knitting needles and double strand of black, cast on 66 sts and work 2 in. (5 cm) of 1/1 ribbing. Bind off loosely.
With crochet hook and single strand, work 1 row of hdc in bound off row, by foll jacquard chart, inc 1 hdc on first row = 67 hdc. Work even foll jacquard chart for 56 rows - 22 in. (56 cm). The total length from beg is 24 in. (61 cm). Fasten off.

FRONT

Work same as back until piece measures 20 in. (51 cm) - 51 rows of jacquard chart. Mark the center 13 sts. Continue jacquard hdc. Work to first marker, ch 2, turn. Work 1 row, ch 2, turn, then work to 3 hdc before marker, leave 3 hdc unworked. Turn, sl st over 2 hdc, ch 2. Work to end of row, ch 2, turn. Work to last hdc, turn, leave last hdc unworked, sl st over 1 hdc. Work to end of row = 56 rows of jacquard chart. Fasten off. Join yarn to 2nd marker, work to end of row. Ch 2, turn, work to last 3 hdc, leave 3 hdc unworked. Turn, sl st over first 2 hdc, ch 2, work to end of row. Then work to last hdc, leave last hdc unworked. Turn, sl st over first hdc, ch 2, continue to end of row. Fasten off.

SLEEVES

With knitting needles and double strand of black, cast on 30 sts and work 2 in. (5 cm) of 1/1 ribbing. Bind off loosely.
With crochet hook and single strand, work hdc in bound off row, by centering jacquard chart, and inc 1 hdc on first row (work 31 hdc + 1 border st at each edge) = 33 hdc. Inc 1 hdc in edge st of every 3rd row 10 times. Inc 1 hdc at each edge of every 4th row, twice = 57 hdc. To inc, work 2 hdc in each edge st. Continue until sleeve measures 17¾ in. (45 cm) from beg. Fasten off.

FINISHING

Block pieces to indicated measurements. Sew 1 shoulder seam. With knitting needles and double strand of black, pick up and knit about 54 sts around neck and work 1½ in. (4 cm) of 1/1 ribbing. Bind off loosely. Sew 2nd shoulder and neckband seam. Sew sleeves to side seams, matching center of sleeve with shoulder seam. Sew side and sleeve seams.

FRONT-BACK   **SLEEVE**

6½ (17)   9¾ (25)   6½ (17)

22 (56)   2 (5)

23¼ (59)

19¾ (50)

15¾ (40)   2 (5)

11 (28)

KEY TO CHART
☐ = dark blue
☑ = light blue
☒ = blue

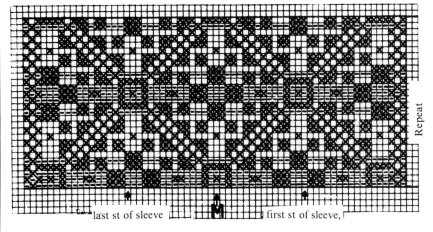

last st of sleeve   first st of sleeve,   Repeat

KEY TO CHART
☒ = black
☐ = yellow
⊟ = pink

41

LUXURIOUS MOHAIR ADDS A SOFT TOUCH TO ANY GARMENT. HERE, BLACK HAS BEEN SUPERIMPOSED ON THE PALEST PINK AND YELLOW FOR A STYLISH EFFECT.

FANCIFUL INTERACTION OF BLUES AND GREEN GIVES THESE JACQUARD PLAID SWEATERS THEIR COLORFUL APPEAL.

CHILD'S JACQUARD CARDIGAN

SIZE

Child's size 8 (10, 12) years, chest 27 (28½, 30) - 69 (72.5, 76) cm. Finished chest measurements: 34 (36¼, 38¾) in. - 86 (92, 97) cm, length: 18 (19¼, 20¼) in. - 46 (49, 51) cm, sleeve seam: 13¼ (14, 15¼) in. - 34 (36, 39) cm.

MATERIALS

3 (4, 4) skeins bulky weight mohair yarn (approx. 110 yds per 50 g skein) color blue, 3 (3, 4) skeins color green and 2 skeins color turquoise. Crochet hook U.S. size H / 8 (U.K. size 6) (Metric size 5) or size needed to obtain gauge. Knitting needles U.S. size 8 (U.K. size 6) (Metric size 5). 5 wooden buttons. **To save time, take time to check gauge!**

GAUGE

11½ hdc and 9 rows = 4 in. (10 cm).

STITCHES

Chain (ch), half double crochet (hdc), slip stitch (sl st).
Jacquard hdc: Work in hdc by foll chart. When changing colors, work the last loop of the last st with the color of the next st. Hold the unused yarn against the wrong side of work. When inserting

KEY TO CHART

☒ = dark blue
⊡ = light blue
☐ = blue

hook, work around the unused yarn so that the new sts hold it against the work. Work the border sts in the same color as the adjacent st in pat. Ch 2 at the beg of each row (= 1 border st).
1/1 ribbing: Row 1: *K1, p1*. Rep * to * across.
Row 2 and all foll rows: Work sts as established in previous row.

BODY

With knitting needles and green, cast on 110 (116, 122) sts and work 1 in. (2.5 cm) in 1/1 ribbing, then make 1 buttonhole 3 sts from right edge. Bind off 2 sts, work to end of row. On foll row, cast on 2 sts over bound off sts. Continue in ribbing until ribbing measures 2 in. (5 cm) from beg. Place 7 sts at each edge on a holder. Bind off rem sts. With crochet hook, work 96 (102, 108) hdc across bound off sts of ribbing foll chart, inc 1 hdc at each edge for border sts. (For inc, work 2 hdc in

each edge st) Work to armholes on chart - 10¾ (11½, 12) in. - 27 (29, 30.5) cm from beg. Now work in 3 parts. Work the first 24 (25, 26) hdc for right front. Inc 1 st at armhole edge for border st. Work 12 (13, 14) rows over these 25 (26, 27) hdc until piece measures 16 (17¼, 18) in. - 40.5 (43.5, 46) cm from beg, then shape neck. At right edge, sl st over 3 sts, work to end of row, turn. Work to last 2 sts, turn, leave 2 sts unworked. Sl st over first st and work to end of row, turn. Work to last st, turn, leaving last st unworked = 18 (19, 20) hdc. After the 37th (40th, 42nd) row from ribbing,

fasten off. Skip 3 sts from right front and work the foll 44 (48, 52) hdc for the back by foll chart, inc 1 st at each edge for border sts = 46 (50, 54) hdc. Work even to same height as right front. Fasten off. Skip 3 sts from back and work left front same as right front, rev shapings.

PIECES

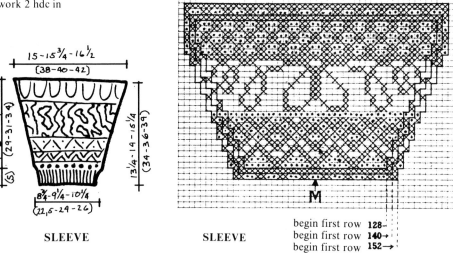

begin first row **128→**
begin first row **140→**
begin first row **152→**

SLEEVE

PIECES

begin first row **128→**
begin first row **140→**
begin first row **152→**

SLEEVES

With knitting needles and green, cast on 28 (30, 32) sts and work 2 in. (5 cm) in 1/1 ribbing. Bind off. With crochet hook, work 26 (28, 30) hdc + 1 border st at each edge from bound off sts of ribbing. Work by foll chart for sleeve. Inc 1 st at each edge of every 2nd row once, inc 1 st at each edge of every 3rd row once (= 2 inc every 3 rows at each edge). (For each inc, work 2 hdc in each edge st.) Work until you have 46 (48, 50) hdc and 26 (28, 31) rows. Fasten off. Piece will measure 13¼ (14, 15¼) in. - 34 (36, 39) cm.

FINISHING

Block pieces to indicated measurements. Front bands: With knitting needles and green, pick up 7 sts from left front holder and inc 1 st at inner edge and work in 1/1 ribbing. Work until band fits to neck. Place 7 sts on holder, dec border st. Work same band on right front, but make 3 buttonholes evenly spaced along band, allowing for 5th buttonhole on neckband. (Space buttonholes about 3¾ (4, 4¼) in. - 9.5 (10, 10.5) cm apart.) Sew bands to fronts. Sew shoulder seams. With knitting needles and green, pick up 53 (55, 57) sts around neck, including sts on holders and work 1/2 in. (1.5 cm) in 1/1 ribbing. Make 1 buttonhole above previous ones. Complete band until it measures 1¼ in. (3 cm) from beg. Bind off loosely. Sew sleeves to armholes, matching center of sleeve with shoulder seams. Sew side and sleeve seams. Reinforce buttonholes and sew on buttons.

CHILD'S PLAID CARDIGAN

SIZE

Child's size 8 (10, 12) years, chest 27 (28½, 30) - 69 (72.5, 76) cm. Finished chest measurements: 34 (36¼, 38¾) in. - 86 (92, 98) cm, length: 19¼ (20¾, 22½) in. - 49 (53, 57) cm, sleeve seam: 13 (14½, 16) in. - 33 (37, 41) cm.

MATERIALS

4 (5, 5) skeins bulky weight mohair yarn (approx. 110 yds per 50 g skein) color green, 3 (3, 4) skeins color blue, and 1 (2, 2) skeins color turquoise. Crochet hook U.S. size K/10 (U.K. size 2) (Metric size 7) or size needed to obtain gauge. Knitting needles U.S. size 10 (U.K. size 4) (Metric size 6). 5 wooden buttons. **To save time, take time to check gauge!**

GAUGE

9½ dc and 7½ rows = 4 in. (10 cm).
1 motif between stripes = 4 in. (10 cm).

STITCHES

Chain (ch), double crochet (dc), slip stitch (sl st).
Pattern stripes: Always use double strand. Beg each row with ch 3 (border st) and end with 1 dc in the 3rd ch of the turning ch of previous row (border st). When

changing colors, work the last st of one color with color of the next st. Work as foll: *3 rows green, 2 rows blue, 2 rows turquoise, 2 rows blue, 3 rows green*, rep * to *.
Vertical lines: Work between the horizontal sts by slip stitching with double strand of yarn. Insert hook from front to back between sts, yo and pull through loop, insert hook in next row and continue as before. Beg at lower edge and work to top edge of each piece. Beg at center back, work as foll: 3 lines green, *2 lines blue, 2 lines turquoise, 2 lines blue, 6 lines green*, rep * to *.
1/1 ribbing: Row 1: *K1, p1*. Rep * to * across.
Row 2 and all foll rows: Work sts as established in previous row.

BODY

Worked in 1 piece, using double strand throughout. With knitting needles and double strand of blue, cast on 89 (95, 101) sts and work 1 in. (2.5 cm) of 1/1 ribbing. At right edge, work 2 sts, bind off 2 sts, work to end of row. On foll row, cast on 2 sts over bound off sts. Continue in ribbing until piece measures 2 in. (5 cm). Place 5 sts at each edge on holder. Bind off rem sts. With crochet hook and double strand of green, work 79 (85, 91) dc across bound off sts of ribbing and work in stripe pat, inc 1 st at each edge

for border sts = 81 (87, 93) sts, leave last 2 sts unworked. Work 11¼ (12½, 13¾) in. - 29 (32, 34.5) cm from beg - 18 (20, 22) rows from top of ribbing. Now work in 3 parts. Work the first 21 (22, 23) sts for right front. Inc 1 st at armhole edge for border st. Work over these 22 (23, 24) sts for 11 (12, 13) rows, then shape neck. At right edge, sl st over 4 sts, work to end of row, turn. Work to last 2 sts. Sl st over first st and work to end of row, turn. Work to last st, turn, leaving last st unworked. After the 33rd (36th, 39th) row from ribbing, fasten off. Work the last 21 (22, 23) sts for right front by rev shapings. Work the center 39 (43, 47) sts in stripe pat, inc 1 st at each edge = 41 (45, 49) sts. Continue until piece measures same as front shoulders. Fasten off.

SLEEVES

With knitting needles and double strand of blue, cast on 25 (25, 27) sts and work 2 in. (5 cm) in 1/1 ribbing. Bind off. With crochet hook work 23 (23, 25) dc + 1 border st at each edge from bound off sts of ribbing. Work in stripe pat. Inc 1 st at each edge of every 3rd row 7 (8, 8) times. (For each inc, work 2 hdc in each edge st.) You now have 39 (41, 43) sts and 21 (24, 27) rows. Fasten off. Piece will measure 13 (14½, 16) in. -33 (37, 41) cm.

FINISHING

Block pieces to indicated measurements. Work vertical lines on body, beg at center back (3 rows green at center). Work vertical lines on each sleeve. Front bands: With knitting needles and double strand of blue, pick up 5 sts from left front holder and inc 1 st at inner edge and work in 1/1 ribbing. Work until band fits to neck. Place 5 sts on holder, dec border st. Work same band on right front, but make 3 buttonholes evenly spaced along band, allowing for 5th buttonhole on neckband. [Space buttonholes about 4 (4¼, 4¾) in. - 10 (11, 12) cm apart.] Sew bands to fronts. Sew shoulder seams. With knitting needles and green, pick up and knit 57 (59, 61) sts total around neck, including sts on holder and work 1/2 in. (1.5 cm) in 1/1 ribbing. Make 1 buttonhole above previous ones. Complete band until it measures 1¼ in. (3 cm) from beg. Bind off loosely. Sew sleeves to armholes, matching center of sleeve with shoulder seams. Sew side and sleeve seams. Reinforce buttonholes and sew on buttons.

PIECES

SLEEVE

FASHION YOUR

SWEATERS INTO CONTEMPORARY
WORKS OF ART. EBONY PLAYS
AGAINST PASTEL BLUE AND
YELLOW FOR UNEXPECTED
DRAMA.

ARTWORK
JACQUARD
JACKET

SIZE

Woman's Small
(Medium, Large), bust
30-32 (33-35, 36-38) in. -
76-81.5 (84-89, 91.5-97)
cm. Finished bust
measurements: 43¼ (46,
49¼) in. - 110 (117, 125)
cm, length: 24½ in.
(62 cm), sleeve seam:
17¼ in. (44 cm).

MATERIALS

7 skeins sport weight
mohair (approx. 135 yds
per 50 g skein) color
black, 4 skeins color light
yellow and 2 skeins color
light blue.
Crochet hook U.S. size
H/8 (U.K. size 6) (Metric
size 5) or size needed to
obtain gauge. Knitting
needles U.S. size 10 (U.K.
size 4) (Metric size 6). 5
buttons. **To save time,
take time to check gauge!**

GAUGE

14½ hdc and 10 rows = 4
in. (10 cm).

STITCHES

**Chain (ch),
single crochet (sc),
half double crochet (hdc),
slip stitch (sl st).
Jacquard hdc:** Work in
hdc by foll chart using
single strand of yarn. The
border sts are not shown
on chart. Beg each row
with ch 2 which counts as
first hdc (= border). Work
the border sts in the same
color as the adjacent st in
pat. When changing
colors, work the last loop
of the last st with the
color of the next st. Hold
the unused yarn against
the wrong side of work.
When inserting hook,
work around the unused
yarn so that the new sts
hold it against the work.

1/1 ribbing: Use double
strand of yarn for knitted
borders. **Row 1:** *K1,
p1*. Rep * to * across.
Row 2 and all foll rows:
Work sts as established in
previous row.
NOTE: The body is
worked in 1 piece. All
jacquard is worked with a
single strand of yarn and
the ribbing is worked
with a double strand of
yarn.

BODY

With knitting needles and
double strand of black,
cast on 139 (147, 155) sts
and work in 1/1 ribbing.
When ribbing measures 1
in. (2.5 cm), make 1
buttonhole 3 sts from
right edge of work. For
buttonhole, bind off 2 sts.
On foll row, cast on 2 sts
over bound off sts. When
ribbing measures 2 in. (5
cm), place 7 sts at each
edge on stitch holders and
bind off rem sts. With
crochet hook and single
strand, work 2 hdc in first
st of center 125 (133, 141)
sts, work in hdc across sts
by foll jacquard chart, inc
29 (32, 35) sts evenly
spaced across the first
row, end with 2 hdc in
last st. For each inc, work
2 hdc in 1 st of bound off
row = 156 (167, 178) hdc.
Work by foll chart for 31
(30, 30) rows. Piece will
measure 14¼ (13¾, 13¾)

in. - 36 (35, 35) cm from
beg.
Divide work as foll for
armholes: work first 36
(39, 42) sts for right front,
working 2 hdc in last st =
37 (40, 43) sts. Work for
19 (20, 20) rows by foll
chart. The armhole will
measure 7½ (8, 8) in. - 19
(20, 20) cm. Shape neck:
with right side facing, sl st
over 3 (3, 4) sts, ch 2,
work hdc to end of row.
On foll row, work to last
2 sts from end, leave last
2 sts unworked, turn. Sl
st over 1 (2, 2) sts, ch 2
and work hdc to end of
row. On foll row, work to
last st from end, leave last
st unworked, turn. Sl st
over 1 st, ch 2, work to
end of row. Work to last
st from end, leave last st
unworked. Turn, work
rem 28 (30, 32) sts until
armhole measures 10¼
(10½, 10½) in. - 26 (27,
27) cm. Fasten off. (Note:
you will have worked 57
rows of chart - 3 repeats.)
Skip 5 hdc from the right
front and work in hdc
over 74 (79, 84) sts for the
back by foll chart, inc 1 st
at each edge for border
sts = 76 (81, 86) hdc.
Work until armhole
measures 10¼ (10½, 10½)
in. - 26 (27, 27) cm.
Fasten off.
Skip 5 hdc from back and
work in hdc over the last
36 (39, 42) hdc, inc 1 st at

armhole edge = 37 (40,
43) hdc by foll chart until
piece measures 7½ (8, 8)
in. - 19 (20, 20) cm. Shape
neck: Work to last 3 (3, 4)
sts, leave these sts
unworked, turn. Sl st
over 2 sts, ch 2 and work
in hdc to end of row.
Work next row to last 1
(2, 2) sts, leave 1 (2, 2) sts
unworked, turn, sl st over
1 st, ch 2, work to end of
row. Turn, ch 2, work to
last st on row, leave last
st unworked, turn, work
to end of row. Turn, ch 2,
work to last st, leave st
unworked. Turn, work
rem 28 (30, 32) sts until
armhole measures 10¼
(10½, 10½) in. - 26 (27,
27) cm. Fasten off.

SLEEVES

With knitting needles and
double strand of black
cast on 28 (30, 32) sts and
work 2 in. (5 cm) of 1/1
ribbing. Bind off loosely.
With crochet hook and
single strand, work hdc in
sts of bound off row by
centering jacquard chart,
inc 19 sts evenly spaced
across row = 47 (49, 51)
hdc. *Inc 1 hdc (work 2
hdc in each edge st) at
each edge of every 2nd
row once, inc 1 hdc at
each edge of every 3rd
row once*, rep * to * 7
times. Inc 1 hdc at each
edge of every 2nd row
once = 77 (79, 81) hdc.
Work until sleeve
measures 18¼ in. - (46
cm) from beg. Fasten off.

20¼ - 20¾ - 21½
(51,5 - 53 - 54,5)

SLEEVE

16¼
(41)

2
(5)

12¼ - 12½ - 13
(31 - 32 - 33,5)

KEY TO CHART

☐ = light yellow
⊡ = black
⊠ = light blue

Repeat

first row

Repeat

2¼ - 2¾ - 3   7 - 7½ - 8   1¼   20 - 21½ - 22¾   1¼   7 - 7½ - 8   2¼ - 2¾ - 3
(6 -7-7,5) (18-19-20,5) (3,5)   (51 - 54,5 - 58)   (3,5) (18-19-20,5) (6-7-7,5)

2¼
(7)

7¼
(19)

10¼ - 10½ - 11
(26 - 27 - 28)

2
(5)

12¼ - 11¾ - 11¾
(31 - 30 - 30)

½
(4)

4¾ - 44½ - 47½
(106 -113,5 - 121)

½
(4)

PIECES

FINISHING

With knitting needles and double strand of black, pick up 7 sts from left front and inc 1 st at inside edge and work until band, slightly stretched, reaches to neck, slightly stretched. Place sts on holder. Work same band along right front, evenly spacing 3 buttonholes as on lower ribbing along the band. [The last buttonhole will be on neckband. Buttonholes will be spaced about 5¼ in. (13.5 cm) apart.] Block pieces to indicated measurements. Sew bands to fronts. Sew shoulder seams. With knitting needles and double strand of black, pick up and knit about 71 (75, 79) sts along neck edge, including the sts from front bands. Work in 1/1 ribbing. When ribbing measures 3/4 in. (2 cm), make the 5th buttonhole above the previous buttonholes. When band measures 1½ in. (4 cm) bind off. Set in sleeves. Sew side and sleeve seams. Reinforce buttonholes. Sew on buttons.

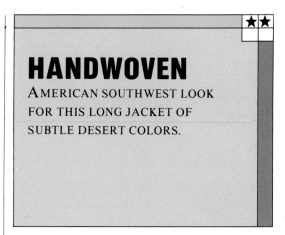

HANDWOVEN

AMERICAN SOUTHWEST LOOK FOR THIS LONG JACKET OF SUBTLE DESERT COLORS.

DESERT JACKET

For the woven look, work the thin strand around a thick strand. During the work, on every row, lay the thick strands along the top of the underlying row and crochet by inserting hook under the thick strand. Be sure to have the turning of the thick yarn showing on the wrong side of work. Check your gauge as you work.

SIZE

Woman's Small (Medium, Large), bust 33-35 (36-38, 39-42) in. - 84-89 (91.5-97) cm. Finished bust measurements: 44 (47, 50½) in. - 112 (120, 128) cm, length: 31½ in. (80 cm), sleeve seam 15 in. (38 cm).

MATERIALS

8 (9, 10) skeins fingering weight alpaca yarn (approx. 206 yds per 50 g skein) color ecru and 9 (9, 10) skeins bulky yarn (approx. 110 yds per 50 g skein) color ecru. Crochet hook U.S. size B/1 (U.K. size 12) (Metric size 2.5) or size needed to obtain gauge. Circular or double pointed knitting needles U.S. size 9 (U.K. size 5) (Metric size 5.5). **To save time, take time to check gauge!**

GAUGE

9 squares (1 sc + ch 3) and 11 rows = 4 in. (10 cm).

STITCHES

Chain (ch), single crochet (sc), slip stitch (sl st). 1/1 ribbing: Row 1: *K1, p1*. Rep * to * across. Row 2 and all foll rows: Work sts as established in previous row.

BACK

With alpaca, ch 204 (220, 236) and work in woven crochet st. Lay 3 strands of bulky yarn on the ch row and crochet around them with alpaca and work in pat st. **Row 1:** 1 sc in the 3rd ch from hook, *ch 3, skip 3, 1 sc in the foll ch*, rep * to *, end with 1 sc in the last ch = 50 (54, 58) squares and 1 border st at each edge. **Row 2:** Ch 2 (border st), 1 sc in the foll sc, *ch 3, 1 sc in the ch-3 sp,* rep * to *, end with ch 1, 1 sc in the foll sc, 1 sc in the turning of the thick yarn (border st). Always rep row 2. Work until piece measures 31½ in. (80 cm) from beg, then fasten off.

POCKET

With alpaca, ch 68 (72, 76) and work in pat st = 16 (17, 18) squares + 1 border st at each edge. When piece measures 9¾ in. (25 cm), fasten off. Make 2.

RIGHT FRONT

With alpaca, ch 104 (112, 120), then work in pat st. After the first row, you will have 25 (27, 29) squares + 1 border st at each edge. Work even until piece measures 11¾ in. (30 cm). On foll row, work 4 (5, 5) squares, skip 16 (17, 18) squares, then substitute the squares of pocket (leaving border sts unworked), work rem 5 (5, 6) squares. Continue for 31½ in. (80 cm), then fasten off.

LEFT FRONT

Work same as right front, rev placement of pocket.

SLEEVES

With alpaca, ch 96 (104, 112) then work in pat st = 23 (25, 27) squares + 1 border st at each edge of first row. At beg of each row, inc 1 st 16 times. Inc 1 st at beg of every 4th and 5th row 5 times. Work inc as foll: at beg of 2nd row, ch 5, 1 sc in the 3rd ch from hook, ch 1, skip 1 ch, 1 sc in the foll ch, ch 3, 1 sc around the foll ch-sp and continue across as on row 3 of pat. Inc at the beg of 3rd row: ch 5, 1 sc in the 3rd ch from the hook, ch 3, skip 1 sc, 1 sc, ch 3, 1 sc around the ch-sp, continue across as on row 3 of pat. Work inc sts = 49 (51, 53) squares + 1 border st at each edge until piece measures 15 in. (38 cm) from beg. Fasten off.

FINISHING

Block pieces to indicated measurements. Sew shoulder seams over 7½ (8, 8¼) in. - 19 (20, 21) cm from armhole edge. Sew sleeves to side seams, matching center of sleeve with shoulder seam. Sew side and sleeve seam. Sew pocket lining in place.

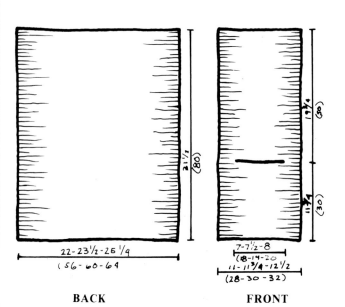

22-23½-25¼
(56-60-64)

BACK

19¾
(30)

7-7½-8
(18-19-20)
11-11¾-12½
(28-30-32)

FRONT

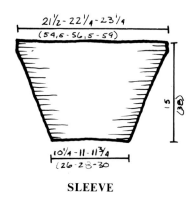

21½-22¼-23¼
(54.5-56.5-59)

15
(38)

10¼-11-11¾
(26-28-30)

SLEEVE

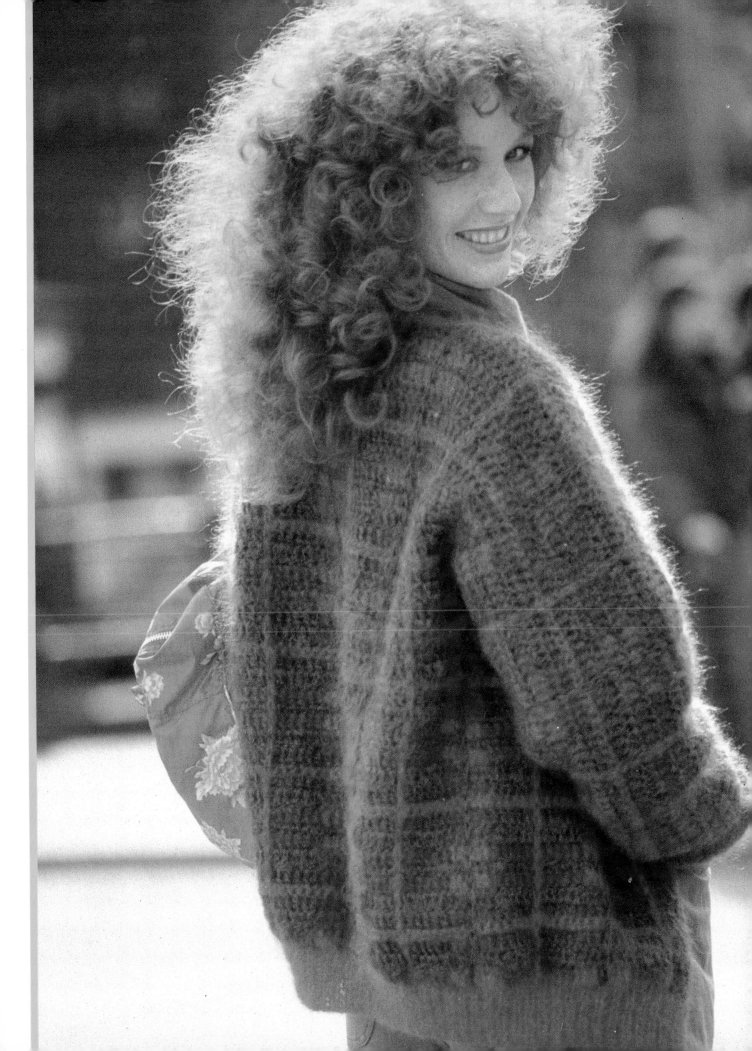

TRAVELING

COMPANION IN GADABOUT PLAID IS A MEMORABLE SWEATER. THIS V-NECK VERSION TAKES SHAPE QUICKLY IN BULKY WEIGHT MOHAIR.

★★

V-NECK PLAID PULLOVER

SIZE
Woman's Small (X Large), bust 30-32 (39-42) in. - 76-81.5 (99-107) cm. Finished bust measurements: 41½ (52) in. - 105 (132) cm, length: 23½ in. (60 cm), sleeve seam: 16½ in. (42 cm).

MATERIALS
3 (4) skeins bulky mohair yarn (approx. 110 yds per 50 g skein) color blue, 5 skeins color petrol and 3 skeins color green. Crochet hook U.S. size F/5 (U.K. size 8) (Metric size 4) or size needed to obtain gauge. Knitting needles and circular needle U.S. size 8 (U.K. size 6) (Metric size 5). **To save time, take time to check gauge!**

GAUGE
13½ dc and 8 rows = 4 in. (10 cm).

STITCHES
Chain (ch), single crochet (sc), half double crochet (hdc), slip stitch (sl st).
Jacquard pattern: Work in dc and sc by foll chart. When changing colors, work the last loop of the last st in 1 color with the color of the next st. Hold the unused yarn against the wrong side of work. When inserting hook, work around the unused yarn so that the new sts hold it against the work. Work the border sts in the same color as the adjacent st in pat. Ch 3 at the beg of each row (= 1 border st). Stripes are crocheted on finished work.
1/1 ribbing: Row 1: *K1, p1*. Rep * to * across.
Row 2 and all foll rows: Work sts as established in previous row.

BACK
With knitting needles and blue, cast on 72 (90) sts and work 2½ in. (6 cm) in 1/1 ribbing. Bind off loosely. With crochet hook, work 1 st in each st of bound off row of ribbing by foll chart = 73 (91) dc. Work until piece measures 22½ in. (57.5 cm) from beg, shape neck. Mark center 23 (25) sts. Work each side separately. With right side facing, work to last st before marker, leave last st unworked, turn. Work rem 24 (32) sts until piece measures 23¾ in. (60 cm) from beg, fasten off. For 2nd half, join yarn to 2nd marker and work across, turn. Work to 1 st before marker, turn, leaving 1 st unworked. Complete as first half.

FRONT
Work same as back until piece measures 15¼ in. (39 cm) from beg. Divide work in half leaving center st unworked. Work each side separately. At neck edge of every row, dec 1 st. (At end of row, work to last st, turn, leaving last st unworked. At beg of row, sl st over first st.) Work until piece measures 23¾ in. (60 cm) from beg, fasten off. Work 2nd half to correspond by rev shapings.

SLEEVES
With knitting needles and blue, cast on 40 sts and work 2 in. (5 cm) in 1/1 ribbing. Bind off loosely. With crochet hook, work 51 dc (inc 11 sts evenly spaced) across bound off row by foll the chart. Inc 1 st at each edge every 2¼ in. (5 cm), 6 times = 63 sts. Continue until sleeve measures 16½ in. (42 cm) from beg. Fasten off.

FINISHING
Block pieces to indicated measurements. Work the vertical stripes on back, front and sleeves as foll: beg at lower edges and alternating blue and green stripes. On the first row, insert hook under the first ch from front to back, then draw through loop, insert hook in the foll row, yo and pull up loop on hook, continue in this way up the front and down the back on all sections. Fasten off. Sew shoulder seams. With circular knitting needle and blue, pick up and knit 120 sts around neck and work 1¼ in. (3 cm) in 1/1 ribbing. Work back and forth beg at center front. Bind off loosely. Lap right side over left and sew in place. Sew sleeves to side seams, matching center of sleeve with shoulder seam. Sew side and sleeve seams.

Border stitches are always worked in the same color as the adjacent stitch. They will be sewn into the seam and are included so that all the stitches on the chart will show on finished work.

FRONT-BACK

7¼-7¾ (18.5-20) 6¾-9 (17-23)

8¼ (21)

21¼ (54)

2½ (6)

20¾-26 (52.5-66)

SLEEVE

17¾ (45)

14½ (37)

2 (5)

14 (36)

KEY TO CHART
⊡ = 1 dc in rust
⊠ = 1 dc in green
⊡ = 1 dc in blue
⊙ = 1 sc in blue
⊞ = 1 sc in green
⊡ = 1 border st
□ = ch 1

TARTAN CARDIGAN IS WORKED IN ONE PIECE. MOHAIR TAKES A HIGHLAND FLING WITH TRADITIONAL COLORS FOR SURPRISING RESULTS.

HIGHLAND TARTAN CARDIGAN

SIZE

Woman's Small (X Large), bust 30-32 (39-42) in. - 76-81.5 (99-107) cm. Finished bust measurements: 41½ (51½) in. - 105 (132) cm, length: 23½ in. (60 cm), sleeve seam: 17¾ in. (45 cm).

MATERIALS

5 skeins mohair yarn (approx. 110 yds per 50 g skein) color rust, 4 skeins color red, and 3 skeins color blue.
Crochet hook U.S. size F/5 (U.K. size 8) (Metric size 4) or size needed to obtain gauge. Knitting needles U.S. size 8 (U.K. size 5) (Metric size 5). 8 leather buttons. **To save time, take time to check gauge!**

GAUGE

13½ dc and 8 rows in jacquard pattern = 4 in. (10 cm).

STITCHES

**Chain (ch),
single crochet (sc),
half double crochet (hdc),
double crochet (dc),
treble crochet (tr),
slip stitch (sl st).**
Jacquard pattern: Work in dc and sc by foll chart. When changing colors, work the last loop of the last st in 1 color with the color of the next st. Hold the unused yarn against the wrong side of work. When inserting hook, work around the unused yarn so that the new sts hold it against the work. Work the border sts in the same color as the adjacent st in pat. Ch 3 at the beg of each row (= 1

border st). The vertical stripes are worked later on finished work.
1/1 ribbing: Row 1: *K1, p1*. Rep * to * across.
Row 2 and all foll rows: Work sts as established in previous row.

BODY

Worked in 1 piece, beg with left front. With red, ch 36 (45) + ch 3 (counts as the first st). Work 1 dc in the 5th ch from hook, continue by foll chart. (At left edge, there will be 1 border st which will be sewn in the seam.) Work until piece measures 10¾ in. (27.5 cm) from beg. At right edge, shape the sleeve: inc 1 st once, inc 2 sts once, inc 1 st once, inc 10 sts 5 times = 90 (99) sts. Work incs at beg of row as foll: To make a single inc, work 2 sts in 1 st. To make a double inc, work 3 sts in 1 st. To add more sts at the end of a row, make an additional chain st for each additional st needed plus the required number of turning chain sts. On the next row crochet a pattern st in each added chain. Work until piece measures 18¼ in. (46.5 cm) from beg, then shape neck. Right side facing, work to last 6 (7) sts, turn, leave last 6 (7) sts unworked, sl st over first 4 sts and work to end of row, work to last st, turn, leaving last st unworked. Turn, sl st over first st, work to end of row. Work rem 78 (85) sts for

3 rows, then inc 1 st at left edge. Leave sts unworked.
Work right front same as left front, rev shapings. Inc at left edge for sleeve and dec at right edge for neck. Work across left front piece, ch 23 (25) for neck, work across right front piece = 181 (199) sts. Continue until piece measures 13¼ in. (34 cm) measured along sleeve end. With right side facing, *sl st across 10 sts at beg of row, work to last 10 sts, turn, leave 10 sts unworked.* Work * to * 5 times. Sl st across first st, work to last st, turn, leaving last st unworked. Sl st across first 2 sts, work to last 2 sts, turn, leaving last 2 sts unworked. Sl st across first st, work to last st, turn, leaving last st unworked = 73 (91) sts. Work even for back until piece measures a total of 62¼ in. (108 cm) from beg. Fasten off.

FINISHING

Block piece to indicated measurements. Crochet vertical stripes as foll: work from lower edge of front. Alternately work red and green stripes, working over the ch sts of jacquard chart. On the first row, insert hook under the first ch from front to back, then draw through loop, insert hook in the foll row, yo and pull up loop and draw

through loop on hook, continue in this way up the front and down the back on all sections. Fasten off.
With crochet hook and red, work 40 sc along lower edge of each sleeve. Fasten off. With knitting needles and red, pick up and knit 1 st from each sc and work 2 in. (5 cm) in 1/1 ribbing. Bind off loosely. With crochet hook and red, work 59 sc along neck edge. Fasten off. With knitting needles and red, pick up and knit 1 st in each sc and work 1¼ in. (3 cm) of 1/1 ribbing. Bind off. Sew side and sleeve seams. With knitting needles and red, pick up and knit 1 st from every crocheted st and work 2½ in. (6 cm) of 1/1 ribbing along lower edge. Bind off. With knitting needles and red, cast on 6 sts and work in 1/1 ribbing until piece fits along left front edge. Bind off. Work same band for right front, making 7 buttonholes as foll: place the first 1¼ buttonhole in. (3 cm) from lower edge. For each buttonhole work 2 sts, k2 tog, yo, work 2 sts. Make 6 more buttonholes spaced about 2¾ in. (7 cm) apart, with the last buttonhole at neckband height. Sew on front bands. Reinforce buttonholes, sew on buttons.

FRONT

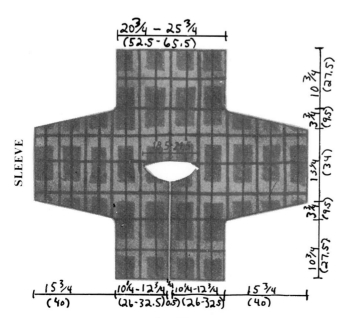

20¾ - 25¾ (52.5 - 65.5)

10¾ (27.5)

3¾ (9.5)

13¼ (34)

3¾ (9.5)

10¾ (27.5)

SLEEVE

10.5 cm

15¾ (40)   10¼-12¾ (26-32.5)   10¼-12¾ (26-32.5)   15¾ (40)

BACK

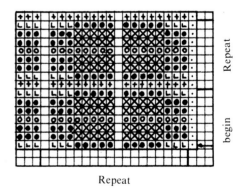

Repeat

begin

Repeat

KEY TO CHART

⊡ = 1 dc in rust
⊠ = 1 dc in green
🄻 = 1 dc in red
⊙ = 1 sc in red
⊞ = 1 sc in green
⊡ = 1 border st
☐ = ch 1

SPARKLING BLENDS OF PASTEL COLORS ARE CROCHETED IN THE BELOVED AFGHAN STITCH TO CREATE THIS CHARMING PAIR OF ALL COTTON SWEATERS.

CHILD'S PASTEL BOATNECK

SIZE

Child's size 6 (8, 10) years, chest 25 (27, 28½) in. -63.5 (69, 72.5) cm. Finished chest measurements: 32 (34, 36) in. - 81 (86, 91) cm, length: 15 (16½, 17½) in. - 38 (41, 45) cm, sleeve seam: 2 in. (5 cm).

MATERIALS

3 skeins "Scheepjeswol Mayflower Cotton 8" (100% cotton - approx. 180 yds per 50 g skein) color light rose, 2 skeins color white, 1 skein each color salmon, gold, green and light blue.
Afghan crochet hook U.S. size E/4 (U.K. size 9) (Metric size 3.5) or size needed to obtain gauge. Knitting needles U.S. size 3 (U.K. size 12) (Metric size 2.5). Double pointed needles U.S. size 3 (U.K. size 12) (Metric size 2.5).
To save time, take time to check gauge!

GAUGE

25 sts and 18 rows = 4 in. (10 cm) = 9 motifs.

STITCHES

Chain (ch), double crochet (dc), treble crochet (tr), slip stitch (sl st).
Brocade afghan stitch: Use afghan crochet hook. Work on a chain base. **Row 1:** Right side of work: with yarn at back of work, insert hook into 3rd ch from hook, yo and draw through loop. Work this way in each ch to end of row. (1 loop remains on hook from each ch.) **Row 2:** Wrong side of work: with yarn at back of work, yo and draw hook through first loop, *yo and draw hook through 2 loops*, rep * to * across row. Work the last loop of the last st of the row with the color of the next row. **Row 3:** Right side of work: the loop on the hook is the border st, *insert hook in first loop, pull through 1 loop = 1 drawn loop, 1 drawn loop, insert hook in next 2 loops, but do not draw through any loops = 2 sl sts, (carry yarn along wrong side of work); 2 drawn loops; insert hook in next loop, yo, draw through loop = dc, 1 dc (2 dc total), yo, insert hook in next loop, draw through loop, yo, draw through 2 loops = 1 tr, 1 tr = 2 tr total, 2 dc*, rep * to * across, end by inserting hook in last st, yo and draw through loop. **Row 4:** Same as row 1. **Row 5:** Same as row 2. **Row 6:** Ch 1 (= border st), *2 dc, 2 tr, 2 dc, 2 drawn loops, sl 2, 2 drawn loops. Rep rows 2 to 6.

Work in stripe pat as foll: **(Alternate 1 row of white between all color rows.)** 0 (2, 4) rows light rose, 0 (1, 1) rows salmon, 1 row gold, 1 row green, 4 rows light rose, 1 row salmon, 1 row green, 1 row light rose, 1 row light blue, 4 rows light rose, 1 row green, 1 row salmon, 4 rows light rose, 1 row salmon, 1 row gold, 1 row light blue, 1 row green, 1 row light rose, 1 row salmon, 3 (3, 4) rows light rose.
1/1 ribbing: Row 1: *K1, p1*, Rep * to * across. **Row 2 and all foll rows:** Work sts as established in previous row.

BACK

With knitting needles and light rose, cast on 72 (78, 84) sts and work 2 in. (5 cm) in 1/1 ribbing. Bind off loosely. With afghan hook and white, pick up 104 (110, 116) sts across bound off sts of ribbing. Continue in brocade st, working first row in white. Work by foll chart, with 1 border st at each edge. Work from point A to C, 8 (9, 9) times, then work from point A to B, 1 (0, 1) time, 1 border st. Work until piece measures 9½ (10¼, 11) in. - 24 (26, 28) cm from beg and 17 (19, 21) brocade motifs are complete. On the foll

row, ch 12 sts at each edge and continue across 128 (134, 140) sts in brocade st until piece measures 14¾ (16½, 17½) in. - 38 (41.5, 45) cm, = total of 30 (33, 36) brocade motifs. End with the 2nd or 4th row of pat st, and 1 row salmon. Work 1 row of sc white, working 1 sc in each loop. Fasten off.

FRONT

Work same as back, working brocade st as foll: 1 border st, work from point B to C, 1 (0, 1) time, then work from point A to C, 8 (9, 9) times, 1 border st. End with 1 row of green, then work 1 row of sc in white, working 1 sc in each loop. Fasten off.

FINISHING

Block pieces to indicated measurements. Sew shoulder seams over 6 (6¼, 6½) in. - 15 (16, 17) cm. Sew side and underarm seams. Work 1 row of sc in white around sleeve ends and fasten off.

For stitch chart, see Child's Pastel Rib Neck

FRONT-BACK

CHILD'S PASTEL RIBNECK

SIZE

Child's size 1 (3, 5) years, chest 20 (22, 24) in. - 51 (56, 61) cm. Finished chest measurements: 24½ (26½, 28) in. - 62 (67, 72) cm, length: 11 (12½, 13) in. - 29 (32, 35) cm, sleeve seam: 2 in. (5 cm).

MATERIALS

2 skeins "Scheepjeswol Mayflower Cotton 8" (100% cotton - approx. 180 yds per 50 g skein) each color white and sea green, 1 skein each color salmon, gold, light pink, lilac and green.
Afghan crochet hook U.S. size E/4 (U.K. size 9) (Metric size 3.5) or size needed to obtain gauge.
Knitting needles U.S. size 3 (U.K. size 12) (Metric size 2.5). Double pointed needles U.S. size 3 (U.K. size 12) (Metric size 2.5).
To save time, take time to check gauge!

GAUGE

25 sts and 18 rows = 4 in. (10 cm) = 9 motifs.

STITCHES

Chain (ch), single crochet (sc), treble crochet (tr), slip stitch (sl st).
Afghan stitch: Use afghan crochet hook. Work on a chain base. **Row 1:** Right side of work: with yarn at back of work, insert hook into 3rd ch from hook, yo and draw through loop. Work this way in each ch to end of row. (1 loop remains on hook from each ch.) **Row 2:** Wrong side of work: with yarn at back of work, yo and draw hook through first loop, *yo and draw hook through 2 loops*, rep * to * across row. **Row 3:** *With yarn at back of work, insert hook through vertical loop of 2nd st of previous row, yo and draw through 1 loop*, rep * to * across to end of row.
Brocade stitch: Use afghan crochet hook. Work on a chain base. **Row 1:** Right side of work: with yarn at back of work, insert hook into 3rd ch from hook, yo and draw through loop. Work this way in each ch to end of row. (1 loop remains on hook from each ch.) **Row 2:** Wrong side of work: with yarn at back of work, yo and draw hook through first loop, *yo and draw hook through 2 loops*, rep * to * across row. Work the last loop of the row with the color of the next row. **Row 3:** Right side of work: the loop on the hook is the border st, *insert hook in first loop, pull through 1 loop = 1 drawn loop, 1 drawn loop, insert hook in next 2 loops, but do not draw through any loops = 2 sl sts, (carry yarn along wrong side of work); 2 drawn loops; insert hook in next loop, yo, pull through loop = 1 dc, 1 dc = 2 dc total, yo, insert hook in next loop, pull through loop, yo, draw through 2 loops = 1 tr, 1 tr = 2 tr total, 2 dc*, rep * to * across, end insert hook in last st, yo and pull through loop. **Row 4:** Same as row 1. **Row 5:** Same as row 2. **Row 6:** Ch 1 (= border st), *2 dc, 2 tr, 2 dc, 2 drawn loops, sl 2, 2 drawn loops. Rep rows 2 to 6.
Work in stripe pat as foll:
(Alternate 1 row of white between all color rows.)

1 (3, 4) rows sea green, 1 row salmon, 1 row gold, 3 rows sea green, 1 row lilac, 1 row green, 1 row light rose, 3 rows sea green, 1 row salmon, 1 row lilac, 3 rows sea green, 1 row gold, 1 row sea green, 1 row light rose, 1 row salmon, 1 (2, 4) rows sea green.

1/1 ribbing: Row 1: *K1, p1*. Rep * to * across.
Row 2 and all foll rows: Work sts as established in previous row.

BACK

With smaller size knitting needles and sea green, cast on 60 (66, 72) sts and work 1½ in. (4 cm) in 1/1 ribbing. Bind off loosely. With afghan hook, pick up 80 (86, 92) sts across bound off sts of ribbing. Continue in brocade st, working first row in white. Work by foll chart, with 1 border st at each edge. Work from point A to C, 6 (7, 7) times, then work from point A to B, 1 (0, 1) time, 1 border st. Work until piece measures 6¼ (7¼, 7¼) in. - 16.5 (18.5, 20.5) cm from beg and 11 (13, 15) brocade motifs are complete. On the foll row, ch 12 sts at each edge and continue across 104 (110, 116) sts in brocade st until piece measures 11 (12½, 12½) in. - 29 (32, 35) cm, = 22 (25, 28) brocade motifs. End with 2nd or 4th row of pat st. Work 1 row of sc in white, working 1 sc in each loop. Fasten off.

FRONT

Work same as back, working brocade st as foll: 1 border st, work from point B to C, 1 (0, 1) time, then work from point A to C, 6 (7, 7) times, 1 border st. Work until piece measures 10¼ (11½, 12¼) in. - 26.5 (29.5, 31.5) cm from beg and 20 (23, 26) brocade motifs have been worked. Mark center 32 (34, 36) sts. Work to first marker, turn. At neck edge, sl st across 3 sts, work to end of row. Turn, work to last 2 sts, leave last 2 sts unworked, turn. Continue in brocade st over the rem 31 (33, 35) sts until 22 (25, 28) motifs are complete, ending with 2nd or 4th row of brocade st. Work 1 row of sc as on back. Fasten off. Work 2nd shoulder to correspond.

FINISHING

Block pieces to indicated measurements. Sew shoulder seams. With double pointed needles and sea green, pickup and knit 96 (100, 104) sts around neck and work 4 rows in 1/1 ribbing. Bind off loosely. Sew side and sleeve seams. With sea green, work 1 row of sc around each sleeve end. Fasten off.

6½ - 6¾ - 7¼
(17-17.5-18.5)

4¾-5¼-5¾ (12.5-14.5-14.5)
4-4¾-5¼ (12.5-14.5-14.5)

12¼-13¼-14
(31-33.5-36)

FRONT-BACK

KEY TO CHART

↑ = drawn loop

− = fasten off 1 loop

⋏ = slip st

⫯ = 1 dc

⫯ = 1 tr

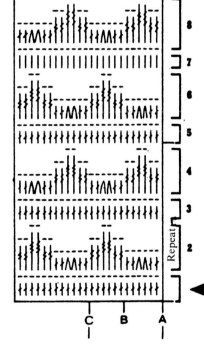

8
7
6
5
4
3
Repeat
2

C   B   A

Row 1 is on the right side of work row.

VERSATILE JACKET

WITH SHAWL COLLAR ESCORTS YOU IN STYLE. THIS PASTEL TWEED WILL TOP ALL YOUR SLACKS AND SKIRTS WITH A TOTALLY NEW LOOK.

PASTEL TWEED JACKET

SIZE

Woman's Small (Medium, Large), bust 30-32 (33-35, 36-38) in. - 76-81.5 (84-89, 91.5-97) cm. Finished bust measurements: 44½ (46¾, 49) in. - 110 (116, 120) cm, length: 26¾ (27, 27½) in. - 68 (69, 70) cm, sleeve seam (with cuff): 17¾ in. (45 cm).

MATERIALS

10 (11, 12) skeins fingering weight yarn (approx. 143 yds per 50 g skein) multicolor, 3 (4, 4) skeins sport weight mohair yarn (approx. 170 yds per 50 g skein) multicolor. Crochet hook U.S. size E/4 (U.K. size 9) (Metric size 3.5) or size needed to obtain gauge. **To save time, take time to check gauge!**

GAUGE

8 squares and 19 rows = 4 in. (10 cm).

STITCHES

Chain (ch), single crochet (sc), half double crochet (hdc), slip stitch (sl st).
Pattern stitch: Worked in pat st around a double strand of mohair. Work on a ch base. Lay the double strand of mohair over the chain base.
Row 1: Lay the double strand of mohair over the ch row and crochet around it. Work 1 sc in the 3rd ch from hook, *ch 2, skip 2 ch, 1 sc*, rep * to *, end with 1 sc in each of the last 2 ch.
Row 2: Lay the double strand of mohair over the last row, leaving a small loop at each edge. Ch 1 (border st), 1 sc, *ch 2, 1 sc*, rep * to *, end with 1 sc in the last sc and 1 sc in the turning ch (border st), Always rep the 2nd row. Be sure to check gauge as you work. Beg each row with ch 1, 1 sc and end with 2 sc.

BACK

Ch 130 (136, 142) and work in pat st = 42 (44, 46) squares + 1 border st at each edge. Work until piece measures 16½ in. (42 cm). Sl st over first 23 sts, work to last 23 sts, turn, leave last 23 sts unworked, work to end of row. Work 1 row even. *Sl st over first st, work to last st, turn, leaving last st unworked, turn and work to end of row. Work 1 row even*. Work * to * 2 times total = 34 (36, 38) squares. Piece will measure 16¾ (17¾, 18¾) in. - 42.5 (45, 47.5) cm across. Work until armhole measures 9¼ (9¾, 10¼) in. - 24 (25, 26) cm. Mark the center 8 squares. Work right shoulder as foll: sl st over 3 (4, 5) squares, work to first marker, turn, work to end of row. Sl st over first 4 squares, work to last square, turn, leaving last square unworked.

Work to end of row. Sl st over first 4 squares, work to last square, turn, leaving last square unworked. Fasten off. For left shoulder, join yarn at 2nd marker and work to end of row. Sl st over 3 (4, 5) squares, work to 2nd marker, turn. Sl st over first square, work to end of row. Turn, sl st over first 4 squares, work to end of row, turn. Sl st over first square, work to end of row. Sl st over first 4 squares, work to end of row, fasten off.

RIGHT FRONT

Ch 82 (85, 88). Work in pat st = 26 (27, 28) squares + 1 border st at each edge. Work until piece measures 15 in. (38 cm) from beg. At beg of right side of work rows, sl st over 1 square 5 times as foll: work 6 squares, skip 1 square, (do not ch over), work next 2 sc. In the foll row, work these 2 sc tog. **At the same time**, after the 8th row from beg of neck dec, shape armhole as on back (work to end of row, leaving last 2 squares unworked, then at armhole edge of next 2 right side of work rows, leave 1 square unworked.) When armhole measures 9¼ (9¾, 10¼) in. - 24 (25, 26) cm, shape shoulder: sl st over 3 (4, 5) squares, work to end of row, turn, and work to end of row. Turn, sl st over first 4 squares, work to end of row, turn, work to end of row. Turn, sl st over first 4 squares, work to end of

row = 6 squares rem. Turn and work to end of row, ch 7, turn. Insert hook in the 3rd ch from hook and work 1 sc = 8 squares total. Work in pat st for 2¾ in. (7 cm). At beg of wrong side of work rows, sl st over first 2 squares 4 times. Fasten off.

LEFT FRONT

Work same as right front, rev neck, armhole and shoulder shapings.

SLEEVES

Ch 76 (79, 82) and work in pat st = 24 (25, 26) squares + 1 border st at each edge. Work even for 4 in. (10 cm). Then at each edge every 2¾ in. (7 cm), inc 1 square 5 times as foll: ch 1, 1 sc, ch 2, 1 sc around the 2nd ch, ch 2, 1 sc in the foll sc, work to the last square, ch 2, 1 sc around the ch 2, 1 sc in the sc and 1 sc in the turning ch. Work these 34 (35, 36) squares until sleeve measures 19¾ in. (50 cm) from beg. Shape sleeve cap: *Sl st over first 2 squares, work to last 2 squares, turn, leaving last 2 squares unworked, turn, slip st over first square, work across to last square, turn, leaving last square unworked.* Rep * to * until you have 8 (9, 10) squares rem. Fasten off.

FINISHING

Block pieces to indicated measurements. Sew shoulder seams and sew collar seam. Sew collar to back neck. Work 1 row of hdc around fronts and back neck edges, beg with ch 2 at lower edge of left front. Work 2 rows in pat st using 3 strands of mohair instead of 2 strands. Fasten off. Fold border in half to outside and sl st in place. Set in sleeves. Sew side and sleeve seams. Fold lower 2 in. (5 cm) of sleeve to outside.

16¾ - 17¾ - 18¾
(42.5 - 45 - 47.5)
2 (5)   6 (15)   2 (5)
9¼-9¾-10¼ (24-25-26)
41½ (42)
20¾-21½-22¾
(52.5-55-57.5)

BACK

2   7-7½-8   1¼
(5) (18-19-20) (3)
3½ (9)
11¾-12-12½ (30-31-32)
15 (38)
11¾-12-12¼   1¼
(29.5-30.5-31.5) (3)

RIGHT FRONT

16¾-17¼-17¾
(42.5-43.5-45)
4¾ (12.5)
15¾ (40)
4 (10)
11¾-12¼-12¾
(30-31-32.5)

SLEEVE

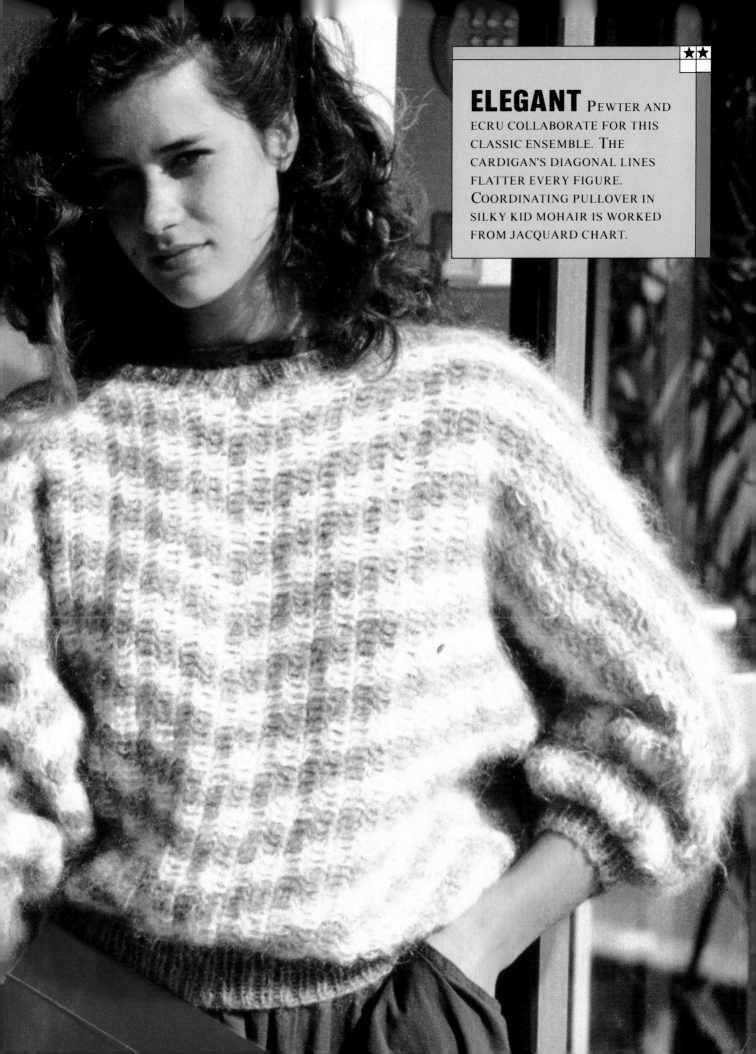

ELEGANT PEWTER AND ECRU COLLABORATE FOR THIS CLASSIC ENSEMBLE. THE CARDIGAN'S DIAGONAL LINES FLATTER EVERY FIGURE. COORDINATING PULLOVER IN SILKY KID MOHAIR IS WORKED FROM JACQUARD CHART.

MOHAIR CARDIGAN

SIZE

Woman's Small (Medium, Large, X Large), bust 30-32 (33-35, 36-38, 39-42) in. - 76-81.5 (84-89, 91.5-97, 99-107) cm. Finished bust measurements: 42½ (45½, 49, 52) in. - 108 (116, 124, 132) cm, length: 25½ in. (65 cm), sleeve seam 17 in. (43 cm).

MATERIALS

7 (7, 7, 8) skeins "Scheepjeswol Selena" (65% kid mohair, 29% mohair, 29% wool, 6% nylon - approx. 110 yds per 50 g skein) color light gray and 6 (6, 7, 7) skeins color ecru.
Crochet hook U.S. size F/5 (U.K. size 8) (Metric size 4) or size needed to obtain gauge. Knitting needles U.S. size 7 (U.K. size 3) (Metric size 4.5). 7 gray buttons. **To save time, take time to check gauge!**

GAUGE

14 dc and 5½ rows = 4 in. (10 cm).

STITCHES

Chain (ch), single crochet (sc), double crochet (dc), slip stitch (sl st).
Jacquard stitch: Center the chart. When changing colors, work the last loop of the last st in 1 color with the color of the next st. Hold the unused yarn against the wrong side of work. When inserting hook, work around the unused yarn so that the new sts hold it against the work. Work the border sts in the same color as the adjacent st in pat. Ch 3 at the beg of each row (= 1 border st).
1/1 ribbing: Row 1: *K1, p1*. Rep * to * across.
Row 2 and all foll rows: Work sts as established in previous row.

BACK

With crochet hook ch 77 (83, 89, 95). **Row 1 (size small and large):** Ch 3 with gray, 1 dc with gray in the 5th ch from hook, *3 dc with ecru, 3 dc with gray*, work * to * 6 (7) times, 1 dc with ecru = center st, **3 dc with gray, 3 dc with ecru**, work ** to ** 6 (7) times, 2 dc with gray. **Row 1 (size medium and X large):** Ch 3 with ecru (= 1 border st), 1 dc with ecru in the 5th ch from hook, 3 dc with gray, *3 dc with ecru, 3 dc with gray*, work * to * 6 (7) times, 1 dc with ecru (= center st), **3 dc with gray, 3 dc with ecru**, work ** to ** 6 (7) times, 3 dc with gray, 2 dc with ecru. **For all sizes:** Work 75 (81, 87, 93) dc + 1 border st at each edge in jacquard dc by centering chart. Work 33 rows. Fasten off.

LEFT FRONT

Ch 38 (41, 44, 47) + ch 3 in gray. **Row 1:** Work same as the first 38 (41, 44, 47) dc as on back (with 1 border st at each edge). The diagonals will go to the right. Work 30 rows, then shape neck. Work to last 9 (10, 11, 12) sts, turn — leave last 9 (10, 11, 12) sts unworked. Work the first 2 sts of foll row tog as foll: in next st, draw through loop, yo, draw through all loops on hook. Work to end of row. On foll row, work to last 2 sts and work 2 tog. Fasten off.

RIGHT FRONT

Work same as left front, rev neck shapings and working last 38 (41, 44, 47) dc as on back so that stripes shift toward left.

SLEEVES

Ch 47 (47, 49, 49) with gray. **Row 1:** Ch 3 with ecru (= 1 border st), 1 dc in the 5th ch from hook, then work 0 (0, 1, 1) dc with ecru, 3 dc in gray, *3 dc with ecru, 3 dc with gray*, work * to * 3 times, 1 dc in ecru (= center st), **3 dc with gray, 3 dc with ecru**, work ** to ** 3 times, 3 dc with gray, 2 (2, 3, 3) dc with ecru = 45 (45, 47, 47) dc + 1 border st at each edge.
Continue jacquard dc by centering chart. Inc 1 dc at each edge of every 2nd row once, then inc 1 dc at each edge of 3rd row once = 4 incs every 3rd row. (For each inc, work 2 dc in each edge st.) Work until you have 69 (69, 71, 71) dc + 1 border st at each edge. Work 21 rows, piece will measure 15 in. (38 cm) from beg. Fasten off.

FINISHING

Block pieces to indicated measurements. With knitting needles and gray, pick up and knit 34 (34, 36, 36) sts from lower edge of each sleeve and work 2 in. (5 cm) in 1/1 ribbing. Bind off loosely. Sew shoulder seams. Sew sleeves to side seams, matching center of sleeve with shoulder seams. Sew side and sleeve seams. Along lower edge with knitting needles and gray, pick up and knit 1 st in every st. Work 2 in. (5 cm) in 1/1 ribbing. Bind off. With knitting needles and gray, pick up and knit 1 st from every st and 2 sts from every row along neck and work 1 in. (2.5 cm) in 1/1 ribbing. Bind off loosely. With knitting needles and gray, pick up and knit 3 sts from every row along left front edge inside border st, and work 1 in. (2.5 cm) of 1/1 ribbing. Bind off loosely. Work the same band along right front, marking positions for 7 buttonholes. When band measures 1/3 in. (1 cm), make buttonholes. For each buttonhole, bind off 2 sts. On foll row, cast on 2 sts over bound off sts. Reinforce buttonholes. Sew on buttons.

center of row, pullover

□ 1 st in ecru, pullover
   1 st in gray, cardigan

☒ 1 st in gray, pullover
   1 st in ecru, cardigan

19¼ - 19¼ - 20 - 20
(49 - 49 - 50.5 - 50.5)

SLEEVE

15
(38)

12½ - 12½ - 13¼ - 13¼
(32 - 32 - 33.5 - 33.5)

23½
(60)

21¼ - 22¾ - 24½ - 26
(54 - 58 - 62 - 66)

BACK

3½ - 4
2¾ - 3¼ - 7 - 8 - 8¼ - 8½
7 - 8 - 9 - 10 (18 - 20 - 21 - 22)

2¾
(6.5)

23½
(59.5)

10¼ - 11 - 11¾ - 12½
(26 - 28 - 30 - 32)

1/2 FRONT

MOHAIR DIAGONAL PULLOVER

SIZE

Woman's Small (Medium, Large, X Large), bust 30-32 (33-35, 36-38, 39-42) in. - 76-81.5 (84-89, 91.5-97, 99-107) cm. Finished bust measurements: 42½ (45½, 49, 52) in. - 104 (112, 120, 128) cm, length: 21½ in. (55 cm), sleeve seam 16½ in. (42 cm).

MATERIALS

6 (6, 6, 7) skeins "Scheepjeswol Selena" (65% kid mohair, 29% mohair, 29% wool, 6% nylon - approx. 110 yds per 50 g skein) color light gray and 5 (5, 6, 6) skeins color ecru. Crochet hook U.S. size F/5 (U.K. size 8) (Metric size 4) or size needed to obtain gauge. Knitting needles U.S. size 7 (U.K. size 7) (Metric size 4.5). **To save time, take time to check gauge!**

GAUGE

14 dc and 5½ rows = 4 in. (10 cm).

STITCHES

Chain (ch), single crochet (sc), double crochet (dc), slip stitch (sl st). Jacquard stitch: Center the chart. When changing colors, work the last loop of the last st of 1 color with the color of the next st. Hold the unused yarn against the wrong side of work. When inserting hook, work around the unused yarn so that the new sts hold it against the work. Work the border sts in the same color as the adjacent st in pat. Ch 3 at the beg of each row (= 1 border st).
1/1 ribbing: Row 1: *K1, p1*. Rep * to * across.
Row 2 and all foll rows: Work sts as established in previous row.

BACK

Worked in 1 piece beg at lower edge of sleeve. With crochet hook and gray, ch 53. **Row 1:** Ch 3 with ecru (= 1 border st), 1 dc with ecru in the 5th ch from hook, *3 dc with gray, 3 dc with ecru*, work * to * 4 times total, 1 dc with gray (= center st), **3 dc with ecru, 3 dc with gray**, work ** to ** 4 times total, 2 dc with ecru. You now have 51 dc with 1 border st at each edge. Continue by foll chart. (Beg with the 2nd row, at each edge of every row, inc 1 st 19 times = 20 rows = 14½ in. (37 cm) from beg.) For each inc, work 2 dc in each edge st. You now have 89 dc + 1 border st at each edge. Work separately, make 2 chains in gray by chaining 25 sts. Join to each edge of sleeve. Work 1 border st, then 24 dc over ch, 91 dc over sleeve, 24 dc over 2nd ch, 1 border st = 139 dc + 1 border st at each edge. Work 6 (7, 8, 9) rows of chart.
Shape Neck: Work 70 dc, turn. Work 7 rows, dec at neck edge of each row as foll: at end of row, work to last st, turn, leaving last st unworked, sl st across the first st of the next row. Work 1 row without dec = center row of pullover which is the 35th (36th, 37th, 38th) row from beg. Piece will measure 25 (25½, 26, 26¾) in. - 63 (65, 67, 69) cm from beg.

Continue in jacquard pat by rev order of diagonals, that is, shift the right diagonals to the left by 1 st every row and shift the left diagonals to the right by 1 st every row. (See photo and small chart.) **At the same time,** inc 1 st at neck edge of next 7 rows by working 2 sts in edge st of every row. Work back the same as front, rev shapings, then work 6 (7, 8, 9) rows even across all sts. Work center 91 sts for sleeve (89 dc + 1 border st at each edge), (leave 25 sts at each edge unworked), dec 1 st at each edge of every row until you have 51 sts with border st at each edge. Piece will measure 50 (51, 52, 53½) in. - 126 (130, 134, 138) cm from beg. Fasten off.

FINISHING

Block piece to indicated measurements. Along the lower edge of each sleeve, work 32 (34 36, 38) sc with gray. Fasten off. With knitting needles, pick up and knit 1 st from every sc and work 2 in. (5 cm) in 1/1 ribbing. Bind off. With knitting needles and gray, around lower edge of back and front, pick up and knit 1 st from the edge dc next to the border sts of every row and work 2 in. (5 cm) in 1/1 ribbing. Bind off loosely. With knitting needles and gray, pick up and knit 1 st from every row (inside the border st) along the back neck edge and 3 sts along each shoulder and work 3/4 in. (2 cm) in 1/1 ribbing. Mark the center 3 sts. On every row, work the center 3 sts as foll: sl 2 tog knitwise, k1, psso. Bind off. Work same border on front neck. Lap front band over back and sew in place. Sew side and sleeve seams.

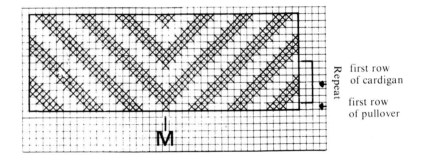

Repeat
first row of cardigan
first row of pullover

M

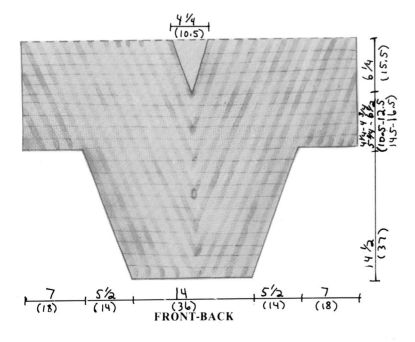

4 ¼ (10.5)

6 ¼ (15.5)

4¼-4¾ (10.5-12.5)

3¾-6½ (9.5-16.5)

14½ (37)

7 (18)　5½ (14)　14 (36)　5½ (14)　7 (18)

FRONT-BACK

PRIMARY APPEAL OF RED, YELLOW AND BLUE ENSURE THIS SWEATER'S POPULARITY FOR SCHOOL OR WEEKENDS. OVERSIZE LOOK IS JUST RIGHT FOR YOUNG JUNIORS.

★★

CHILD'S GEOMETRIC PULLOVER

SIZE

Child's size 8 (10, 12) years, chest 27 (28½, 30) in. - 69 (72.5, 76) cm. Finished chest measurements: 31½ (34, 36½) in. - 80 (86, 93) cm, length: 18 (19¾, 21¼) in. - 46 (50, 54) cm, sleeve seam: 12¾ (14, 15) in. - 32 (35, 38) cm.

MATERIALS

8 (9, 10) skeins worsted weight yarn (approx. 80 yds per 50 g skein) color gold, 5 skeins color black, 3 (4, 4) skeins color blue and 1 skein color red. Crochet hook U.S. size F/5 (U.K. size 8) (Metric size 4) or size needed to obtain gauge. Knitting needles U.S. size 6 (U.K. size 8) (Metric size 4). **To save time, take time to check gauge!**

GAUGE

15 hdc and 10 rows in jacquard pat = 4 in. (10 cm).

STITCHES

Chain (ch), single crochet (sc), half double crochet (hdc), slip stitch (sl st). Jacquard hdc: Foll the chart in hdc. When changing colors, work the last loop of the last st of one color with the color of the next st. Hold the unused yarn against the wrong side of work. When inserting hook, work around the unused yarn so that the new sts hold it against the work. Work the border sts in the same color as the adjacent st in pat. Beg each row with ch 2, which counts as the first hdc.
2/2 ribbing: Row 1: *K2, p2*. Rep * to * across.
Row 2 and all foll rows: Work sts as established in previous row.

BACK

With knitting needles and black, cast on 70 (74, 78) sts and work in 2/2 ribbing as foll: 1 row black, 2 rows red, 2 rows black, 2 rows red, 2 rows black, 2 rows red, 2 rows black. Bind off. With crochet hook and black, work 62 (66, 72) hdc across the bound off row of ribbing. Continue by foll chart 1, beg at point A (B, C). Work until piece measures 16½ (18¼, 19¾) in. - 42 (46, 50) cm from beg. Fasten off. With knitting needles and black, pick up and knit 78 (86, 94) sts along last row of crochet. Then work in 2/2 ribbing as foll: 3 rows black, 2 rows red, 2 rows black, 2 rows red and 2 rows in black. Bind off in black.

FRONT

Work same as back.

SLEEVES

With knitting needles and black, cast on 30 (34, 38) sts and work ribbing same as back. Bind off. With crochet hook, work 65 (71, 79) hdc across bound off row of ribbing and work by centering chart 2 (center is at point G). Inc 1 st at each edge of every 2nd row 12 (14, 15) times. (For each inc, work 2 hdc in each edge st.) Work inc in jacquard hdc. You now have 59 (65, 71) hdc. Work until piece measures 12¾ (14, 15) in. - 32 (35, 38) cm from beg. Fasten off.

FINISHING

Block pieces to indicated measurements. Sew shoulder seams, leaving center 8 (8¼, 8¾) in. - 20 (21, 22.5) cm open for neck. Sew sleeves to armholes, matching center of sleeve with shoulder seams. Sew side and sleeve seams.

FRONT-BACK

SLEEVE

Chart 1

Chart 2

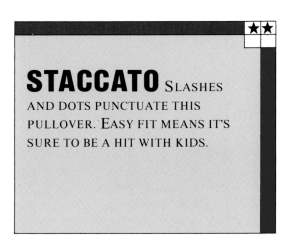

STACCATO SLASHES
AND DOTS PUNCTUATE THIS PULLOVER. EASY FIT MEANS IT'S SURE TO BE A HIT WITH KIDS.

CHILD'S RED PULLOVER

SIZE
Child's size 8 (10, 12) years, chest 27 (28½, 30) in. - 69 (72.5, 76) cm. Finished chest measurements: 32½ (35, 37½) in. - 83 (89, 96) cm, length: 18¾ (20¼, 21¾) in. - 47 (51, 55) cm, sleeve seam: 13½ (14¾, 15¾) in. - 34 (37, 40) cm.

MATERIALS
8 (9, 10) skeins worsted weight yarn (approx. 80 yds per 50 g skein) color red, 4 (4, 5) skeins color black.
Crochet hook U.S. size F/5 (U.K. size 8) (Metric size 4) or size needed to obtain gauge. Knitting needles U.S. size 4 (U.K. size 8) (Metric size 4). **To save time, take time to check gauge!**

GAUGE
15 hdc and 10 rows in jacquard hdc = 4 in. (10 cm).

STITCHES
Chain (ch), single crochet (sc), half double crochet (hdc), slip stitch (sl st).
Jacquard hdc: Foll the chart in hdc. When changing colors, work the last loop of the last st of 1 color with the color of the next st. Hold the unused yarn against the wrong side of work. When inserting hook, work around the unused yarn so that the new sts hold it against the work. Work the border sts in the same color as the adjacent st in pat. Beg each row with ch 2, which counts as the first hdc.
2/2 ribbing: Row 1: *K2, p2*. Rep * to * across.
Row 2 and all foll rows: Work sts as established in previous row.

BACK
With knitting needles and black, cast on 74 (78, 82) sts and work in 2/2 ribbing as foll: 1 row black, 2 rows red, 2 rows black, 2 rows red, 2 rows black, 2 rows red, 2 rows black. Bind off. With crochet hook and black, work 64 (68, 74) hdc across the bound off row of ribbing. Continue by foll chart 1. Work until piece measures 17½ (19, 20½) in. - 44 (48, 52) cm from beg. Fasten off. With knitting needles and black, pick up and knit 82 (90, 98) sts along last row of crochet. Then work in 2/2 ribbing as foll: 2 rows black, 2 rows red, 2 rows black and 2 rows red. Bind off in black.

FRONT
Work same as back.

SLEEVES
With knitting needles and black, cast on 34 (38, 42) sts and work ribbing same as back. Bind off. With crochet hook, work 38 (40, 44) hdc across bound off row of ribbing. Continue work by foll chart 2. Inc 1 st at each edge of every 2nd row 12 (14, 15) times. (For each inc, work 2 hdc in each edge st.) Work inc in jacquard hdc. You now have 62 (68, 74) sts. Work until piece measures 13½ (14¾, 15¾) in. - 34 (38, 42) cm from beg. Fasten off.

FINISHING
Block pieces to indicated measurements. Sew shoulder seams, leaving center 8½ (8¾, 9¼) in. - 21 (22.5, 24) cm open for neck. Sew sleeves to armholes, matching center of sleeve with shoulder seams. Sew side and sleeve seams.

Here is the perfect opportunity to use up "leftover" yarn. Make the back, front, sleeves, even ribbing using contrasting colors of yarn, but always work the motifs and stripes in the same color to unify the entire design.

KEY TO CHART
□ = red
⊠ = black

Repeat

Chart 2

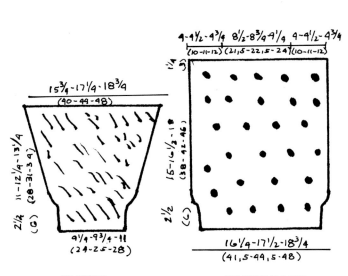

SLEEVE

FRONT-BACK

Repeat

Repeat

Chart 1

VIVID AUTUMN IMAGES
FORM WHEN BURNISHED COPPER,
RUST AND GOLD MOHAIR ARE
BLENDED. THE CARDIGAN
FEATURES SPACIOUS POCKETS
AND A DESIGNER FLAIR.

FOLKLORE MOTIFS IN CONTEMPORARY COLORS MAKE REAL SHOWSTOPPERS. SOFT MOHAIR ADDS FEATHERWEIGHT WARMTH.

★★

FOLKLORE CARDIGAN

SIZE

Woman's Small (Medium, Large), bust 30-32 (33-35, 36-38) in. - 76-81.5 (84-89, 91.5-97) cm. Finished bust measurements: 42½ (46¼, 49½) in. - 108 (117, 126) cm, length: 28 in. (71 cm), sleeve seam: 16½ in. (42 cm).

MATERIALS

4 (5, 5) skeins sport weight kid mohair (approx. 110 yds per 50 g skein) each color gray and black and 1 skein each color light green, green, light lilac, pale yellow, dark pink, light gray, dark lilac and salmon.
Crochet hook U.S. size F/5 (U.K. size 8) (Metric size 4) or size needed to obtain gauge. Knitting needles U.S. size 4 (U.K. size 9) (Metric size 3.5). 9 buttons. Stitch holder. **To save time, take time to check gauge!**

GAUGE

15 hdc and 10½ rows = 4 in. (10 cm).

STITCHES

**Chain (ch),
half double crochet (hdc),
slip stitch (sl st).
Jacquard pattern st:**
Work in hdc by foll chart. When changing colors, work the last loop of the last st with the color of the next st. Use small bobbins of yarn for each section of color and beg each row with ch 2 = first hdc.
1/1 ribbing: Row 1: *K1, p1*. Rep * to * across.
Row 2 and all foll rows: Work sts as established in previous row.

BODY

Worked in 1 piece to armholes. With knitting needles and black, cast on 169 (183, 197) sts and work 2 in. (5 cm) in 1/1 ribbing, beg and end on right side of work with k1. Make 1 buttonhole on right edge by binding off the 3rd and 4th sts from right edge. On foll row, cast on 2 sts over bound off sts. Work until border measures 2½ in. (6 cm), then place 5 sts at each edge on holder. Bind off center 159 (173, 187) sts.
Foundation row: With crochet hook and black, work 1 hdc in each bound off st, inc 1 st at each edge = 161 (175, 189) hdc. Work in jacquard st by foll chart. Work jacquard chart from point C (B, A) to point D (E, F). Work for 44 (43, 42) rows = point I (H, G). Piece will measure 19 (18½, 18) in. - 48 (47, 46) cm from beg. Divide work for armholes. Work right front over 40 (44, 47) sts, inc 1 st at left edge (leave rem sts unworked). Work these sts to point J on chart. The armhole now measures 7 (7½, 8) in. -18 (19, 20) cm. Shape neck. At right edge, with right side facing, sl st over 4 sts, work to end of row,

turn. Work to last 2 sts, turn, leave last 2 sts unworked. Sl st over first st, work to end of row, turn. Work to last st, turn, leave last st unworked. Sl st across first st and work to last row of chart. Fasten off. Work the 40 (44, 47) sts of left front, rev shapings. Fasten off.
Work over the center 81 (87, 95) sts, inc 1 st at each edge. Work by foll chart. When chart is complete, fasten off.

SLEEVES

With knitting needles and black, cast on 45 (47, 49) sts and work 1½ in. (4 cm) in 1/1 ribbing. Fasten off. With crochet hook and black, work 45 (47, 49) hdc across the bound off sts of ribbing. Beg jacquard hdc st by foll chart with point C (B, A), end at point D (E, F). At each edge every 1¼ in. (3 cm), inc 1 st 12 times total (to inc, work 2 sts in each edge st). Work inc sts in jacquard hdc. You now have 69 (71, 73) sts. When last row of chart is complete, fasten off. Piece will measure 16½ in. (42 cm) from beg. Work the 2nd sleeve by rev the order of the chart, beg at left edge of point D (E, F) and ending at point C (B, A).

FINISHING

Block pieces to indicated measurements. Front bands: With knitting needles and black, pick up 5 sts from left front and inc 1 st at body edge for border st. Work in 1/1 ribbing until band reaches neck. Dec the border st, then place rem sts on holder. Work the right band the same, making buttonholes when piece measures 5½, 9, 12½, 16, 19¾ and 23¼ in. (14, 23, 32, 41, 50 and 59 cm) from beg. For each buttonhole, bind off 2 sts. On foll row, cast on 2 sts. Sew bands to fronts. Sew shoulder seams. With knitting needles and black, pick up and knit 75 sts around neck and work in 1/1 ribbing, beg and end with k1 on right side of work row. Work 1/3 in. (1 cm), then make 1 buttonhole above previous ones. When band measures 1¼ in. (3 cm), bind off all sts. Reinforce buttonholes and sew sleeves to armholes, matching center and sleeve with shoulder seam. Sew side and sleeve seam. Sew on buttons. Make small bobbles in each color to sew to flower motifs as you desire.

PIECES

SLEEVE

AUTUMN JACQUARD CARDIGAN

SIZE

Woman's Medium, bust 33-35 in. (84-89 cm). Finished bust measurements: 45 in. (114 cm), length: 31 in. (79 cm), sleeve seam: 17¾ in. (45 cm).

MATERIALS

7 skeins mohair yarn (approx. 130 yds per 50 g skein) color orange, 2 skeins each color ecru and blue-green, and 1 skein each color pink, light gold, green, rust and brown.
Crochet hook U.S. size F/5 (U.K. size 8) (Metric size 4) or size needed to obtain gauge. Knitting needles U.S. size 4 (U.K. size 9) (Metric size 3.5). 8 buttons. Stitch holder. **To save time, take time to check gauge!**

GAUGE

14½ hdc and 10 rows in jacquard hdc = 4 in. (10 cm).

STITCHES

**Chain (ch),
half double crochet (hdc),
slip stitch (sl st).
Jacquard hdc:** Work by foll chart in hdc. The border sts are not shown on the chart. When changing colors, work the last loop of the last st in 1 color with the color of the next st. Hold the unused yarn against the wrong side of work. When inserting hook, work around the unused yarn so that the new sts hold it against the work. Work the border sts in the same color as the adjacent st in pat. Beg each row with ch 2 which counts as the first hdc. Use a separate ball of yarn for each section of color.
1/1 ribbing: Row 1: *K1, p1*. Rep * to * across.
Row 2 and all foll rows: Work sts as established in previous row.

POCKET LININGS

With crochet hook and orange, ch 19 + ch 2 to turn. **Foundation Row:** 1 hdc in the 4th ch from hook, hdc across. Work in hdc = 19 hdc until piece measures 6¼ in. (16 cm). Fasten off. Make 2.

BODY

Worked in 1 piece beg at lower edge. With knitting needles and orange, cast on 171 sts and work 3/4 in. (2 cm) in 1/1 ribbing. At right edge, work 2 sts, bind off 2 sts, then work to end of row in 1/1 ribbing. On foll row, cast on 2 sts over bound off sts and continue in 1/1 ribbing until piece measures 2½ in. (6 cm). Place 5 sts at each edge on stitch holders. Bind off center 161 sts. Crochet across these sts in hdc foll jacquard chart, inc 1 st at each edge for border sts. (Work 2 sts in each edge st = 163 sts). Work for 8½ in. (22 cm) from beg, then work as foll: work first 14 sts, skip 19 sts of body and work 19 hdc of 1 pocket lining, work to last 33 sts, skip 19 hdc of body and work 19 sts of 2nd pocket lining, work last 14 sts. Work these sts until piece measures 21¼ in. (54 cm) from beg, that is to point C on chart. Now work the first 37 sts, leaving rem sts unworked. Inc 1 st at left edge (work 2 sts in edge st) (= 1 border st). Work these 38 dc, shaping raglans as foll: with right side facing, work to last 2 sts, turn, leave last 2 sts unworked. Sl st over first 2 sts, work to end of row, turn. Work to last st of row, leaving last st unworked, turn. Sl st over first st and work to end of row. You are now at point D on chart. Fasten off. Work last 37 sts at left edge, inc 1 st at right edge = 38 sts, by rev shapings. Fasten off. 9 sts from the end of the right front, work 71 sts in hdc (ending 9 sts from the beg of the left front). Inc 1 st at each edge for border sts. Work these 73 sts in hdc foll the chart, working raglan shapings as foll: sl st over first 2 sts of row, work to last 2 sts of row, turn, leave last 2 sts unworked. Sl st over first 2 sts of row, work to last 2 sts of row, turn, leave last 2 sts unworked. Sl st over first st, work to last st on row, turn, leaving last st unworked. Sl st over first st, work to last st on row, turn, leaving last st unworked. You are now at point D on chart. Fasten off.

RIGHT SLEEVE

With knitting needles and orange, cast on 40 sts and work 2 in. (5 cm) in 1/1 ribbing. Bind off. With crochet hook work in hdc by foll jacquard chart for right sleeve, across the bound off sts of ribbing, inc 5 sts across first row = 43 hdc + 1 border st at each edge. *At each edge of every 3rd row, work 2 sts in each edge st, then work 2 sts in each edge st of every 4th row.* = 8 incs every 7 rows. Work inc sts in jacquard pat. Work * to * until you have 65 sts. Continue until sleeve measures 17¾ in. (45 cm) from beg which is point C on chart. Then shape raglan: sl st over the first 4 sts, work to last 4 sts, leaving last 4 sts unworked, turn. *Sl st over first 2 sts, work to last 2 sts, leave last 2 sts unworked, turn*, work * to * 3 times total. Sl st over first st, work to last st, turn, leaving last st unworked. Leave rem sts unworked (point D on chart). Fasten off.

LEFT SLEEVE

Work same as right sleeve, but rev jacquard chart by beg at point A and working to point B, then follow chart.

YOKE

Work in hdc (foll chart from point D) over the sts of the right front, right sleeve, back, left sleeve and left front as foll: *work to 3 sts before raglan edge, 2 hdc tog: (yo, inserting hook in first hdc, yo and draw up loop, insert hook in 2nd hdc and draw through loop, yo and draw through all loops on hook), 2 hdc, 2 hdc tog*, rep * to * 4 times total = 8 dec. Rep these dec every row 18 times. On the last 2 dec rows, eliminate the 2 hdc between the dec. **At the same time,** on the same row as the 13th dec row, beg neck shapings. At beg of row, sl st over the first 6 sts, then work to last 6 sts, turn, leaving last 6 sts unworked. Sl st over first 2 sts, work to last 2 sts, leave last 2 sts unworked, turn. *Sl 1, work to last st, turn, leaving last st unworked.* Work * to * twice total. Fasten off.

FINISHING

Block pieces to indicated measurements. Sew the raglan and sleeve seams. With knitting needles and orange, pickup and knit 21 sts along top of each pocket and work 1 in. (2.5 cm) of 1/1 ribbing. Bind off in ribbing. Sew pocket lining and bands in place. Front bands: with knitting needles, pick up and knit 5 sts from left front holder and inc 1 st at inner edge and work in 1/1 ribbing until piece reaches to neck. Dec 1 st at inner edge and place 5 sts on holder. Work right band same as left band, making 6 buttonholes as the first, placed 5, 9, 13, 17, 21, 25 in. (13, 23, 33, 43, 53, 63 cm). Sew bands to fronts. With knitting needles and orange, pick up and knit 75 sts around neck and work 1/3 in. (1 cm) of 1/1 ribbing, then work 3/4 in. (2 cm) more in 1/1 ribbing, forming buttonhole above previous ones. Bind off loosely.
Reinforce buttonholes.
Sew on buttons.

SLEEVE

PIECES

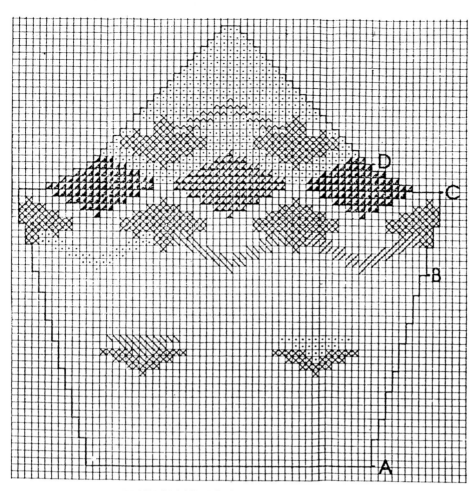

SLEEVE (RIGHT) AUTUMN JACQUARD CARDIGAN

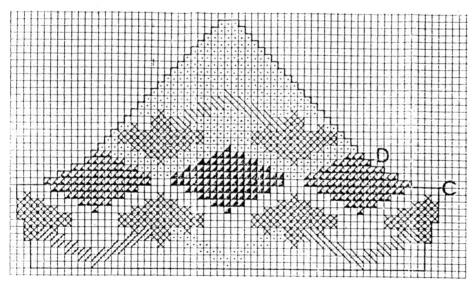

SLEEVE (LEFT) AUTUMN JACQUARD CARDIGAN

KEY TO CHART

☐ = orange
⊡ = ecru
⊠ = blue-green
◩ = green
◪ = pink
◤ = brown
◣ = rust
⧄ = light gold

74

KEY TO CHART

⊞ = light green
Ⅲ = salmon
⊠ = gray
◪ = black
⊡ = green
⧄ = pale lilac
⊡ = light yellow
⊙ = dark pink
⊟ = light gray
⊙ = dark lilac

black

gray

black

CBA

SLEEVE
FOLKLORE CARDIGAN

KEY TO CHART

- ☐ = orange
- ☐ = ecru
- ☒ = blue-green
- ◩ = green
- ◪ = pink
- ◩ = brown
- ◪ = rust
- ◪ = light gold

KEY TO CHART

- ⊞ = light green
- Ⅲ = salmon
- ☒ = gray
- ◪ = black
- L = green
- ◪ = pale lilac
- · = light yellow
- ⊙ = dark pink
- ⊟ = light gray
- ⊙ = dark lilac

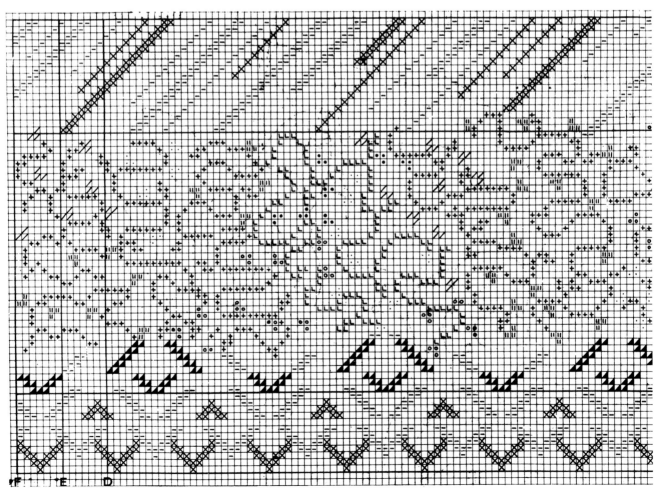

BACK AND FRONT (FOLKLORE CARDIGAN)

COVETED HANDWOVEN

LOOK IS EASY ONCE YOU MASTER THIS CROCHET TECHNIQUE USING TWO STRANDS OF YARN. ALPACA INTERACTS WITH BULKY WOOL ON OUR SHAWL COLLAR PULLOVER.

PULLOVER

For the woven look, work the thin strand around a thick strand. During the work, on every row, lay the thick strands along the top of the underlying row and crochet by inserting hook under the thick strand. Be sure to have the turning of the thick yarn showing on the wrong side of work. **Check your gauge as you work.**

SIZE

Woman's Small (Medium, Large), bust 30-32 (33-35, 36-38) in. - 76-81.5 (84-89, 91.5-97) cm. Finished bust measurements: 41 (44½, 48) in. - 104 (113, 122) cm, length: 25½ in. (65 cm), sleeve seam 17¼ in. (44 cm).

MATERIALS

5 (6, 6) skeins fingering weight alpaca yarn (approx. 206 yds per 50 g skein) color ecru and 8 (9, 10) skeins bulky yarn (approx. 110 yds per 50 g skein) color ecru. Crochet hook U.S. size B/1 (U.K. size 12) (Metric size 2.5) or size needed to obtain gauge. Circular or double pointed knitting needles U.S. size 9 (U.K. size 5) (Metric size 5.5). **To save time, take time to check gauge!**

GAUGE

9 squares (1 sc + ch 3) and 11 rows = 4 in. (10 cm).

STITCHES

Chain (ch), single crochet (sc), slip stitch (sl st).
1/1 ribbing: Row 1: *K1, p1*. Rep * to * across.
Row 2 and all foll rows: Work sts as established in previous row.

BACK

With crochet hook and alpaca, ch 192 (208, 224) and work in woven crochet st as foll: lay 2 strands of bulky yarn on the ch row and crochet around them with alpaca.
Row 1: 1 sc in the 3rd ch from hook, *ch 3, skip 3, 1 sc in the foll ch*, rep * to *, end with 1 sc in the last ch = 47 (51, 55) squares and 1 border st at each edge. **Row 2:** Ch 2 (border st), 1 sc in the foll sc, *ch 3, 1 sc in the ch-3 sp,* rep * to *, end with ch 1, 1 sc in the foll sc, 1 sc in the turning of the thick yarn (border st).
Row 3: Ch 2 (border st), 1 sc in the foll sc, ch 3, *1 sc in the ch-3 sp, ch 3*, rep * to *, end with 1 sc in the foll sc, 1 sc in the turning of the thick yarn (border st). Always rep rows 2 and 3. Work until piece measures 23½ in. (60 cm) from beg, then fasten off.

FRONT

Work same as back until piece measures 18¾ (18½, 18) in. - 48 (47, 46) cm, then mark the center 15 (17, 19) squares. Work right side, inc 1 st at neck edge, then work for 4¾ (5, 5½) in. - 12 (13, 14) cm from beg, then fasten off. (To inc, work 2 sts in edge st.) Work left side the same, inc 1 st at neck edge. Fasten off.

SLEEVES

With alpaca, ch 96 (104, 112) then work in pat st = 23 (25, 27) squares + 1 border st at each edge of first row. At beg of 2nd and 3rd rows, inc 1 st 7 times. At beg of 4th and 5th row inc 1 st 6 times. Work inc as foll: at beg of 2nd row, ch 5, 1 sc in the 3rd ch from hook, ch 1, skip 1 ch, 1 sc in the foll ch, ch 3, 1 sc around the foll ch-sp and continue across as on row 3 of pat. Inc at the beg of 3rd row: ch 5, 1 sc in the 3rd ch from the hook, ch 3, skip 1 sc, 1 sc, ch 3, 1 sc around the ch-sp, continue across as on row 3 of pat. Work inc sts = 49 (51, 53) squares + 1 border st at each edge until piece measures 15¾ in. (40 cm) from beg. Fasten off.

FINISHING

Block pieces to indicated measurements. Sew shoulder seams. With double pointed needles and bulky yarn, along back and side of front neck edges, pick up and knit 92 (96, 100) sts and work 7 in. (18 cm) in 1/1 ribbing, working back and forth. Bind off loosely. Lap right collar over left and sew in place. With knitting needles and bulky yarn, pick up and knit 112 (114, 116) sts along back edge and work 2 in. (5 cm) in 1/1 ribbing. Bind off loosely. Work same band along front edge. With knitting needles and bulky yarn, pick up and knit 28 (30, 32) sts along each sleeve edge and work 1½ in. (4 cm) in 1/1 ribbing. Bind off loosely. Sew sleeves to side seams, matching center of sleeve with shoulder seam. Sew side and sleeve seams.

6½-7½-8¼
(17-19-21)

4¾-5-5½
(12-13-14)

10¼-18½-18
(48-47-46)

21½-22¼-23¾

6¾
(10)

2
(5)

½
(4)

20½-22¼-24
(52-56,5-61)

10¼-11-11¾
(26-28-30)

FRONT-BACK   **SLEEVE**

COOL OFF IN THIS DELICIOUS SUMMER COOLER MADE FROM BUTTERY-SOFT COTTON. BASKETWEAVE STITCH LENDS AN AIR OF DISTINCTION.

★★

PULLOVER

SIZE

Woman's Medium (Large, X Large), bust 33-35 (36-38, 39-42) in. - 84-89 (91.5-97, 99-107) cm. Finished bust measurements: 41½ (44½, 47) in. - 106 (113, 120) cm, length: 23½ in. (60 cm), sleeve seam 17 in. (43 cm).

MATERIALS

24 (25, 26) skeins "Scheepjeswol Mayflower Helarsgarn" (100% cotton - approx. 88 yds per 50 g skein) color yellow. Crochet hooks U.S. sizes B/1 and E/4 (U.K. sizes 12 and 9) (Metric sizes 2.5 and 3.5) or size needed to obtain gauge. Knitting needles U.S. size 3 (U.K. size 10) (Metric size 3). **To save time, take time to check gauge!**

GAUGE

12 relief dc motifs and 13 rows in pat st = 4 in. (10 cm) using larger size hook.

STITCHES

Chain (ch), single crochet (sc), half double crochet (hdc), double crochet (dc).
Front Relief dc: Worked around the post of the st of the previous row. Yo over hook insert hook back to front between next 2 sts, then back again between the st worked and the foll st, hook is now placed horizontally in front of st, complete the dc.
Back Relief dc: Worked around the post of the st of the previous row. Yo over hook, insert hook front to back between next 2 sts, then back again between the st worked and the foll st, hook is now placed horizontally in back of st, complete the dc.
Front Relief sc: Worked around the post of the st of the previous row. Insert hook back to front between next 2 sts, then back again between the st worked and the foll st, hook is now placed horizontally in front of st, complete the sc.
Back Relief sc: Worked around the post of the st of the previous row. Insert hook front to back between next 2 sts , then back again between the st worked and the foll st, hook is now placed horizontally in back of st, complete the sc.
Pattern stitch: Row 1: 1 hdc in the 6th ch from hook, *ch 1, skip 1 ch, 1 hdc*. Rep * to *.
Row 2: Ch 3 (= 1 border st + ch 1), skip 1 ch, *1 front relief dc, ch 1, skip 1 ch, 1 back relief dc, ch 1, skip 1 ch*, rep * to *, end 1 hdc (= 1 border st).

Row 3: Ch 3 (= 1 border st + ch 1, skip 1 ch, *1 back relief dc, ch 1, skip 1 ch, 1 front relief dc, ch 1, skip 1 ch*, rep * to *, end 1 hdc (= 1 border st). Rep rows 2 and 3 to stagger the motif, that is, work 1 front relief over 1 front relief and vice versa.
1/1 ribbing: Row 1: *K1, p1*. Rep * to * across.
Row 2 and all foll rows: Work sts as established in previous row.

BACK

With larger size hook, ch 131 (139, 147) + ch 2 (= 1 border st) + ch 1. continue in pat st as foll:
Row 1: Work * to * of row 1, 64 (68, 72) times.
Row 2: Work * to * of row 2, 32 (34, 36) times = 64 (64, 72) relief sts + 1 border st at each edge. Work in pat st until piece measures 21¼ in. (54 cm) from beg. Change to smaller size hook and work 1 row of pat st as foll: Ch 2 (= border st), ch 1, skip 1 ch, *1 front relief sc, ch 1, skip 1 ch, 1 back relief sc, ch 1, skip 1 ch,* rep * to *, end 1 sc (= border st). Fasten off.

FRONT

Work same as back.

SLEEVES

With larger size hook, ch 75 + ch 2 (= border st) + ch 1. Work in pat st. On row 1, rep * to * 36 times. On row 2: rep * to * 18 times = 36 relief dc + 1 border st at each edge. *Inc 1 dc and ch 1 at each edge of every 3rd row once, inc 1 dc and ch 1 at each edge of every 4th row once*, rep * to * 6 times (for each inc, work 1 dc and ch 1) = 60 relief dc + 1 border st at each edge. When piece measures 15 in. (38 cm) from beg, change to smaller size hook and work last row same as back. Fasten off.

FINISHING

Block piece to indicated measurements. With knitting needles, pick up and knit 72 (76, 80) sts from lower edge of back and work 2½ in. (6 cm) of 1/1 ribbing. Bind off. Work same border on front. With knitting needles, pick up and knit 38 sts from lower edge of each sleeve and work 2 in. (5 cm) of 1/1 ribbing. Bind off. Sew shoulder seams over 5 (5½, 6) in. - 13 (14, 15) cm. Sew sleeves to armholes, matching center of sleeve with shoulder seams. Sew side and sleeve seams.

19¾ (50)
15 (38)
11¾ (30)
2 (5)

SLEEVE

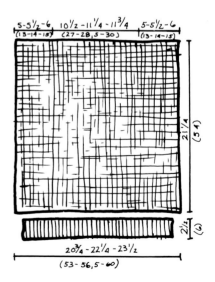

5-5½-6 (13-14-15) 10½-11¼-11¾ (27-28,5-30) 5-5½-6 (13-14-15)
21¼ (54)
2¼ (6)
20¾ - 22¼ - 23½ (53 - 56,5 - 60)

FRONT-BACK

GLOWING Apricot

PULLOVER IS A SUMPTUOUS
SAMPLER OF BOBBLE AND RELIEF
STITCHES. SCOOP NECK AND
BATWING SLEEVES HEIGHTEN THE
SUMMERY LOOK.

BATWING PULLOVER

SIZE

Woman's size Small (Medium, Large), bust 30-32 (33-35, 36-38) in. - 76-81.5 (84-89, 91.5-97) cm. Finished bust measurements: 41 (44, 47¼) in. - 104 (112, 120) cm, length: 21½ in. (55 cm), sleeve seam: 15¾ (40 cm).

MATERIALS

10 (11, 12) skeins sport weight boucle cotton yarn (approx. 153 yds per 50 g skein) color tangerine. Crochet hook U.S. size H/8 (U.K. size 6) (Metric size 5) or size needed to obtain gauge. Knitting needles U.S. size 3 (U.K. size 10) (Metric size 3). **To save time, take time to check gauge!**

GAUGE

14 dc and 10 rounds = 4 in. (10 cm).

STITCHES

Chain (ch),
single crochet (sc),
half double crochet (hdc),
double crochet (dc),
slip stitch (sl st).
Front Relief stitch:
Worked in dc by working around the post of the st below. For front relief sts, yo, and insert hook from right to left around the post of the indicated st at front of work. Yo, and draw through loop, then continue as you would for a dc.
Back Relief stitch:
Worked in dc by working around the post of the st below. For back relief sts, yo, and insert hook from right to left around the post of the indicated st in back of work. Yo, and draw through loop, then continue as you would for a dc.

Relief pattern stitch:
Row 1: wrong side of work: Ch 3 (counts as first dc), 1 dc in the 5th ch from the hook, 1 dc in each of the foll ch sts.
Row 2: Ch 2, front relief dc across, end with 1 hdc as last st.
Row 3: Ch 2, back relief dc across, end with 1 hdc as last st.
Always rep rows 2 and 3.
1/1 ribbing: Row 1: *K1, p1*. Rep * to * across.
Row 2 and all foll rows: Work sts as established in previous row.

BODY

Worked from side to side. The front V neck is deeper than the back. Beg with the lower edge of the right sleeve. Ch 40 (42, 44) + ch 3. Work in relief pat st. At each edge of 4th row, inc 1 st at each edge (work 2 relief sts in each edge st). At each edge of every 2nd row, inc 1 st 5 times, inc 2 sts 4 times, inc 3 sts twice, inc 4 sts 3 times, inc 6 (6, 5)

sts twice, inc 8 (7, 8) sts once. (Inc by extending a chain from the side edge, then work back along the chain on the next row.) After inc, the piece will have 38 rows and will measure 15 in. (38 cm) = 144 sts. Work even for 9 (11, 13) rows. Divide work in half. Work the first 71 sts for front. At neck edge of every 2nd row, dec 1 st once, dec 2 sts once, dec 1 st once, dec 2 sts once, dec 1 st once, dec 2 sts 3 times. (For each dec, sl st over required number of sts.) Work rem 58 sts until 26 (28, 30) rows from beg of front. You are now at center of work. Work 2nd half by rev shapings: work 10 (12, 14) rows even, then at neck edge of every 2nd row, inc 2 sts 3 times, inc 1 st once, inc 2 sts once, inc 1 st once, inc 2 sts once, inc 1 st once. Piece will have 43 (45, 47) rows. Now, beg 2 sts after neck edge of front, work back across. At neck edge of every 2nd row, dec 2 sts once, dec 3 sts once, dec 2 sts once, dec 3 sts once, dec 2 sts once, dec 3 sts once, dec 2 sts twice. Work rem 52 sts until you have 26 (28, 30) rows from beg of back. You are now at center of back neck. Work 2nd half to correspond by rev shapings: work 10 (12, 14) rows even, then at neck

edge of every 2nd row, inc 2 sts twice, inc 3 sts once, inc 2 sts once, inc 3 sts once, inc 2 sts once, inc 3 sts once. Work these 71 sts for a total of 43 (45, 47) rows. Work across all sts, ch 2 at center = 144 sts. Work 9 (11, 13) rows, then shape 2nd sleeve by rev shapings of first sleeve: at each edge of every 2nd row, dec 8 (7, 8) sts once, dec 6 (6, 5) sts twice, dec 4 sts 3 times, dec 3 sts twice, dec 2 sts 4 times, dec 1 st 5 times. (For each st dec at beg of row, sl st over specified number of sts. At end of row, leave the specified number of sts unworked and turn.) You now have 40 (42, 44) sts and 38 rows on sleeve. Fasten off.

FINISHING

Block pieces to indicated measurements. With knitting needles, pick up and knit 28 (30, 32) sts from each sleeve end and work 3/4 in. (2 cm) of 1/1 ribbing. Bind off. With knitting needles, pick up and knit 60 (64, 68) sts from front and back and work 1½ in. (4 cm) of 1/1 ribbing. Bind off. With knitting needles, pick up and knit 61 sts from each side of neck, beg at center front and end at back neck and work 3/4 in. (2 cm) of 1/1 ribbing. Bind off loosely. Lap right end over left end and sew in place. Sew side and sleeve seams.

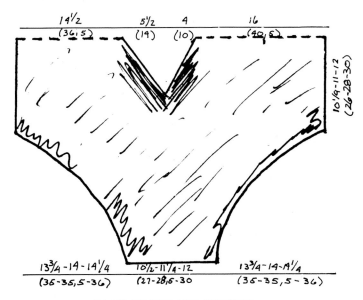

BACK, FRONT AND SLEEVES

CORAL PULLOVER

SIZE

Woman's Small (Medium, Large), bust 30-32 (33-35, 36-38) in. - 76-81.5 (84-89, 91.5-97) cm. Finished bust measurements: 41 (44, 47) in. - 104 (112, 120) cm, length: 23¼ in. (59 cm), sleeve seam 17 in. (43 cm).

MATERIALS

13 (14, 15) skeins "Scheepjeswol Voluma" (85% acrylic, 15% kid mohair - approx. 209 yds per 50 g skein) color coral.
Crochet hooks U.S. sizes C/2 and E/4 (U.K. sizes 11 and 9) (Metric sizes 3 and 3.5) or size needed to obtain gauge. **To save time, take time to check gauge!**

GAUGE

20 dc and 13 rows = 4 in. (10 cm) using larger size hook.

STITCHES

**Chain (ch),
single crochet (sc),
half double crochet (hdc),
double crochet (dc),
slip stitch (sl st).
Front Relief stitch:**
Worked in dc by inserting hook from right to left around the post of the st below. For front relief sts, yo, and insert hook from right to left around the post of the indicated st at front of work. Yo, and draw through loop, then continue as you would for a dc.
Back Relief stitch:
Worked in dc by inserting hook from right to left around the post of the st below. For back relief sts, yo, and insert hook from right to left around the post of the indicated st in back of work. Yo, and draw through loop, then continue as you would for a dc.
Post stitch: Row 1: Ch 3 (counts as first st) 1 dc in each st.

KEY TO CHART

☑ = 1 front relief st on right side of work, 1 back relief st on wrong side of work row.

☐ = 1 back relief st on right side of work, 1 front relief st on wrong side of work row.

Row 2: *1 front relief dc, 1 back relief dc*, rep * to * across row.
Row 3: Work opposite st of the previous row, that is, work 1 relief dc in the front of the st above a back relief st so that the border alternates front and back relief sts on both sides of the work.
Zigzag stitch: Worked by foll chart in front and back relief st. Chart shows sts as they appear on the right side of work. Beg each row with ch 2 and end with 1 hdc.

BACK

With larger size hook, ch 106 (114, 122). **Row 1:** Ch 3 (counts as first st), 1 dc in the 5th ch from hook, 1 dc in each ch = 106 (114, 122) dc. Work by foll chart, beg sizes Small (Medium, Large) as indicated on chart by S (M, L) as foll: right side of work: ch 2, 104 (112, 120) relief dc, 1 hdc. Continue by foll chart until piece measures 20 in. (50 cm) from beg, then work 1¼ in. (3 cm) in post st, beg with 1 front relief st, 1 back relief st (omit Row 1). Fasten off.

FRONT

Work same as back.

SLEEVES

With larger crochet hook, ch 64 (66, 68). **Row 1:** Ch 3 (counts as first st), 1 dc in 5th ch from hook, 1 dc in each ch = 64 (66, 68) dc. Work by foll chart, beg with point 1 (2, 3) on chart. Work 1 row without inc, then work 2 sts in each edge st of next 2 rows = 4 incs every 3 rows 8 times. Work until you have 96 (98, 100) sts + 1 border st at each edge. Work inc sts in zigzag pattern. When piece measures 15¾ in. (40 cm) from beg, fasten off.

FINISHING

Block pieces to indicated measurements. Hold the back and front pieces with right sides tog and join with 1 row of sc, using smaller crochet hook. (Insert hook through corresponding sts of back and front and work across 5¼ (6, 6½) in. - 13.5 (15, 16.5) cm at armhole edge for each shoulder, leaving center open for neck. Crochet sleeves to side seams, matching center of sleeves with shoulder seam. (With right sides tog, work 2 sc every row, working through both thicknesses.) Crochet side and sleeve seams in the same way. With smaller crochet hook, work 32 (34, 36) sc around lower edge of each sleeve, joining round with a sl st. Work 1¼ in. (3 cm) in rounds of post st, joining each round with a sl st. With smaller size crochet hook, work 170 (184, 198) sc around lower edge of back and front, joining round with a sl st. Work 2 in. (5 cm) in post st, joining rounds with a sl st. Fasten off.

FRONT-BACK   **SLEEVE**

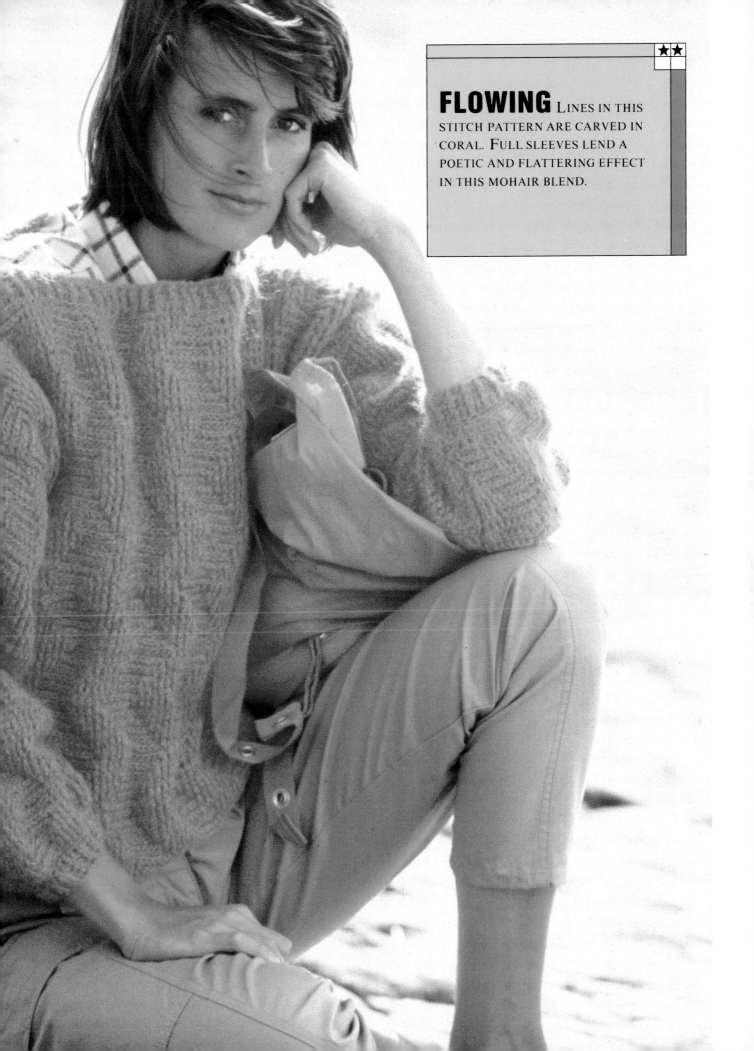

FLOWING LINES IN THIS STITCH PATTERN ARE CARVED IN CORAL. FULL SLEEVES LEND A POETIC AND FLATTERING EFFECT IN THIS MOHAIR BLEND.

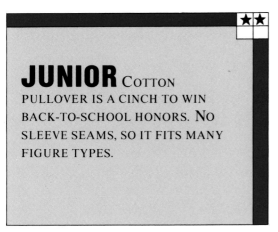

JUNIOR COTTON

PULLOVER IS A CINCH TO WIN
BACK-TO-SCHOOL HONORS. NO
SLEEVE SEAMS, SO IT FITS MANY
FIGURE TYPES.

TEEN
PULLOVER

SIZE

Woman's X Small (Small,
Medium), bust 30-32 (33-
35, 36-38) in. - 76-82.5
(84-89, 91.5-97) cm.
Finished bust measure-
ments: 41½ (43, 45) in. -
106 (110, 114) cm, length:
23¾ in. (58 cm), sleeve
seam 15¾ in. (40 cm).

MATERIALS

21 (22, 22) skeins
"Scheepjeswol Mayflower
Helarsgarn" (100% cotton
- approx. 88 yds per 50 g
skein) color gold.
Crochet hook U.S. size
E/4 (U.K. size 9) (Metric
size 3.5) or size needed to
obtain gauge. Knitting
needles U.S. size 3 (U.K.
size 11) (Metric size 3).
**To save time, take time to
check gauge!**

GAUGE

12 groups (1 dc + ch 1)
and 11½ rows = 4 in.
(10 cm).

STITCHES

**Chain (ch),
single crochet (sc),
half double crochet (hdc),
double crochet (dc),
slip stitch (sl st).**
Relief dc: Worked around
the post of the st of the
previous row. Yo over
hook, insert hook back to
front between next 2 sts,
then back again between
the st worked and the foll
st, hook is now placed
horizontally in front of st,
complete the dc.
Relief pattern stitch:
Multiple of 2 + 1.
Row 1: Ch 3 (counts as 1
hdc + ch 1), 1 hdc in the
6th ch from the hook, *ch
1, skip 1 ch, 1 hdc*.
Row 2: Ch 2 (= 1 border
st), ch 1, sk 1 ch, *1 relief
dc, ch 1, skip 1 ch*, rep *
to *, end with 1 hdc (= 1

border st). Always rep
row 2.
1/1 ribbing: Row 1: *K1,
p1*. Rep * to * across.
Row 2: Work sts as
established in previous
row.

BODY

**Worked from lower end
of left sleeve to lower end
of right sleeve.** With
crochet hook ch 75 and
work in relief pat st = 36
groups + 1 border st at
each edge. At each edge
of every 4th row, inc 1
group (1 hdc, ch 1 in the
st next to the border sts)
4 times. At each edge of
every 3rd row, inc 1
group 4 times. At each

edge of every row, inc 1
group 10 times = 72
groups + 1 border st at
each edge. Work until
piece measures 14 in. (36
cm) from first row of
relief pat st (diagram
shows 1½ in. (4 cm) of
knitted ribbing added
later). At right edge, ch
58. Fasten off.
Working separately, ch 58
and join to left edge.
Work as foll: 1 border st,
ch 1, skip 1 ch, 1 hdc,
rep * to * 28 times, work
74 groups of sleeve, *ch 1,
skip 1 ch, 1 hdc*, 1
border st. On the foll
row, work 130 groups + 1
border st at each edge for
5 (5½, 6) in. - 13 (14, 15)
cm. **Back:** Work the first
65 groups only for 11¾
(12¼, 12½) in. - 30 (31,
32) cm, end on wrong
side of work. Working
separately, work the last
65 groups for the front
for 11¾ (12¼, 12½) in. -
30 (31, 32) cm, leaving 5
groups at the center
unworked. End on wrong
side of work. Now work
across all sts, ch 11 across
center for neck. On the
foll row, work in relief
pat st to center 11 chains
as foll: skip 1 ch, *1 hdc,

ch 1, skip 1 ch*, rep * to
* 4 times, then work
across rem sts in relief pat
st, end with 1 border st.
Work until piece
measures 20¾ (21½, 22½)
in. - 53 (55, 57) cm from
beg. Break yarn. Work
over the center 72 groups
in relief pat st with 1
border st at each edge.
Dec 1 group every row 10
times, dec 1 group every
3rd row 4 times, dec 1
group every 4th row 4
times = 36 groups + 1
border st at each edge.
Fasten off.

FINISHING

Block piece to indicated
measurements. With
knitting needles, pick up
and knit 38 sts from
lower edge of each sleeve
and work 1½ in. (4 cm) of
1/1 ribbing. Bind off.
With knitting needles,
pick up and knit 72 (74,
76) sts from lower edge of
back and work 1½ in. (4
cm) of 1/1 ribbing. Bind
off. Work same border on
lower front. Sew side and
sleeve seams. Work 1
round of sc around neck;
sl st to join. Fasten off.

*Sweaters which are
worked from sleeve to
sleeve have a
tendency to stretch,
especially at the
shoulders and sleeves.
Take extra care to
measure the sleeve
length, allowing for
the natural give of the
stitch. You may want
to use knitting elastic
in the sleeve cuffs as
well to ensure a
comfortable fit.*

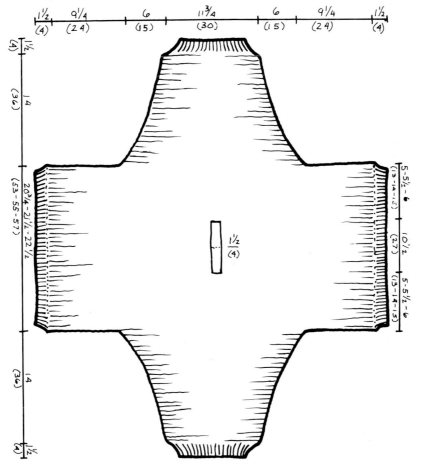

IMPECCABLE

STYLING IS ASSISTED BY A TWEED TEXTURE AND A SHAWL COLLAR. THIS FLEXIBLE MOHAIR JACKET WORKS ON THE JOB OR AFTER HOURS.

★★

MOHAIR JACKET

SIZE

Woman's Large (X Large), bust 36-38 (39-42) in. - 91.5-97 (99-107) cm. Finished bust measurements: 49¼ (51½) in. - 125 (131) cm, length: 27½ (28¾) in. 70 (73) cm, sleeve seam: 18¾ (19¼) in. - 48 (49) cm.

MATERIALS

34 (36) skeins bulky weight fancy mohair yarn (approx. 71 yds per 50 g skein) color green tweed. Crochet hook U.S. size I/9 (U.K. size 5) (Metric size 5.5) or size needed to obtain gauge. **To save time, take time to check gauge!**

GAUGE

15 dc and 9 rows in relief pat = 4 in. (10 cm).

STITCHES

**Chain (ch),
single crochet (sc),
half double crochet (hdc),
double crochet (dc),
slip stitch (sl st).
Front Relief stitch:**
Worked in dc by working around the post of the st below. For front relief sts, yo, and insert hook from right to left around the post of the indicated st at front of work. Yo, and draw through loop, then continue as you would for a dc.
Back Relief stitch:
Worked in dc by working around the post of the st below. For back relief sts, yo, and insert hook from right to left around the post of the indicated st in back of work. Yo, and draw through loop, then continue as you would for a dc.
Post stitch: Row 1: 1 dc in each st.

Row 2: Ch 2 (= 1 border st) *1 front relief dc, 1 back relief dc*, rep * to * across row, end with 1 front relief dc, 1 hdc (= 1 border st).
Row 3: Ch 2, *1 back relief dc, 1 front relief dc*, rep * to * across row, end with 1 back relief dc, 1 hdc.
Always rep rows 2 and 3.

BACK

Ch 95 (99), then work in post st = 91 (95) sts with 1 border st at each edge (the border sts are not included in the final measurements on the chart). When piece measures 6 (6¼) in. - 15 (16) cm from beg, dec 1 st at each edge of work as foll: work border st, work 2 sts tog in relief, work to last 3 sts, work 2 sts tog in relief, work border st. (To work 2 sts tog, insert hook in first st, draw through loop, insert hook in 2nd st, draw through loop, yo, draw through 2 loops, yo, draw through 2 loops. On foll row work in relief dc as established.) Work these dec every 2½ in. (6 cm) 4 times = 83 (87) dc. Work until piece measures 18½ (19¼) in. - 47 (49) cm from beg. Shape armholes: Sl st over first 8 sts, ch 2, work 1 hdc, work to last 9 sts, 1 hdc, leave last 8 sts unworked = 67 (71) dc. Turn. Continue in relief st until piece measures 9 (9¼) in. - 23 (24) cm from armhole. Fasten off.

RIGHT FRONT

Ch 57 (59) and work in relief st = 53 (55) dc + 1 border st at each edge. When piece measures 6 (6¼) in. - 15 (16) cm from beg, dec 1 st at left edge every 2½ in. (6 cm) 4 times. Work until piece measures 18½ (19¼) in. - 47 (49) cm from beg. Shape armhole: Work to

last 9 sts, 1 hdc, turn, leaving last 8 sts unworked. Ch 2, work the rem 41 (43) dc in relief until piece measures 9 (9¼) in. - 23 (24) cm from armhole. Shape shoulder: Work to last 22 (23) dc, then turn and work on rem 19 (20) dc for 3 (3¼) in. - 7.5 (8) cm, end on right side of work. Work 14 (15) sts, turn, work 5 hdc, 9 (10) relief dc, turn, work 4 (5) relief dc. fasten off.

LEFT FRONT

Work same as right front, rev shapings.

SLEEVES

Ch 33 (35), Work in relief st until piece measures 3¼ in. (8 cm) from beg = 29 (31) dc + 1 border st at each edge. In 8 front relief dc, evenly spaced across row, work 1 back relief dc, 1 front relief dc, 1 back relief dc = 45 (47) dc. 1 st in from each edge every 1¼ in. (3 cm), inc 1 st 11 (12) times = 67 (71) dc. Piece will measure 19¾ (20¼) in. - 50 (51) cm from beg. Fasten off.

POCKET

Ch 25. Work in relief st for 6¼ in. (16 cm). Fasten off. Make 2.

FINISHING

Block pieces to indicated measurements. Sew the seam of the shawl collar and sew to center of back. Sew shoulder and side seams. Sew sleeves to armhole, matching upper 2 in. (5 cm) of each sleeve edge to body underarm edges. Sew sleeve seams. Sew pockets to front 2¾ in. (7 cm) from lower edge and 3¼ in. (8 cm) from side seams.

17½ - 18½ (49,5 - 47)

3¾ (8)

14½ - 15 (37-39)

a (5)

11¾ - 12½ (30 - 32)

SLEEVE

5¾ - 6 (19,6 - 15) 6 - 6½ (15 - 16,5) 5¾ - 6 (14,5 - 15)

9 - 9¼ (23 - 24)

12½ - 13 (32 - 33)

6 - 6¼ (15 - 16)

23½ - 24¾ (60 - 63)

BACK

5¾ - 6 (19,5 - 15) 4¾ - 5 (12,5 - 13)

4¼ - 4½ (11 - 11,5)

27½ - 28¾ (70 - 73)

11¾ - 12¼ (30 - 31,5) 2 (5)

RIGHT FRONT

LATTICE PULLOVER

SIZE

Woman's Small (Medium, Large), bust 30-32 (33-35, 36-38) in. - 76-81.5 (84-89, 91.5-97) cm. Finished bust measurements: 44 (48, 52) in. - 112 (122, 132) cm, length: 24¾ in. (63 cm), sleeve seam 17¼ in. (44 cm).

MATERIALS

22 (24, 26) skeins worsted weight yarn (approx. 99 yds per 50 g skein) color gray.
Crochet hooks U.S. sizes E/4 and F/5 (U.K. sizes 9 and 8) (Metric sizes 3.5 and 4) or size needed to obtain gauge. **To save time, take time to check gauge!**

GAUGE

16 sts and 8½ rows = 4 in. (10 cm) in lattice st using larger size hook.

STITCHES

**Chain (ch),
single crochet (sc),
half double crochet (hdc),
double crochet (dc),
treble crochet (tr),
slip stitch (sl st).**
Front Relief dc: Worked in dc by working around the post of the st below. For front relief sts, yo, and insert hook from right to left around the post of the indicated st at front of work. Yo, and draw through loop, then continue as you would for a dc.
Back Relief dc: Worked in dc by working around the post of the st below. For back relief sts, yo, and insert hook from right to left around the post of the indicated st in back of work. Yo, and draw through loop, then continue as you would for a dc.

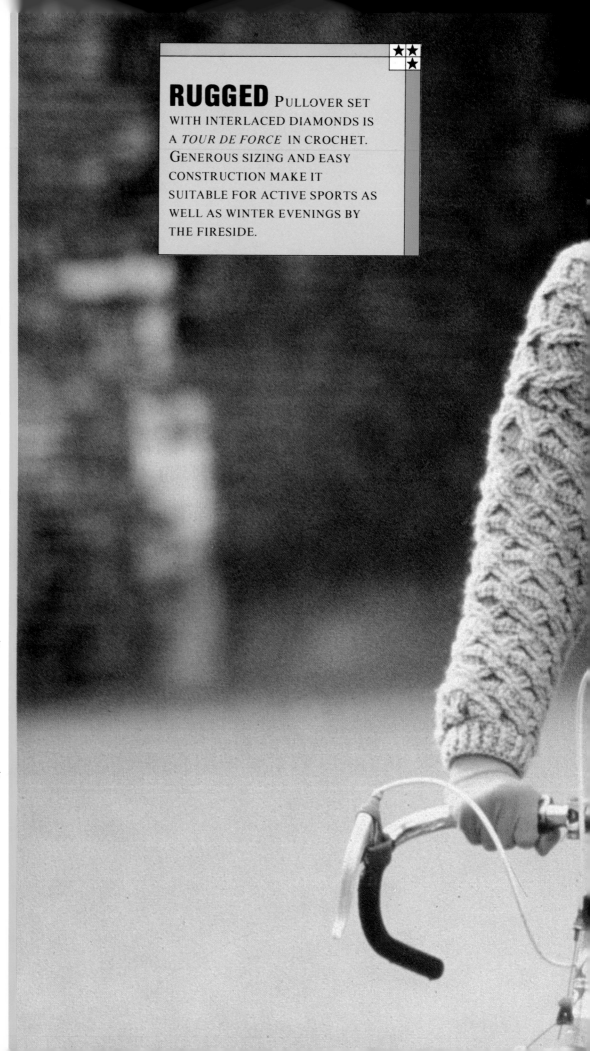

RUGGED PULLOVER SET WITH INTERLACED DIAMONDS IS A *TOUR DE FORCE* IN CROCHET. GENEROUS SIZING AND EASY CONSTRUCTION MAKE IT SUITABLE FOR ACTIVE SPORTS AS WELL AS WINTER EVENINGS BY THE FIRESIDE.

Front Relief tr: Worked in tr by working around the post of the st below. For front relief sts, yo twice, and insert hook from right to left around the post of the indicated st at front of work. Yo, and draw through loop, then continue as you would for a tr.

Back Relief tr: Worked in tr by working around the post of the st below. For back relief sts, yo twice, and insert hook from right to left around the post of the indicated st in back of work. Yo, and draw through loop, then continue as you would for a tr.

Lattice stitch: Multiple of 8 + 10.

Row 1: Right side of work: ch 3 (counts as first dc), 1 dc in the 5th ch and the 6th ch from hook, *skip 2 sts, 2 dc, 2 front relief dc in the skipped sts, 4 dc*, rep * to *, end with 3 dc instead of 4 dc.

Row 2: Ch 3 (counts as first dc), *skip 2 sts, 2 back relief tr, 2 dc in skipped sts (pass hook in front of the back relief tr), skip 2 sts, 2 dc, 1 back relief tr in the skipped sts*, rep * to *, end 1 dc.

Row 3: Ch 3 (counts as first dc), skip 1 st, 1 front relief tr, 1 front relief tr in the skipped st, 2 dc, *2 dc, 1 front relief tr in the 3rd and 4th skipped sts, 2 dc*, rep * to *, skip 1 st, 1 front relief tr in the first skipped st, 1 dc.

Row 4: Ch 3 (counts as first dc), *2 back relief dc, 4 dc, 2 back relief dc*, rep * to *, end 1 dc.

Row 5: Work same as row 3.

Row 6: Ch 3 (counts as first dc), *skip 2 sts, 1 dc in the 3rd and 4th st, 1 back relief tr in the first and 2nd skipped, sts, then skip 2 sts, 1 back relief tr in the 7th and 8th sts, 1 dc in the skipped sts by passing the hook in front of the 7th and 8th sts, 2 dc*, rep * to *, end 1 dc.

Row 7: Ch 3 (counts as first dc), *2 dc, skip 2 sts, 1 front relief tr in the 3rd and 4th sts, 1 front relief tr in the first and 2nd sts (around the skipped sts), 2 dc*, rep * to *, end 1 dc.

Row 8: Ch 3 (counts as first dc), *2 dc, 4 back relief dc, 2 dc* rep * to *, end 1 dc.

Row 9: Work same as row 7.
Always rep rows 2 to 9.

Post stitch: Row 1: Dc.
Row 2: *1 front relief dc, 1 back relief dc*, rep * to * across row.

Row 3: Work opposite st of the previous row, that is, work 1 front relief dc in the front of the st above a back relief st so that the border alternates front and back relief sts on both sides of the work.

BACK

With larger hook, ch 90 (98, 106) + ch 3 (counts as first dc). Work in lattice st by foll chart. Beg first row with 1 dc in the 5th ch from hook, *1 dc in the foll ch, skip 2 sts, 2 dc, 1 front relief dc in skipped sts, 3 dc*, rep * to * 10 (11,12) times = 11 (12, 13) lattice motifs. Continue in lattice st until piece measures 23½ in. (60 cm) from beg. Fasten off.

FRONT

Work same as back for 46 rows. Mark center 28 (30, 32) sts and work each side separately. At neck edge of first 3 rows, work 2 dc tog (insert hook in first dc to be worked tog, draw through loop and insert hook in 2nd dc, yo and draw through loop, yo and draw through 4 loops on hook). You now have 28 (31, 34) sts. Continue in lattice st until piece measures 23½ in. (60 cm) from beg. Fasten off.

SLEEVES

With larger hook ch 58 + ch 3 (counts as first dc). Work in lattice st across = 7 lattice motifs. Inc 1 dc at each edge of every 2nd row 12 (14, 16) times (work 2 dc in each edge st). Work new sts in lattice st. You now have 82 (86, 90) sts. When sleeve measures 16 in. (41 cm) from beg, fasten off.

FINISHING

Block pieces to indicated measurements. Sew shoulder seams. Sew sleeves to side seams, matching center of sleeve with shoulder seams. Sew side and sleeve seams. With smaller hook work 34 (36, 38) sc along edge of each sleeve, skipping 1 st in each group of crossed sts. Join round with a sl st, then work in rounds of post st, joining each round with a sl st and beg each round with ch 3. Work post st for 1¼ in. (3 cm). Fasten off. Work 1 round of sc around lower edge of body, skipping 1 st in each group of crossed sts. Join round with a sl st, then work in rounds of post st, joining each round with a sl st and beg each round with ch 3. Work post st for 1¼ in. (3 cm). Fasten off. Work 34 (36, 38) sc around neck, skipping 1 st in each group of crossed sts. Join round with a sl st, then work 2 rounds of post st, joining each round with a sl st and beg each round with ch 3. Then work 1 round of dc and 1 round of post st. Fasten off.

KEY TO CHART

- • = ch 1
- | = 1 dc
- ↓ = 1 relief dc
- ↓ = 1 relief tr

The chart shows sts as they appear on right side of work.

FRONT-BACK   **SLEEVE**

ELABORATE CABLES

EMBELLISH THE YOKE OF THIS JACKET IN THE ARAN TRADITION. A CHALLENGE TO CROCHET, BUT A SHOWCASE FOR YOUR SKILLS!

ARAN-STYLE CABLE CARDIGAN

SIZE

Woman's Small/ Medium (Large/ X Large), bust 30-35 (36-42) in. - 76-89 (91.5-107) cm. Finished bust measurements: 44½ (52) in. - 113 (132) cm, length: 25¼ (26) in. - 64 (66) cm, sleeve seam: 17 in. (43 cm).

MATERIALS

21 (23) skeins worsted weight yarn (approx. 99 yds per 50 g skein) color ecru.
Crochet hooks U.S. sizes E/4 and F/5 (U.K. sizes 9 and 8) (Metric sizes 3.5 and 4) or size needed to obtain gauge. 7 buttons.
To save time, take time to check gauge!

GAUGE

16 dc and 8 rows = 4 in. (10 cm) in cable lattice using larger size hook.

STITCHES

**Chain (ch),
single crochet (sc),
half double crochet (hdc),
double crochet (dc),
treble (tr),
slip stitch (sl st).
Relief stitches:** Worked in dc or tr by working around the post of the st below. For front relief sts, yo, and insert hook from right to left around the post of the indicated st at front of work. Yo, and draw through loop, then continue as you would for a dc or tr. For back relief sts, yo, and insert hook from right to left under the post of the indicated st at back of work. Yo, and draw through loop, then continue as you would for a dc or tr.

Right Cable: Row 1: 1 dc in 5th ch from hook, *1 dc in foll ch; skip 2 ch; 1 tr in foll 2 ch; passing hook in front of 2 tr, work 1 tr in each of 2 skipped sts; 1 dc in each of foll 3 ch*, rep * to * across, 1 dc = 1 border st.
Row 2: Ch 3 = 1 border st, *1 dc in each of foll 3 dc, 1 back relief dc around each of foll 4 tr, 1 dc*, rep * to * across, 2 dc (last dc = border st).
Row 3: Ch 3 = 1 border st, 1 dc, *1 dc, skip 2 sts, work 1 relief tr in front and around next 2 sts (= 2 front relief tr), 1 front relief tr in each of 2 skipped sts, 1 dc in each of next 3 dc*, rep * to * across, 1 dc (= border st). Always rep rows 2 and 3.
Lattice Cable: Worked 3 times at top of sweater. Rep top 8 rows of chart twice for lattice cable, end with last 4 rows of chart.

KEY TO CHART

| | = tr
| = relief tr
| = relief dc
· = ch
| = dc

first row of lattice cable →
2nd row right cable →
← first row right cable
Repeat
Repeat
Repeat

Post stitch: Row 1: 1 dc in each st.
Row 2: *1 relief dc in the front of the st, 1 relief dc in the back of the st*, rep * to * across.
Row 3: Work opposite st of the previous row, that is, work 1 relief dc in the front of the st above a back relief st so that the border alternates front and back relief sts on both sides of the work.

BACK

With larger size crochet hook, ch 90 (106) + ch 3 to turn. Work in right cable st foll chart. You will have 11 (13) cables across + 1 border st at each edge. Work 27 (29) rows of cable, ending with 3rd row of pat repeat. Then work in lattice cable pat, rep rows 1 to 8 for a total of 20 rows, ending with the 4th row of lattice cable. Fasten off.

RIGHT FRONT

With larger size crochet hook, ch 42 (50) + ch 3 to turn. Work in right cable st foll chart. You will have 5 (6) cables across + 1 border st at each edge. Work for 27 (29) rows of cable, ending with the 3rd row of pat repeat. Continue in lattice cable pat. On the 16th row of lattice pat rep, sl st over the first 11 (14) sts, work to end of row. On foll row, work to last 2 sts, yo, insert hook in next st, yo and draw through loop, yo, draw through 2 loops, yo, insert hook in next st, yo and draw through loop, yo and draw through 2 loops, yo, draw through 3 loops on hook (= 1 dec). Turn and work 1 dec over the first 2 sts. Work to end of row. Fasten off.

LEFT FRONT

Work same as right front, rev neck shapings.

SLEEVES

With larger size crochet hook, ch 58 + ch 3 to turn (counts as first dc). Work in right cable st foll chart. You will have 7 cables + 1 border st at each edge. At each edge of every 2nd row, work 2 dc in each edge st 12 (15) times. Work inc sts in right cable sts as you inc. You now have 82 (88) sts. After the 31st row of right cable st, fasten off.

FINISHING

Block pieces to indicated measurements. Sew shoulder seams. Sew sleeves to side seams, matching center of sleeve with shoulder seam. Work top 2 rows of sleeve and edge st of body armhole in seam allowance. Sew sleeve and side seams. With smaller size crochet hook, work 30 (32) sc along lower edge of sleeve and join with sl st: Then work 1 round alternating back relief dc and front relief dc. Join with sl st. Work 1½ in. (4 cm) in post st. Fasten off. With smaller size crochet hook, work 1 row of sc along lower edge of body as foll: work 1 sc in each st, but skip 1 st on each cable. Be sure to work an odd number of sts. Work 2 in. (5 cm) in post st. Fasten off.
With smaller size crochet hook, work 1 row of sc along neck edge, skipping 1 st every cable. (Be sure to work an odd number of sts.) Work 1 row of dc, 1 row of post st. With larger size crochet hook, work 1 row of sc along left front border, working 3 sc every 2 rows. Work 3 (2) rows of sc, then change to smaller size crochet hook and work 1 row of sc. Work same border on right front, but on the 2nd row, mark positions for 7 evenly spaced buttonholes. For each buttonhole, ch 2 and ship 2 sts. On foll row, work 2 sc over ch-2 space. Fasten off. Reinforce buttonholes. Sew on buttons.

7¼-8-8½ 3¼-3½-4
(18.5-20-21.5 (8.5-9-10)

19-19¾-20¼
(48.5-50-51.5)

15¼
(39)

1½
(4)

2½
(55)

19¼
(49)

2
(5)

2
(5)

21¼ - 22¾ - 24¼
(54 - 58 - 61.5)

10½-11½-12¼
(27-29-31.5)

11¾-12¼-13
(30-31.5-33)

BACK   RIGHT FRONT   SLEEVE

BOBBLE CABLES MADE FROM A WORSTED YARN IN WINTER WEIGHT MAKES THIS CARDIGAN A FAVORITE SWEATER IN COLD WEATHER.

BOBBLE CARDIGAN

SIZE

Woman's Small (Medium, Large), bust 30-32 (33-35, 36-38) in. - 76-81.5 (84-89, 91.5-97) cm. Finished bust measurements: 43 (46, 49) in. - 109 (117, 125) cm, length: 23½ in. (60 cm), sleeve seam 17 in. (43 cm).

MATERIALS

18 (19, 20) skeins worsted weight yarn (approx. 91 yds per 50 g skein) color ecru.
Crochet hooks U.S. sizes E/4 and F/5 (U.K. sizes 9 and 8) (Metric sizes 3.5 and 4) or size needed to obtain gauge. 7 buttons.
To save time, take time to check gauge!

GAUGE

14 sts and 7 rows = 4 in. (10 cm) in pat sts using larger size hook.

STITCHES

**Chain (ch),
single crochet (sc),
half double crochet (hdc),
double crochet (dc),
treble (tr),
slip stitch (sl st).**
Relief stitches: Worked in dc or tr by working around the post of the st below. For front relief sts, yo, and insert hook from right to left around the post of the indicated st. Yo, and draw through loop, then continue as you would for a dc or tr.
Bobble: All in 1 st: *yo, insert hook in st, yo, draw through loop*, rep * to * 5 times total so that you have 11 loops. Yo and draw through 10 loops, yo and draw through last 2 loops.
Cable motif: worked over 8 sts. Foll the chart and work as foll:
Row 1: Right side of work: 1 dc in the first and 2nd st, skip 2 sts, 1 tr relief st in the 5th and 6th sts, skip 2 sts, 1 front tr relief st in the 3rd and 4th sts, 1 dc in the 7th and 8th sts.
Row 2: Wrong side of work: skip the next 2 dc, 1 back tr in the 3rd and 4th sts, 1 front tr in the 2nd st, 1 front tr in the 7th and 8th dc, skip 2 sts, 1 back tr relief st in the 5th and 6th sts.

Row 3: 1 bobble in the first st, 1 dc in the foll st, skip 2 sts, front tr relief st in the 3rd and 4th sts, 2 front tr relief sts in the 2 skipped sts, 1 dc in the 7th st, 1 bobble in the 8th st. Rep the 2nd and 3rd row.
Post stitch: Row 1: Dc.
Row 2: *1 front relief dc, 1 back relief dc*, rep * to * across row.
Row 3: Work opposite st of the previous row, that is work 1 front relief dc in the st above a back relief st so that the border alternates front and back relief sts on both sides of the work.

BACK

With larger size crochet hook, ch 76 (81, 86) + ch 2 to turn (counts as the first hdc). **Row 1:** 1 hdc in the 4th ch from the hook = 76 (81, 86) hdc, ch 3.
Row 2: 4 dc, *8 sts in cable motif, 4 (5, 6) dc*, work * to * 5 times total, 8 sts in cable motif, 4 dc.
Row 3: Ch 3 = first st, 5 dc, *skip 2 sts, 1 front tr relief st in the foll 2 hdc, 1 front tr relief st in each of the foll 2 skipped hdc, 8 (9, 10) dc*, rep * to * 6 times, end with 6 dc. You have 6 repeats of the cable motif horizontally with 4 (5, 6) dc between them and 4 dc at each edge. Work Rows 2 and 3 until piece measures about 21½ in. (55 cm) from beg, ending with the 3rd row (with bobbles) of the cable motif. Fasten off.

RIGHT FRONT

Ch 38 (41, 44) + ch 2 to turn (= first hdc). **Row 1:** 1 hdc in the 4th ch from the hook = 38 (41, 44) hdc. **Row 2:** 2 (3, 4) dc, then *8 sts of cable motif, 4 (5, 6) dc*, work * to * twice, end with 8 sts of cable motif, 4 dc. Work until piece measures about 19¼ in. (49 cm) from beg (4 rows less than back).
Shape Neck: At right edge, right side facing, sl st over first 10 (11, 12) sts. Work to end of row, turn and continue to last st of foll row. Turn, leaving last st unworked. Sl st over first st, work to end of row. Work 1 row over 26 (28, 30) sts. Fasten off.

LEFT FRONT

Work same as right front, but rev order of pat st as foll: 4 dc, *8 sts of cable motif, 4 (5, 6) dc*, work * to * twice, end with 8 sts of cable motif, 2 (3, 4) dc. Complete same as right front, working neck shaping as foll: work to last 10 (11, 12) sts, turn. Work to last st, turn. Sl st over first st, work to end of row. Work 1 row over rem 26 (28, 30) sts. Fasten off.

SLEEVES

Ch 42 (44, 46) + ch 2 to turn (= first hdc). **Row 1:** 1 hdc in the 4th ch from the hook = 42 (44, 46) hdc. **Row 2:** 5 dc, *8 sts of cable motif, 4 (5, 6) dc*, work * to * twice, end with 8 sts of cable motif, 5 dc. At each edge of every 2nd row, work 2 dc in each edge st 13 times. Work inc sts in pat = 68 (70, 72) sts. When piece measures about 15¼ in. (39 cm) from beg, ending with row 3 of pat. Fasten off.

FINISHING

Block pieces to indicated measurements. Sew shoulder seams. Sew sleeves to side seams, matching center of sleeve with shoulder seam. Sew side and sleeve seams. With smaller size hook, work 28 (30, 32) sc along lower edge of each sleeve, join the end of round to first st of round with 1 sl st. Work in post st joining each round with a sl st and beg each round with a ch 3. Work for 1½ in. (4 cm), then fasten off. With smaller size crochet hook, work 1 row of sc along lower edge of body, skipping every 5th st. (Be sure to work odd number of sts.) Work in post st for 2 in. (5 cm). Fasten off. With smaller size crochet hook, work 1 sc in each st and 2 sc at each corner of neck edges. (Be sure to work an odd number of sts.) Work 2 rows of post st. Fasten off. With smaller size crochet hook, work 3 sc every 2 rows along the left front edge. Work 3 rows of post st. Fasten off. Work same band along the right front edge, but on the 2nd row, make 7 buttonholes. Mark positions for buttonholes evenly spaced along edge. For each buttonhole, ch 2, skip 2 sc. On foll row, work 2 sc over each ch-2 space. Fasten off. Reinforce buttonholes. Sew on buttons.

FRONT

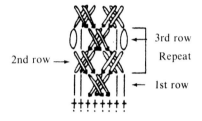

2nd row → ← 3rd row
Repeat
← 1st row

KEY TO CHART

- • = ch
- O = bobble
- ◊ = relief dc
- ◊ = relief quad
- + = hdc
- | = dc

BACK

SLEEVE

MOTIFS ARE EASY WHEN YOU FOLLOW A CHART. THE THUNDERBOLT MOTIF ON THIS BOATNECK SWEATER ADDS REAL DISTINCTION. A GOLD PULLOVER IS SHOWN, BUT TRY IT ALSO IN BLUE.

BOATNECK PULLOVERS

SIZE

Woman's Small (Medium, Large), bust 30-32 (33-35, 36-38) in. - 76-81.5 (84-89, 91.5-97) cm. Finished bust measurements: 41 (44, 47) in. - 104 (112, 120) cm, length: 23¼ in. (59 cm), sleeve seam 17 in. (43 cm).

MATERIALS

14 (15, 16) skeins "Scheepjeswol Voluma" (85% acrylic, 15% kid mohair - approx. 209 yds per 50 g skein) color blue or gold.
Crochet hooks U.S. sizes C/2 and E/4 (U.K. sizes 11 and 9) (Metric sizes 3 and 3.5) or size needed to obtain gauge. **To save time, take time to check gauge!**

GAUGE

20 dc and 13 rows = 4 in. (10 cm) in relief stitch using larger size hook.

STITCHES

**Chain (ch),
single crochet (sc),
half double crochet (hdc),
slip stitch (sl st).
Front Relief stitch:**
Worked in dc by working around the post of the st below. For front relief sts, yo, and insert hook from right to left around the post of the indicated st at front of work. Yo, and draw through loop, then continue as you would for a dc.
Back Relief stitch:
Worked in dc by working around the post of the st below. For back relief sts, yo, and insert hook from right to left around the post of the indicated st in back of work. Yo, and

draw through loop, then continue as you would for a dc.
Pattern stitch: Foll the chart. The chart shows sts as they appear on right side of work. At each edge of every row, work 1 border st at each edge: ch 2 at beg of each row and 1 hdc at end of each row. The border sts are not shown on chart.
BLUE PULLOVER: Foll chart for blue pullover. Beg back and front at point A (B, C). Beg sleeve at points D (B, E). Beg wrong side rows with point Z.
GOLD PULLOVER: Foll chart for gold pullover. Beg back and front with points A (B, C). Beg sleeve at points D (B, E). Beg wrong side of work rows with point Z. Repeat lower part of chart until piece measures 11½ in. (29 cm) from beg, then work 6 rows reversing direction of diagonals as shown on chart. Work top part of chart until piece measures 20 in. (50 cm) from beg, end with the last row of chart. Beg sleeve with points D (B, E). Work the lower part of chart (left to right diagonals) for about 13¾ in. (35 cm), then work center 6 rows of chart (right to left diagonals).
Post stitch: Row 1: Dc.
Row 2: *1 front relief dc, 1 back relief dc*, rep * to * across row.
Row 3: Work opposite st of the previous row, that is, work 1 front relief dc above a back relief st so that the border alternates front and back relief sts on both sides of the work.

BACK

With larger size crochet hook, ch 106 (114, 122).
Foundation row: Ch 3 (counts as first st), 1 dc in the 5th ch from hook, dc across = 106 (114, 122) dc, continue by foll chart for blue or gold pullover. With right side facing, ch 2 (first st), 104 (112, 120) relief sts, 1 hdc. Continue by foll chart until piece measures 20 in. (51 cm) from beg. Work 1¼ in. (3 cm) in post st. Fasten off.

FRONT

Work same as back.

SLEEVES

With larger size crochet hook, ch 64 (66, 68).
Foundation Row: Ch 3 (counts as first st), 1 dc in 5th ch from hook, dc across = 64 (66, 68) dc. Work by foll chart, beg on right side of work: ch 2, 62 (64, 66) relief, 1 hdc. Continue by foll chart. **At the same time**, at each edge of 2nd row and each edge of every 3rd row, inc 1 st 17 times (4 incs every 3 rows) = 96 (98, 100) relief dc + 1 border st at each edge. For each inc work 2 sts in edge sts. Work inc sts in relief st by foll chart. When piece measures 15¾ in. (40 cm) from beg, fasten off.

FINISHING

Block pieces to indicated measurements. With smaller size crochet hook, sc the shoulders tog: hold the back and front with right sides tog. Insert hook through both thicknesses in corresponding sts and sc across for 5¼ (6, 6½) in. - 13.5 (15, 16.5) cm at each armhole edge. Fasten off. With smaller size crochet hook, sc the sleeves to the side seams, matching center of sleeve with shoulder seam and sc sleeve and side seams: hold the piece with right sides tog. Insert hook through both thicknesses in corresponding sts and work across in sc, working 2 sts every row. Fasten off. With smaller size hook, crochet 32 (34, 36) sc along lower edge of each sleeve and sl st into round. Work 1¼ in. (3 cm) of post st. Join each round with a sl st and begin each round with ch 3. Fasten off. With smaller size hook, work 170 (184, 198) sc along lower edge of body and sl st into round. Work 2 in. (5 cm) of post st. Fasten off.

Your choice of color can make the same sweater look strikingly different. For another look, try changing the color when the direction of the diagonals change to further emphasize the relief pattern.

5¼-6-6½ 9¾-10¼-10½ 6¼-6-6½
(13.5-15-16.5) (25-26-27) (13.5-15-16.5)

20
(51)

3

FRONT-BACK

20½-22-23½
(52-56-60)

2 (3)

18¾-19¼-19¾
(48-49-50)

15¾
(40)

SLEEVE

12¼-12½-13
(31-32-33)

2 (3)

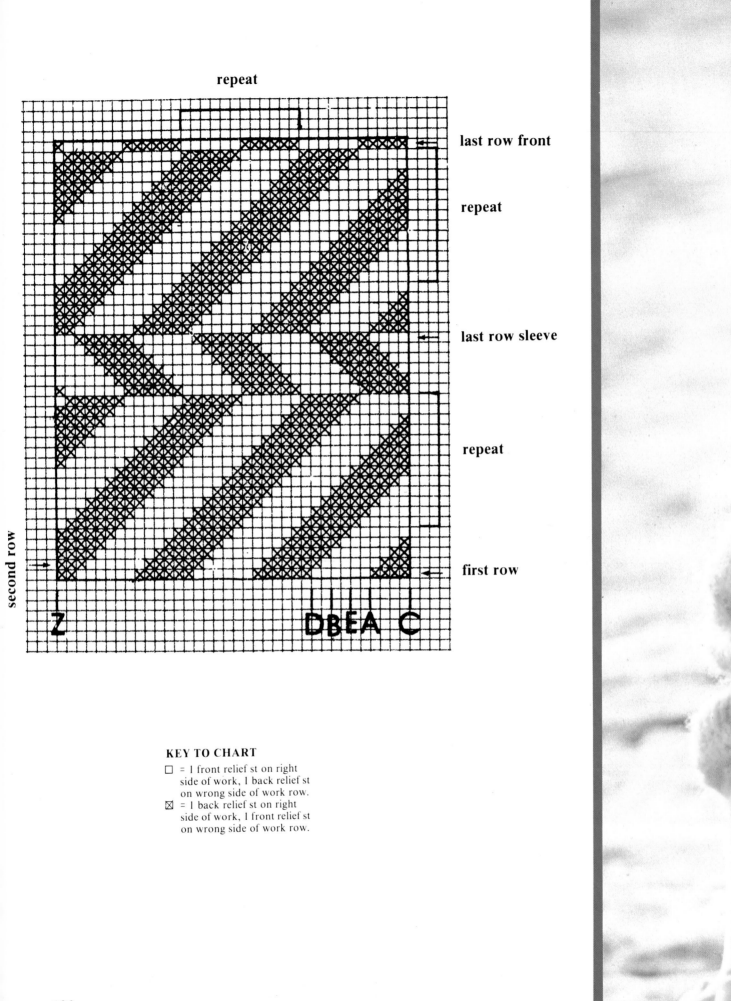

repeat

last row front

repeat

last row sleeve

repeat

first row

second row

Z

DBEA C

KEY TO CHART

☐ = 1 front relief st on right
side of work, 1 back relief st
on wrong side of work row.

☒ = 1 back relief st on right
side of work, 1 front relief st
on wrong side of work row.

BASKET-WEAVE PULLOVER

SIZE

Woman's Small (Medium, Large), bust 30-32 (33-35, 36-38) in. - 76-81.5 (84-89, 91.5-97) cm. Finished bust measurements: 41 (44, 47) in. - 104 (112, 120) cm, length: 23½ in. (60 cm), sleeve seam 17 in. (43 cm).

MATERIALS

18 (18, 20) skeins sport weight cotton yarn (approx. 120 yds per 50 g skein) color blue. Crochet hook U.S. size C/2 (U.K. size 11) (Metric size 3) or size needed to obtain gauge. Knitting needles U.S. size 2 (U.K. size 12) (Metric size 2.5). **To save time, take time to check gauge!**

GAUGE

5 groups of 3 relief dc and 13 rows = 4 in. (10 cm).

STITCHES

**Chain (ch),
single crochet (sc),
half double crochet (hdc),
double crochet (dc),
slip stitch (sl st).**
Relief stitches: Worked in dc by working around the post of the st below. For front relief dc, yo, and insert hook from right to left around the post of the indicated st. Yo, and draw through loop, then continue as you would for a dc. For back relief dc, work the same as above, but work under the post of the st of the previous row, but work in back of st.

Pattern stitch: Worked over 8 + 1.
Row 1: Ch 3 (counts as first dc), 1 dc in the 5th ch from hook, 2 dc, *ch 1, skip ch-1 sp, 3 dc*, rep * to * across, end with 1 dc in the last ch.
Row 2: Ch 2 (= border st), *3 front relief dc, skip ch-1 sp, ch 1, 3 back relief dc, ch 1, skip ch-1 sp*, rep * to * across, end the last rep with 1 hdc instead of ch 1, skip ch-1 sp = 1 border st.
Row 3: Work same sts as established in previous row, with 1 border st at each edge.
Row 4: Ch 2 (= border st), *3 back relief dc, skip ch-1 sp, ch 1, 3 front relief dc, ch 1, skip ch-1 sp*, rep * to * across, end the last rep with 1 hdc instead of ch 1, skip ch-1 sp = 1 border st.
Row 5: Work same sts as established in previous row, with 1 border st at each edge.
Rep rows 2 to 5.
1/1 ribbing: Row 1: *K1, p1*. Rep * to * across.
Row 2 and all foll rows: Work sts as established in previous row.

BACK

With crochet hook, ch 105 (113, 121), then continue in pat st, beg row 1 with ch 3. After the first row, you will have 26 (28, 30) groups of 3 dc + 1 border st at each edge. Continue until piece measures 20¾ in. (53 cm) from beg, ending with the 3rd or 5th row of pat st. Mark the center 14 groups for the neck. Shape shoulders: Work the first 6 (7, 8) groups in pat st. After the last group of 3, ch 1, then 1 hdc in the first st of the foll group (= border st). Work 1 row in pat st, then fasten off. Work 2nd shoulder to correspond.

FRONT

Work same as back.

SLEEVES

Ch 53 (57, 61). Work in pat st, beg row 1 with ch 3. You will have 13 (14, 15) groups of 3 dc + 1 border st at each edge. At each edge of every 2nd row, work 2 sts in each edge st until you have 23 (24, 25) groups of 3 dc + 1 border st at each edge. Work the edge sts in pat as you inc. When sleeve measures 15 in. (38 cm) from beg, fasten off.

FINISHING

Block pieces to indicated measurements. With knitting needles, pick up and knit 30 (34, 38) sts along lower edge of sleeves and work 2 in. (5 cm) of 1/1 ribbing. Bind off loosely. With knitting needles, pick up and knit 70 (78, 86) sts along lower edge of back and front and work 2 in. (5 cm) of 1/1 ribbing. Bind off loosely. Crochet shoulder seams tog: with right sides facing, hold the pieces tog and work 1 row of sc along each shoulder, working 1 sc in each st, skipping the ch sts between the groups of dc. Fasten off. Sew sleeves to side seams, matching center of sleeve with shoulder seam. Sew side and sleeve seams using mattress st: lay the pieces tog, right sides facing. Insert needle around the strand after the border st, then insert needle around the strand after the border st on the next piece, but 1 row above. Continue to work from piece to piece, joining the 2 edges. With crochet hook, work 1 row of sc around neck, working 1 sc in each st, skipping the ch sts between the groups. Fasten off.

FRONT-BACK

SLEEVE

INTENSE INDIGO COTTON IS A BOLT FROM THE BLUE. THE BASKETWEAVE STITCH, EASILY MASTERED, ADDS IMPACT TO THIS SIMPLE SILHOUETTE.

CABLE CARDIGAN

SIZE

Woman's Small (Medium, Large), bust 30-32 (33-35, 36-38) in. - 76-81.5 (84-89, 91.5-97) cm. Finished bust measurements: 42½ (45½, 49) in. - 108 (116, 124) cm, length: 23½ in. (60 cm), sleeve seam: 17¾ in. (45 cm).

MATERIALS

9 (9, 10) skeins worsted weight yarn (approx. 100 yds per 50 g skein) color ecru.
Crochet hook U.S. size F / 5 (U.K. size 8) (Metric size 4) or size needed to obtain gauge. 7 leather buttons. **To save time, take time to check gauge!**

GAUGE

14 dc and 10 rows = 4 in. (10 cm).

STITCHES

Chain (ch), single crochet (sc), half double crochet (hdc), double crochet (dc), slip stitch (sl st).
Front Relief stitches: Worked in dc by working around the post of the st below. For front relief sts, yo, and insert hook from right to left around the post of the indicated st at front of work. Yo, and draw through loop, then continue as you would for a dc.

Back Relief stitch: Worked in dc by working around the post of the st below. For back relief sts, yo, and insert hook from right to left around the post of the indicated st at back of work. Yo, and draw through loop, then continue as you would for a dc.

Pattern stitch:
Row 1: Ch 2 (counts as first hdc), 1 hdc in the 4th ch from the hook, hdc across, ch 2 to turn.
Row 2: wrong side of work: *2 hdc, 2 back relief dc, 2 hdc*, rep * to * across, ch 2 to turn.
Row 3: right side of work: *2 hdc, 1 front relief dc around the 2nd relief dc, 1 front relief dc around the first dc, 2 hdc*, rep * to * across row, ch 2 to turn.
Row 4: *2 hdc, 1 back relief dc in each of the crossed relief dc of the previous row, 2 hdc*, rep * to * across, ch 2 to turn. Always rep rows 3 and 4.
Post stitch: Row 1: 1 dc in each st.
Row 2: *1 front relief dc, 1 back relief dc*, rep * to * across row.
Row 3: Work opposite st of the previous row, that is, work 1 front relief dc above a back relief st so that the border alternates front and back relief sts on both sides of the work.

BACK

Ch 78 (84, 90). Work in pat st as foll: **Row 1:** Ch 2, 1 hdc in the 4th ch from the hook, 76 (82, 88) hdc = 78 (84, 90) hdc.
Row 2: *2 hdc, 2 back relief dc, 2 hdc*, rep * to * 13 (14, 15) times = 13 (14, 15) cables + 2 hdc at each edge and 4 hdc between each cable. When piece measures 21½ in. (55 cm) from beg, fasten off.

RIGHT FRONT

Ch 38 (41, 44). Work in pat st as foll: **Row 1:** Ch 2, 1 hdc in the 4th ch from hook, 36 (39, 42) hdc across row = 38 (41, 44) hdc. **Row 2:** *2 hdc, 2 back relief dc, 2 hdc*, rep * to * 6 (6, 7) times, end 2 hdc, 0 (2, 0) back relief dc, 0 (1, 0) hdc = 6 (7, 7) cables + 4 (1, 4) hdc at right edge and 2 hdc after last cable at left edge. Work until piece measures 19¼ in. (49 cm) = 6 rows less than back. Shape neck: at right edge, sl st over 7 (8, 9) sts, work to end of row. Work foll row to last 3 sts, turn. Sl st over first 2 sts, ch 2, work to end of row. Work 3 more rows over rem 26 (28, 30) sts. Fasten off.

LEFT FRONT

Ch 38 (41, 44). Work in pat st as foll: **Row 1:** Ch 2, 1 hdc in the 4th ch from hook, 36 (39, 42) hdc across row = 38 (41, 44) hdc. **Row 2:** Ch 2, 0 (1, 0) hdc, 0 (2, 0) back relief dc, *2 hdc, 2 back relief dc, 2 hdc*, rep * to * 6 (6, 7) times, end with 0 (1, 0) hdc = 6 (7, 7) cables + 4 (1, 4) hdc at left edge and 2 hdc after last cable at right edge. Work until piece measures 19¼ in. (49 cm) = 6 rows less than back.
Shape neck: work to last 7 (8, 9) sts, turn. Sl st over first 3 sts, work to end of row, turn, ch 2. Work to last 2 sts, turn. Work 3 more rows over rem 26 (28, 30) sts. Fasten off.

SLEEVES

Ch 44 (46, 48). Work in pat st as foll: **Row 1:** Ch 2, 1 hdc in the 4th ch from hook, 42 (44, 46) hdc = 44 (46, 48) hdc.
Row 2: Ch 2, *2 hdc, 2 back relief dc, 2 hdc*, rep * to * 7 (7, 8) times = 7 (8, 8) cables with 4 hdc between each cable. At beg edge you will have 2 hdc and at end you will have 4 (0, 2) hdc.
Continue in pat st. At each edge of every 3rd row, inc 1 st 12 times. (For each inc, work 2 sts in each edge st) = 68 (70, 72) sts = 11 (12, 12) cables and 2 hdc at 1 edge and 4 (0, 2) hdc. Work until piece measures 15¾ in. (40 cm) from beg. Fasten off.

FINISHING

Block pieces to indicated measurements. Sew shoulder seams. Work 32 (34, 36) sc along lower edge of each sleeve, then 1 row of dc, then work 4 rows of post st. Join each round with a sl st and begin each round with ch 3. Fasten off. Sew sleeves to side seams, matching center of sleeve with shoulder seam. Sew side and sleeve seams. Along lower edge of body, work 1 sc in every st, skipping every 4th st, being sure to have an uneven number. Work 1 row of dc, then 4 rows of post st. Fasten off. Work 63 (65, 67) sc around neck and then work 1 row of dc, then 1 row of post st. Fasten off. Along the left front edge, work in sc, working 3 sc every 2 rows. Work 2 more rows in sc. Fasten off.
Along right front edge work as foll: **Row 1:** Work 3 sc every 2 rows. **Row 2:** Mark positions for 7 buttonholes. Work in sc and for each buttonhole, ch 2 and skip 2 sc. **Row 3:** Sc across, working sc in the ch sts of previous row. Fasten off. Reinforce buttonholes. Sew on buttons.

BACK

21½ (55)

21¼-22¾-24½ (54-58-62)

RIGHT FRONT

6¾-7¼-8 (17,5-18,5-20) 3¼-3¾-9 (8,5-9,35 ? 10)

19¼ (49)

10¼-11-11¾ (26-28-30)

SLEEVE

18½-19-19¾ (47-48,5-50)

15¾ (40)

11¾-12¼-13 (30-31,5-33)

104

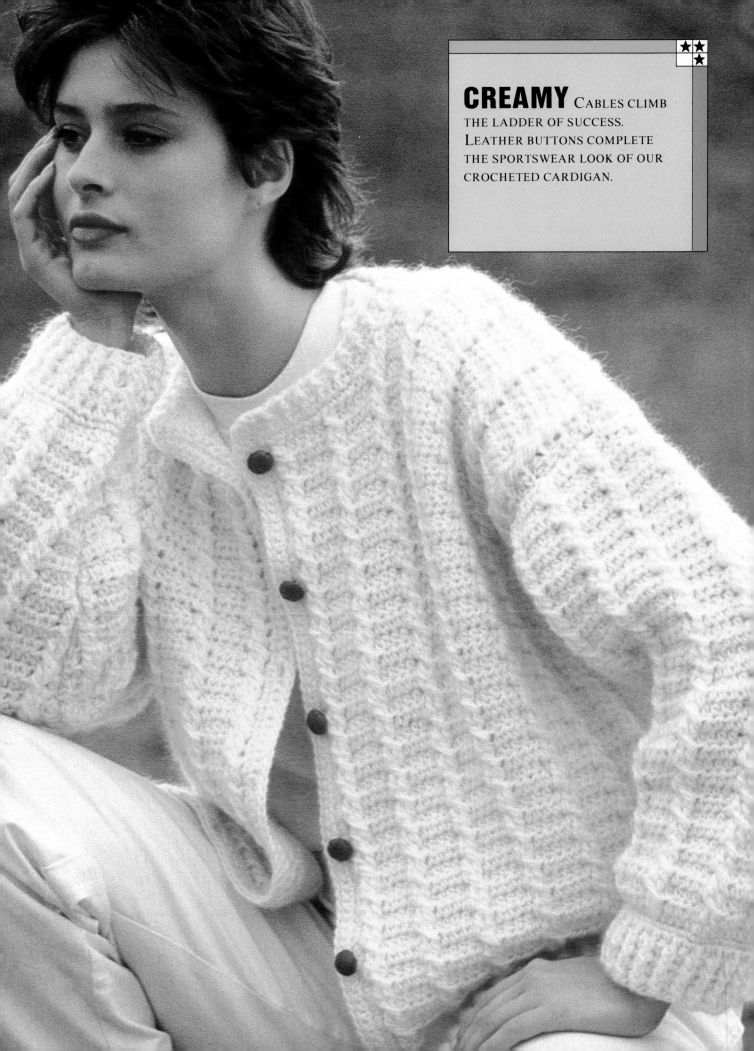

CREAMY CABLES CLIMB
THE LADDER OF SUCCESS.
LEATHER BUTTONS COMPLETE
THE SPORTSWEAR LOOK OF OUR
CROCHETED CARDIGAN.

STREAKS OF
LIGHTNING-LIKE PASTEL COLORS
ELECTRIFY THIS WHITE BOATNECK
PULLOVER. THE COOL, COTTON
YARN MAKES IT COMFORTABLE
ALL SUMMER LONG.

ZIG-ZAG PULLOVER

SIZE

Woman's Small (Medium, Large, X Large), bust 30-32 (33-35, 36-38, 39-42) in. - 76-81.5 (84-89, 91.5-97, 99-107) cm. Finished bust measurements: 43 (47, 51, 54) in. - 110 (120, 129, 138) cm, length: 25½ in. (65 cm), sleeve seam 17¾ in. (45 cm).

MATERIALS

13 (14, 15, 16) skeins double strand "Scheepjeswol Mayflower Cotton 8" (100% cotton yarn -approx. 187 yds per 50 g skein) or "Scheepjeswol Mayflower Helarsgarn" (100% cotton yarn -approx. 88 yds per 50 g skein) color white, 1 skein each color gold, green, pink and blue. Crochet hook U.S. size F/5 (U.K. size 8) (Metric size 4) or size needed to obtain gauge. Knitting needles U.S. size 3 (U.K. size 10) (Metric size 3).

To save time, take time to check gauge!

GAUGE

13 sc and 11 rows = 4 in. (10 cm).

STITCHES

Chain (ch),
single crochet (sc),
slip stitch (sl st).
Relief sc: work in sc by working around the post of the st below. Insert hook from right to left around the post of the indicated st at front of work. Yo, and draw through loop.
Relief pattern: Worked over 6 sts + 1 border st at each edge.
Row 1: Sc across.
Row 2: Ch 1 (= border st), *1 sc in each of the foll 3 sc, 1 relief sc in each of the foll 3 sc*, rep * to * across, end with 1 sc (= border st).

Row 3 and all foll rows:
Ch 1, *1 sc in each of the foll 3 relief sc, 1 relief sc in each of the foll 3 sc*, rep * to *, end with 1 sc.
Stripes: 4 rows white, *2 rows green, 8 rows white, 2 rows gold, 8 rows white, 2 rows blue, 8 rows white, 2 rows pink. 8 rows white*, rep * to *. Ch 3 at the beg of each row (= 1 border st).
2/2 ribbing: Row 1: *K2, p2*. Rep * to * across.
Row 2 and all foll rows:
Work sts as established in previous row.

18-18-20-20
(46-46-50.5-50.5)

15¾
(40)

2
(5)

10¾-10¾-12½-12½
(27.5-27.5-32-32)

SLEEVE

6-6½-7¼-8   9¾-10¼-10¾-11½   6-6½-7¼-8
(15-17-18.5-20) (25-26-27.5-29) (15-17-18.5-20)

23½
(60)

2
(5)

21½-23½-25½-27
(55-60-64.5-69)

FRONT-BACK

ICE CREAM COLORS
MAKE AN APPEALING TOP TO
COORDINATE WITH SISTER'S
PULLOVER. THE WOVEN STITCHES
PROVIDE A PLEASING CONTRAST
IN TEXTURE.

BACK

With knitting needles and white, cast on 86 (90, 94, 98) sts and work 2 in. (5 cm) in 2/2 ribbing. Bind off. With crochet hook, work 72 (78, 84, 90) sc along bound off edge of ribbing and work in relief pat in stripes with 1 border st at each edge. When piece measures 25½ in. (65 cm) from beg, fasten off.

FRONT

Work same as back.

SLEEVES

With knitting needles and white, cast on 34 (34, 38, 38) sts and work 2 in. (5 cm) in 2/2 ribbing. Bind off loosely.
With crochet hook, work 36 (36, 42, 42) sc + 1 border st at each edge along top edge of ribbing and work in relief pat in stripes as foll: 4 rows white, 2 rows blue, 8 rows white, 2 rows pink, 8 rows white, 2 rows green, 2 rows gold, then complete sleeve in white. **At the same time**, at each edge of every 3rd row, inc 1 st by working 2 sc in each edge st. Work incs 12 times. Work inc sts in pat st. You now have 60 (60, 66, 66) sts + 1 border st at each edge. When sleeve measures 17¾ in. (45 cm) from beg, fasten off.

FINISHING

Block pieces to indicated measurements. Sew shoulder seams along 6 (6½, 7¼, 8) in. - 15 (17, 18.5, 20) cm from each armhole edge. Sew sleeves to side seams, matching center of sleeve with shoulder seam. Sew side and sleeve seams.

CHILD'S STRIPED PULLOVER

SIZE

Child's size 4 (6, 8, 10) years, chest 23 (25, 27, 28½) in. - 58.5 (63.5, 69, 72.5) cm. Finished chest measurements: 26½ (28, 29½, 31½) in. - 67 (71, 75, 80) cm, length: 13¼ (15, 16½, 18) in. - 34 (38, 42, 46) cm.

MATERIALS

1 (2, 2, 2) skeins "Scheepjeswol Mayflower Cotton 8" (100% cotton - approx. 187 yds per 50 g skein) color white, 1 skein each color blue, pink, gold and green.
Crochet hook U.S. size C/2 (U.K. size 11) (Metric size 3) or size needed to obtain gauge. Knitting needles U.S. size 2 (U.K. size 10) (Metric size 2.5). **To save time, take time to check gauge!**

GAUGE

18 sts (= 9 motifs) and 16 rows ≐ 4 in. (10 cm).

STITCHES

Chain (ch), single crochet (sc), double crochet (dc), slip stitch (sl st).
Pattern stitch: Ch 3 at the beg of each row (= 1 border st).
Row 1: with white, right side of work: ch 3 (= 1 border st), *2 dc in the foll sc, skip 1 sc*, rep * to * across, end 1 dc in the last dc (= 1 border st). Do not turn, leave the white strand dangling.
Row 2: with blue, right side of work: 1 sc in the ch 3 at beg of row, *1 sc between the 2 dc, ch 1*, rep * to * across, end with 1 sc between the 2 dc, 1 sc in the last st using the dangling strand of white. Cut the blue thread and draw through loop on hook. Turn.
Row 3: with white, wrong side of work, ch 3, *2 dc in ch-1 sp*, rep * to *, end 1 dc in the last sc. Turn and leave the white strand dangling.
Row 4: with pink, right side of work, 1 sc in the dc and the white loop, *ch 1, 1 sc between the 2 dc of the group*, rep * to * across, end with 1 sc in the 3rd ch of the turning ch. Do not turn. Cut the pink strand and draw through the loop on hook.
Row 5: with white, right side of work, ch 3, *2 dc in the ch-1 sp*, rep * to * across, end with 1 dc in the last sc. Do not turn, leave the white strand dangling.
Row 6: with gold, right side of work, 1 sc in the 3rd ch, *1 sc between the 2 dc of the group, ch 1*, rep * to * across, end 1 sc in the last dc using the loose strand of white, turn and cut gold yarn and draw through loop on hook.
Row 7: with white, wrong side of work, ch 3, *2 dc in the ch-1 sp*, rep * to *, end 1 dc in the last sc. Turn and leave the white strand dangling.

Row 8: with green, right side of work, 1 sc in the dc at end of previous row, *ch 1, 1 sc between the group of 2 dc*, rep * to *, end 1 sc in the 3rd ch. Do not turn. Cut the yarn and draw through loop on hook.
Row 9: with white, right side facing, ch 3, *2 dc in the ch-1 sp*, rep * to *, end 1 dc in the last sc, leave the white strand dangling and do not turn. Always rep rows 2 to 9.
2/2 ribbing: Row 1: *K2, p2*. Rep * to * across.
Row 2 and all foll rows: Work sts as established in previous row.

BACK

With knitting needles and gold, cast on 70 (74, 78, 82) sts and work in 2/2 ribbing for 5 rows, then work 6 rows in green. Bind off. With green and crochet hook, work 60 (64, 68, 72) sc along bound off edge of ribbing. Continue in pat st beg row 1 working 1 border st at each edge (= 30 (32, 34, 36) motifs) until piece measures 13 (14½, 15¼, 17¾) in. - 33 (37, 41, 46) cm from beg. Fasten off. With knitting needles and pink, pick up and knit 92 (96, 100, 104) sts and work 3/4 in. (2 cm) in 2/2 ribbing as foll: k1, *k2, p2*, end with k3. Bind off loosely.

FRONT

Work same as back, but work top ribbing in blue.

FINISHING

Block pieces to indicated measurements. Lap the back top border over the front top border for 2 (2¼, 2½, 2¾) in. - 5 (5.5, 6.7) cm and sew in place. With knitting needles and green, cast on 74 (78, 82, 86) sts and work in 2/2 ribbing as foll: 12 rows of green and 6 rows of gold. Bind off loosely. Sew to center 11 (12, 12½, 13) in. - 28 (30, 32, 34) cm side seams with seam showing on right side of work, the bound off edge on right side of body. Fold borders in half to inside and sl st in place. Sew side seams.

2-2¼-2½-2¾   9-9½-10-10¼   2-2¼-2½-2¾
(5-5,5-6-7) (23,5-24,5-25,5-26) (5-5,5-6-7)

5½-6-6¼-6½ (14-15-16-17)

¾ (2)

11¾-13¾-15-16½ (30-34-38-42)

1¼ (3)

13¼-14-14¾-16¾ (33,5-35,5-37,5-40)

FRONT-BACK

EXUBERANT

PATTERNED PULLOVERS ADD
SPICE TO COLLEGE LIFE. THE
TRIANGLE STITCH IS A
FASCINATING GEOMETRY LESSON.

RELIEF STITCH PULLOVER

SIZE

Woman's Small (Medium/Large, X Large), bust 30-32 (33-38, 39-42) in. - 76-81.5 (84-97, 99-107) cm. Finished bust measurements: 41½ (47¼, 53) in. - 105 (120, 135) cm, length: 27½ in. (70 cm), sleeve seam 18½ (19¼, 20) in. - 47 (49, 51) cm.

MATERIALS

11 (13, 15) skeins sport weight mohair blend yarn (approx. 190 yds per 50 g skein) color red. Crochet hooks U.S. sizes C/2 and E/4 (U.K. sizes 11 and 9) (Metric sizes 3 and 3.5) or size needed to obtain gauge. **To save time, take time to check gauge!**

GAUGE

14 sts and 8 rows = 3 in. (7.5 cm) wide x 2½ in. (6 cm) high using larger size hook.

STITCHES

Chain (ch), single crochet (sc), half double crochet (hdc), double crochet (dc), slip stitch (sl st).
Front Relief dc: Worked in dc by working around the post of the st below. For front relief sts, yo, and insert hook from right to left around the post of the indicated st at front of work. Yo, and draw through loop, then continue as you would for a dc.
Back Relief dc: Worked in dc by working around the post of the st below. For back relief sts, yo, and insert hook from right to left around the post of the indicated st in back of work. Yo, and draw through loop, then continue as you would for a dc.
Post stitch: Row 1: 1 dc in each st.
Row 2: *1 front relief dc, 1 back relief dc*, rep * to * across row.
Row 3: Work opposite st of the previous row, that is, work 1 relief dc in the front of the st above a back relief st so that the border alternates front and back relief sts on both sides of the work.

Triangle stitch: Worked in rounds by foll the chart in relief st. Each square equals 1 relief st. Ch 2 at the beg of each round instead of 1 relief st. Join rounds with sl st. When working 1 back relief st at beg of round, work in back of ch 2 of previous round. When working 1 front relief st at beg of round, work in front of ch 2 of previous round.

BODY

With larger size crochet hook, ch 196 (224, 253) and join in ring with sl st. Work 1 round of dc, begin with ch 3 = 195 (223, 251) dc. Join with sl st in the 3rd ch. **Round 2:** Work by foll chart, beg as indicated on chart: ch 2 (counts as the first back relief dc), *13 front relief dc, 1 back relief dc*, work * to * 13 (15, 17) times, end with 13 front relief dc. Join round with sl st. Work 1 back relief dc in the ch st at beg of round. **Round 3:** Ch 3 for the first back relief dc, 1 back relief dc, *11 front relief dc, 3 back relief dc*, rep * to *, end with 11 front relief dc, 1 back relief st. Join rounds with sl st. Work by foll chart, creating 6 rounds of triangle motifs until piece measures 14 in. (36 cm) from beg.
Divide for armholes: Work 7 (8, 9) triangles and work back and forth by foll chart. Beg each row with ch 2 for border st (above the first st of the previous row) = first st of chart. End each row with 1 hdc = 1 border st (work in triangle st). Work these 99 (113, 127) sts for 4 rows of triangle motifs and piece measures 23½ in. (60 cm) from beg. Now work 2 rows of post st, working 1 st in each st of last row. Work 2nd half the same.
With wrong side facing, join the back and front shoulders tog by working through 2 thicknesses in sl st over 6 (6¾, 8) in. - 15 (17.5, 20) cm.

Sleeves: With larger size crochet hook, work 98 sts along armholes edges, beg between the 49th and 50th sts from the shoulder seam and work 1 round of dc, then continue in rounds of triangle st. You will have 7 triangles. On every round, dec 1 st at underarm until you have 5 complete triangles. When 7 triangle motifs have been worked and sleeve measures about 16½ in. (42 cm) from beg, fasten off. Work 2nd sleeve.

FINISHING

Block pieces to indicae measurements. With smaller size crochet hook, work 160 (180, 200) sc along lower edges of body and work 3¼ in. (8 cm) of post st. Join each round with a sl st and begin each round with ch 3. Fasten off. With smaller size crochet hook, work 38 (42, 46) sc along lower edges of each sleeve and work 2 (2¾, 3½) in. - 5 (7, 9) cm of post st. Join round with sl st. Fasten off.

KEY TO CHART

⊠ = 1 back relief dc

☐ = 1 front relief dc

Repeat

ANGELIC TRIO OF GIRL'S
SHIRT COLLAR PULLOVERS IS
HEAVEN SENT FOR CROCHETERS.
THREE STITCH PATTERNS OFFER
VARIATIONS ON A THEME: EYELET
IN LILAC, YELLOW CABLED LACE;
OR GREEN FILET CROCHET.

KEY TO CHART
- ● = Ch 1
- V = 1 sc
- † = 1 dc

CHILD'S LILAC POLO TOP

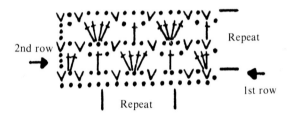

2nd row ← ... Repeat

Repeat ... 1st row

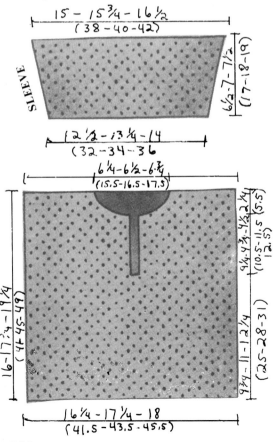

15 – 15¾ – 16½
(38 – 40 – 42)

SLEEVE

6¼ – 7 – 7½
(17 – 18 – 19)

12½ – 13¼ – 14
(32 – 34 – 36)

6¼ – 6½ – 6¾
(15.5 – 16.5 – 17.5)

9¼ – 9¾ – 9¾ – 10¼
(10.5 – 11.5 – 12.5)

16 – 17¾ – 19¾
(44 – 54 – 44)

9¾ – 11 – 12¼
(25 – 28 – 31)

16¼ – 17¼ – 18
(41.5 – 43.5 – 45.5)

SIZE

Child's size 8 (10, 12) years, chest 27 (28½, 30) in. - 69 (72.5, 76) cm. Finished chest measurements: 32½ (34½, 36) in. - 83 (87, 91) cm, length: 17¼ (19, 20½) in. - 44 (48, 52) cm, sleeve seam: 7¼ (7¾, 8¼) in. - 19 (20, 21) cm.

MATERIALS

6 (7, 7) skeins fingering weight yarn (approx. 220 yds per 50 g skein) color lilac.
Crochet hook U.S. size B/1 (U.K. size 12) (Metric size 2.5) or size needed to obtain gauge. Knitting needles U.S. size 2 (U.K. size 13) (Metric size 2). 3 buttons. **To save time, take time to check gauge!**

GAUGE

42 sts and 18 rows in pat st = 4 in. (10 cm).

STITCHES

Chain (ch), single crochet (sc), double crochet (dc), slip stitch (sl st).
1/1 ribbing: Row 1: *K1, p1*. Rep * to * across.
Row 2 and all foll rows: Work sts as established in previous row.

BACK

With crochet hook ch 177 (185, 193) + ch 1 to turn.
Row 1: right side of work: 1 sc in the 2nd ch from the hook, ch 1, skip 1, 1 sc, *ch 3, skip 3, 1 sc*, rep * to *, end with ch 1, skip 1, 1 sc in the last ch. **Row 2:** Ch 3, 2 dc in the ch-1 sp, *ch 1, 1 dc in the ch-3 sp, ch 1, 4 dc in the ch-3 sp*, rep * to *, end with ch 1, 1 dc in the ch-3 sp, ch 1, 2 dc in the last ch-1 space, 1 dc in the sc. Continue in pat st by foll chart, rep rows 2 to 5 until piece measures 16 (17¾, 19¼) in. - 41 (45, 49) cm from beg. Fasten off.

FRONT

Work same as back until piece measures 9¾ (11, 12¼) in. - 25 (28, 31) cm from beg. Divide work for front opening. Work the first 85 (89, 93) sts and work even for 4¼ (4½, 4¾) in. - 10.5 (11.5, 12.5) cm from beg, then shape neck. *With right side facing, work to last 6 (6, 7) sts, leave these sts unworked, turn, work to end of row*, rep * to * 4 times total. With right side facing, work to last 5 (7, 5) sts, turn, work to end of row. Continue on rem 56 (58, 60) sts until piece measures 16 (17¾, 19¼) in. - 41 (45, 49) cm. Fasten off.
Work over last 85 (89, 93) sts and work by rev shapings. (For neck dec, sl st over specified number of sts on right side of work.) Leave the 7 sts between the 2 halves unworked.

SLEEVES

Ch 137 (145, 153) + ch 1 to turn. Work by foll chart. At each edge of every 4th (5th, 5th) row, inc 2 sts 6 times. (For each inc, work 3 sts in each edge st.) Work inc sts in pat. You now have 161 (169, 177) sts. When piece measures 6½ (7, 7½) in. - 17 (18, 19) cm from beg, fasten off.

FINISHING

Block pieces to indicated measurements. With knitting needles, pick up and knit 110 (118, 126) sts along lower edge of back and work 1¼ in. (3 cm) in 1/1 ribbing. Bind off loosely. Work same ribbing on front. With knitting needles, pick up and knit 94 (100, 106) sts along lower edge of each sleeve and work 1¼ in. (3 cm) in 1/1 ribbing. Bind off loosely. With knitting needles, pick up and knit 33 (36, 39) sts along left front opening and work 3/4 in. (2 cm) in st (knit right side of work rows, purl wrong side of work rows.) Bind off loosely. Work same band on right front, making 3 buttonholes evenly spaced when band measures 1/3 in. (1 cm). Place the first and 3rd buttonholes 1/3 in. (1 cm) from each edge of band, space second buttonhole evenly between them. For each buttonhole, bind off 2 sts. On foll row, cast on 2 sts over bound off sts. Sew shoulder seams. With knitting needles, pick up and knit 115 (121, 127) sts around neck, not including front bands and work 1¼ in. (3 cm) in 1/1 ribbing. Bind off. With crochet hook work 1 row of sc around front bands and collar, working 1 sc, ch 1, 1 sc in each corner. Fasten off. Lap right border over left and sew end in place. Sew on buttons. Sew sleeves to armholes, matching center of sleeve with shoulder seams. Sew side and sleeve seams.

CHILD'S YELLOW POLO PULLOVER

SIZE

Child's size 3 (5, 7) years, chest 22 (24, 26) in. - 56 (61, 66) cm. Finished chest measurements: 26½ (28½, 31½) in. - 67 (73, 80) cm, length: 11¾ (13¼, 14¾) in. - 30 (34, 38) cm, sleeve seam: 4½ (4¾, 5¼) in. - 11 (12, 13) cm.

MATERIALS

3 (4, 5) skeins fingering weight yarn (approx. 220 yds per 50 g skein) color yellow.
Crochet hook U.S. size B/1 (U.K. size 12) (Metric size 2.5) or size needed to obtain gauge. Knitting needles U.S. size 2 (U.K. size 13) (Metric size 2). 3 buttons. **To save time, take time to check gauge!**

GAUGE

31 sts and 18 rows in pat st = 4 in. (10 cm).

STITCHES

Chain (ch), single crochet (sc), double crochet (dc), slip stitch (sl st).
Cross 4 on right side: Skip 1, 3 dc, 1 dc in the skipped st by passing hook behind the 3 dc.
Cross 4 on wrong side: Skip 1, 3 dc, 1 dc in the skipped st by passing hook in front of the 3 dc.
Pattern stitch: Row 1: right side of work: 1 dc in the 7th ch from hook, *ch 1, skip 1, 1 dc*, rep * to *, end with 1 dc in the last st.
Row 2: Ch 1, 1 sc in each st.
Row 3: right side of work: ch 3, *4 sts crossed on right side*, rep * to *, end with 1 dc.
Row 4: wrong side of work: ch 3, *4 sts crossed on wrong side*, rep * to *, end with 1 dc.
Row 5: Same as row 2.
Row 6: Same as row 1. Rep rows 1 to 6.
1/1 ribbing: Row 1: *K1, p1*. Rep * to * across.
Row 2 and all foll rows: Work sts as established in previous row.

BACK

Worked side to side. With crochet hook ch 90 (102, 114) + ch 4. Work in pat st for 60 (66, 72) rows.

Piece will measure 13¼ (14¼. 15¾) in. - 33.5 (36.5, 40) cm from beg. Fasten off.

FRONT

Work same as back until piece measures 4¼ (4½, 5) in. - 10.5 (11.5, 13) cm - 19 (21, 23) rows. *At the end of the next row (neck edge), leave 4 sts unworked. Work 1 row even.* Work * to * 4 times total = 74 (86, 98) sts and a total of 28 (31, 34) rows. On foll row, leave 28 (28, 32) sts unworked at neck edge. Work rem 46 (58, 66) sts for 3 rows, then ch 28 (28, 32) sts at neck edge and work in pat st = 74 (86, 98) sts. Rev neck shapings on 2nd half by ch 4 at neck edge every 2nd row 4 times and work these sts in pat st = 90 (102, 114) sts for a total of 60 (66, 72) rows from beg, fasten off.

SLEEVES

Worked side to side. Ch 10 (14, 18) + ch 4 to turn. Work by foll chart. At beg of 4th and 6th row, ch 8 sts and work these 26 (30, 34) sts until piece measures 9¾ (10½, 11½) in. - 25 (27, 29) cm at left edge of right side of work row. With wrong side facing, sl over 8 sts on first and 3rd row. Work 3 rows even, then fasten off.

FINISHING

Block pieces to indicated measurements. With knitting needles, pick up and knit 68 (74, 80) sts along lower edge of each sleeve and work ¾ in. (2 cm) in 1/1 ribbing. Bind off loosely. With knitting needles, pick up and knit 100 (108, 116) sts along lower edge of back and work 1¼ in. (3 cm) in 1/1 ribbing. Bind off loosely. Work same ribbing on front. With knitting needles, pick up and knit 28 (28, 32) sts along left front opening and work ¾ in. (2 cm) in st (knit right side of work rows, purl wrong side of work rows.) Bind off loosely. Work same band on right front, making 3 buttonholes evenly spaced when border measures 1/3 in. (1 cm). Place the first and 3rd buttonholes 1/3 in. (1 cm) from each edge of band. Space 2nd buttonhole between these 2. For each buttonhole, bind off 2 sts. On foll row, cast on 2 sts over bound off sts. Sew shoulder seams. With knitting needles, pick up and knit 77 (83, 89) sts around neck, not including front bands and work 1¼ in. (3 cm) in 1/1 ribbing. Bind off. With crochet hook work 1 row of sc around front bands and collar, working 1 sc, ch 1, 1 sc in each corner. Fasten off. Lap right band over left and sew end in place. Sew on buttons. Sew sleeves to armholes, matching center of sleeve with center of shoulder seams. Sew side and sleeve seams.

4¾-5-5½ | 4¼-4½-5
(12-13-14) (10.5-11.5-13)

3½-3½-4 (9-9-10)

11-12½-14 (28-32-36)

13¼ - 14¼ - 15¾
(33.5-36.5-40)

FRONT-BACK

12¼ - 13 - 13¾
(31-33-35)

3½-3½-4 (9-9-10)

9¾-10½-11½
(25-27-29)

SLEEVE

KEY TO CHART

- • = Ch 1
- v = 1 sc
- ↑ = 1 dc
- ⋔ = cross 4 on right side
- ⋔ = cross 4 on wrong side

2nd row →

← 1st row

Repeat

Repeat

CHILD'S GREEN POLO TOP

SIZE

Child's size 6 (8, 10) years, chest 25 (27, 28½) in. - 63.5 (69, 72.5) cm. Finished chest measurements: 30 (32, 34½) in. - 76 (82, 88) cm, length: 15¼ (16¾, 18) in. - 40 (44, 47) cm, sleeve seam: 5½ (6, 6¼) in. - 14.5 (15.5, 16.5) cm.

MATERIALS

5 (5, 6) skeins fingering weight yarn (approx. 220 yds per 50 g skein) color green. Crochet hook U.S. size B / 1 (U.K. size 12) (Metric size 2.5) or size needed to obtain gauge. Knitting needles U.S. size 2 (U.K. size 13) (Metric size 2). 3 buttons. **To save time, take time to check gauge!**

GAUGE

33 sts and 22 rows in pat st = 4 in. (10 cm).

STITCHES

Chain (ch), single crochet (sc), double crochet (dc), slip stitch (sl st). 1/1 ribbing: Row 1: *K1, p1*. Rep * to * across. **Row 2 and all foll rows:** Work sts as established in previous row.

BACK

Worked side to side. With crochet hook ch 124 (136, 148) + ch 3 to turn. **Row 1:** right side of work: 1 dc in the 5th ch from the hook, 1 dc, *ch 1, skip 1, 2 dc*, rep * to *, end with 1 dc in the last ch. **Row 2:** Ch 1, sc across, inserting hook in the back loop of each st. Continue in pat st by foll the chart, always working in the back loop of the sts of the previous row until piece measures 15 (16, 17¼) in. - 38 (41, 44) cm from beg. End with 1 row of dc. Fasten off.

FRONT

Work same as back until piece measures 4¾ (5, 5½) in. - 12 (13, 14) cm from beg. Shape neck. With wrong side facing, sl st over first 6 sts, work to end of row, turn, work 1 row even. *Sl st over first 3 sts, work to end of row, turn, work 1 row even*, rep * to * 3 times total. Work rem 109 (121, 133) sts until piece measures about 2½ (2½, 2¾) in. - 6 (6.5, 7) cm from beg of neck. Leave 33 (36, 39) sts unworked at neck edge. Work rem 76 (85, 94) sts for 4 rows. At neck edge, ch 33 (36, 39) sts and work over 109 (121, 133) sts in pat st. **At the same time**, work 2nd half of neck shapings by inc at neck edge to correspond to dec. Work even on 124 (136, 148) sts for 4¾ (5, 5½) in. - 12 (13, 14) cm, ending with 1 row of dc. Fasten off.

SLEEVES

Worked side to side. Ch 16 (19, 22) + ch 3 to turn. Work these sts in pat st by foll chart. At end of 2nd, 4th and 6th row, ch 9 and work over these sts in pat st = 43 (46, 49) sts. Continue in pat st until piece measures 11¾ (12½, 13¼) in. - 30 (32, 34) cm, measured after edge inc. At right edge of every 2nd row, sl st over 9 sts 3 times. Work 1 row over rem 16 (19, 22) sts. Fasten off.

FINISHING

Block pieces to indicated measurements. With knitting needles, pick up and knit 118 (126, 134) sts along lower edge of back and work 1¼ in. (3 cm) in 1/1 ribbing. Bind off loosely. Work same ribbing on front. With knitting needles, pick up and knit 88 (94, 100) sts along lower edge of each sleeve and work 1¼ in. (3 cm) in 1/1 ribbing. Bind off loosely. With knitting needles, pick up and knit 30 (33, 36) sts along left front opening and work ¾ in. (2 cm) in st (knit right side of work rows, purl wrong side of work rows) Bind off loosely. Work same band on right front, making 3 buttonholes evenly spaced when band measures 1/3 in. (1 cm). Place the first and 3rd buttonholes evenly spaced when band measures 1/3 in. (1 cm). Place the first and 3rd buttonholes 1/3 in. (1 cm) from each edge of ends of band, evenly spacing 2nd buttonhole. For each buttonhole, bind off 2 sts. On foll row, cast on 2 sts over bound off sts. Sew shoulder seams. With knitting needles, pick up and knit 109 (115, 121) sts around neck, not including front bands and work 1¼ in. (3 cm) in 1/1 ribbing. Bind off. With crochet hook work 1 row of sc around front bands

and collar, working 1 sc, ch 1, 1 sc in each corner. Fasten off. Lap right band over left and sew ends in place. Sew on buttons. Sew sleeves to armholes, matching center of sleeve with shoulder seams. Sew side and sleeve seams.

KEY TO CHART

● = Ch 1

V = 1 sc

† = 1 dc

SEASIDE SENSATION OF KHAKI COTTON WITH CAP SLEEVES. THE INDIAN BASKET PATTERN STITCH MAKES THIS PULLOVER A BEACHCOMBER'S TREASURE.

WOMAN'S TOP

SIZE
Woman's Small (Medium, Large), bust 30-32 (33-35, 36-38) in. 76-81.5 (84-89, 91.5-97) cm. Finished bust measurements: 37 (41½, 45½) in. - 94 (106, 116) cm, length: 22½ (22½, 23½) in. - 57 (57, 60) cm.

MATERIALS
10 (12, 14) skeins sport weight cotton yarn (50 g skein) color khaki. Crochet hook U.S. size C/2 (U.K. size 11) (Metric size 3) or size needed to obtain gauge. Knitting needles U.S. size 2 (U.K. size 12) (Metric size 2.5). **To save time, take time to check gauge!**

GAUGE
22 sc and 16 rows = 4 in. (10 cm).

STITCHES
**Chain (ch),
single crochet (sc),
half double crochet (hdc),
treble crochet (tr),
double treble crochet (dtr),
slip stitch (sl st).
Triangle stitch:** Worked in tr, but wrap yarn around hook 3 times, yo and draw through 2 loops 4 times = dtr.

Pattern stitch: Worked on a multiple of 6 + 2.
Rows 1, 2 and 3: 1 sc in each st, ch 1, turn.
Row 4: Ch 4 instead of ch 1 (counts as first tr), *skip 3 sc, then work 3 triangle sts in the foll 3 sc, work 3 triangle sts in the 3 skipped sc by working behind the first 3 sts*, rep * to *, end with 1 tr in the last sc, ch 1, turn. Always rep these 4 rows.
1/1 ribbing: Row 1: *K1, p1*. Rep * to * across.
Row 2 and all foll rows: Work sts as established in previous row.

BACK
Ch 12 for the sleeve. Fasten off and save this piece.
With knitting needles, cast on 100 (112, 145) sts and work 2 in. (5 cm) in 1/1 ribbing. Bind off. With crochet hook, work 1 sc in each st of bound off edge, inc 4 sts by working 2 sc in 4 sts evenly spaced across. You now have 104 (116, 128) sc. Work in pat st. You will have 17 (19, 21)

motifs across. Work 44 (44, 48) rows, when piece measures about 12½ (12½, 13¾) in. - 32 (32, 35) cm, ch 12 at end of row. On foll row, work across in pat st, place the ch 12 piece previously made at left edge and work across in pat st = 128 (140, 152) sc on the first row of pat st, 21 (23, 25) pat motifs on 4th row of pat st. Work a total of 84 (84, 88) rows. Work 1 row of sc across all sts and fasten off.

FRONT
Work same as back for 80 (80, 84) rows. Mark the center 34 sts and work right shoulder separately for 6 rows. Leave rem sts unworked. On the first row, you will have 47 (53, 59) sc on shoulder. On each of the next 5 rows, dec 2 sts at neck edge of every row. (At end of row at neck edge, leave 2 sts unworked. At beg of row at neck edge, sl st over 2 sts.) You now have 37 (43, 49) sc on shoulder. Fasten off. Work 2nd shoulder, rev shapings.

FINISHING
Block pieces to indicated measurements. Sew 1 shoulder seam. With knitting needles, pick up and knit 112 sts around neck and work 1¼ in. (3 cm) in 1/1 ribbing. Bind off loosely. Sew 2nd shoulder and neckband seam. Along each sleeve end, pick up and knit 100 (108, 116) sts and work 1¼ in. (3 cm) in 1/1 ribbing. Bind off loosely. Sew side and sleeve seams.

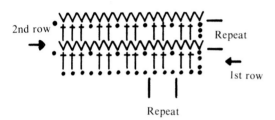

2nd row → Repeat

1st row →

Repeat

FRONT-BACK

1¾-4-4¼-4¾ 9¼-10-10½
(4.5) (10-11-12) (21-25.5-27)

4¾-5-5½
(12-13-14)

5½-6-6¼
(14-15-16)

15-16-17¼
(38-41-44)

14½-16-17¼
(37-41-44)

SLEEVE

14-15-15¾
(36-38-40)

4¾-5¼-5½
(12.5-13.5-14.5)

11¾-12½-13¼
(30-32-34)

FRONT-BACK

6½-8-8¾   9¼   6½-8-8¾
(17-20-22.5) (24)   (17-20-22.5)

¼   9¾
(.5,5) (25)

2¼
(.5,6)

2
(5)

10½-10½-11¾
(27-27-30)

18½-20¾-22¾
(47-53-58)

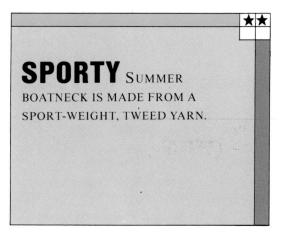

SPORTY SUMMER

BOATNECK IS MADE FROM A
SPORT-WEIGHT, TWEED YARN.

WHITE BOATNECK PULLOVER

SIZE

Woman's Small
(Medium, Large), bust
30-32 (33-35, 36-38) in.
76-81.5 (84-89, 91.5-97)
cm. Finished bust
measurements: 41½
(44, 47¼) in. - 105
(112, 120) cm, length:
23¼ in. (59 cm), sleeve
seam: 18½ (47 cm).

MATERIALS

12 (13, 14) skeins sport
weight yarn (50 g skeins)
color white tweed.
Crochet hook U.S. size
B/1 (U.K. size 12)
(Metric size 2.5) or size
needed to obtain gauge.
Knitting needles U.S. size
2 (U.K. size 12) (Metric
size 2.5). **To save time,
take time to check gauge!**

GAUGE

5½ fan sts and 10 rounds
= 4 in. (10 cm).

STITCHES

Chain (ch),
single crochet (sc),
double crochet (dc),
slip stitch (sl st).
Fan stitch: Multiple of 4
+ 5 worked on a ch base.
Row 1: Work 5 dc in the
7th ch from the hook,
*skip 4 ch, 5 dc in foll ch
(fan st)*, rep * to * 28
(30, 32) = 29 (31, 33) fans,
skip 2 ch, 1 dc in the last
2 ch. Turn.
Row 2: Ch 3 (counts as
first dc), 5 dc in the
middle dc of the fan st*,
rep * to * across, end
with 1 dc in 3rd ch from
end.
Row 3 and all foll rows:
Work same as 2nd row,
end with 1 dc in top of
turning ch of previous
row.
1/1 ribbing: Row 1: *K1,
p1*. Rep * to * across.
Row 2 and all foll rows:
Work sts as established in
previous row.

BACK

With crochet hook ch 147
(157, 167) + ch 3 (counts
as first st). Work in fan st
until piece measures 21¼
in. (54 cm) from beg.
Fasten off. With knitting
needles, pick up and knit
147 (157, 167) sts from
last row of crochet and
work 3/4 in. (2 cm) in 1/1
ribbing. Bind off loosely.

FRONT

Work same as back.

SLEEVES

With crochet hook ch 82
+ ch 3 (counts as first st).
Continue in fan st = 16
fan sts with 1 border st at
each edge. At each edge
of every 6th row, inc 1
fan st at each edge as foll:
at beg of 6th row, ch 3 to
turn, work 1 fan st in the
first st, *1 fan st in the
center of the foll fan st*,
rep * to * across 15 times,
work 6 dc in the last st (=
1 fan st in 1 dc), turn.
Continue in fan st, inc 1
fan st at each edge of
every 6th row until you
have 28 fan sts across and
sleeve measures 15¾ in.
(40 cm). Fasten off. With
knitting needles, pick up
and knit 142 sts across
last crochet row and work
3/4 in. (2 cm) in 1/1
ribbing. Bind off loosely.

FINISHING

Block pieces to indicated
measurements. With
crochet hook work 88
(94, 100) sc along lower
edge of front and back
pieces. Fasten off. With
knitting needles, pickup
and knit 1 st from each sc
and work 1¼ in. (3 cm) in
1/1 ribbing. Bind off
loosely. Work 40 sc along
lower edge of sleeves.
Fasten off. With knitting
needles, pick up and knit
1 st from each sc and
work 2 in. (5 cm) in 1/1
ribbing. Bind off loosely.
Sew shoulder seams over
5 (5¾, 6¼) in. - 13 (14.5,
16) cm from armhole
edge. Sew sleeves to side
seams, matching center of
sleeve with shoulder
seam. Sew side and sleeve
seams.

GILDED LACE SETS A NEW

GOLD STANDARD. LIGHTWEIGHT
COTTON PULLOVER HAS THREE-
QUARTER LENGTH SLEEVES FOR
ALL-SEASON COMFORT.

GOLD LACE PULLOVER

SIZE

Woman's Small
(Medium, Large, X
Large), bust 30-32 (33-35,
36-38, 39-42) in. - 76-81.5
(84-89, 91.5-97, 99-107)
cm. Finished bust
measurements: 42 (45, 47,
50) in. - 108 (114, 120,
126) cm, length: 23¼ in.
(59 cm), sleeve seam:
17 in. (43 cm).

MATERIALS

4 skeins "Chat Botte"
(100% cotton - approx.
175 yds per 50 g skein)
color gold.
Crochet hook U.S. size
B/1 (U.K. size 12)
(Metric size 2.5) or size
needed to obtain gauge.
Knitting needles U.S. size
2 (U.K. size 11) (Metric
size 2.5). **To save time,
take time to check gauge!**

GAUGE

1 pattern repeat = 1¼ in.
(3 cm)
10 rows = 4 in. (10 cm).

SLEEVE

FRONT-BACK

FRONT-BACK

SLEEVE

STITCHES

Chain (ch),
single crochet (sc),
double crochet (dc),
triple crochet (tr),
slip stitch (sl st).
3 Dc sts tog: work 1 dc in each of the foll 3 sts, but leave the last loop of each dc on the hook: after the first dc, there will be 2 loops on the hook, after the 2nd dc, there will be 3 loops on the hook, after the 3rd dc, there will be 4 loops on the hook. Yo and draw through the 4 loops on hook.
Pattern stitch: Worked on a base of sc.
Row 1: Ch 3 (counts as first st), *3 sc, work 3 tr, ch 1, 1 dc in next st; ch 3, 3 dc tog over next 3 sts, ch 1*. Rep * to *, end with 1 dc in the last st after the last 3 dc tog instead of ch 1.
Row 2: Ch 3, *insert hook in ch-1 space between dc and the 3 tr of the previous row and work 3 tr, ch 1, 1 dc in next st; ch 3, 3 dc tog over next 3 tr, ch 1*. Rep * to *, end with 1 dc in the 3rd turning ch of the previous row.
Always rep row 2.
2/2 ribbing: Row 1: *K2, p2*. Rep * to * across.
Row 2 and all foll rows: Work as established in previous row.

BACK

With knitting needles, cast on 118 (126, 130, 138) sts and work 2 in. (5 cm) in 2/2 ribbing, beg and end with k2. Bind off.
With crochet hook, work 119 (126, 132, 139) sc in the bound off row of ribbing. Continue in pat st, having 18 (19, 20, 21) motifs and 1 border dc at each edge. (On first row, alternately skip 3 sts, then 2 sts between *'s of pat rep.) Work until piece measures 23¼ in. (59 cm) from beg. Fasten off.

FRONT

Work same as back, until you have 1 less row than the back. **Last row:** Work 4½ (5, 5½, 6) motifs, end with 1 dc. Fasten off. Skip the foll 9 motifs and join yarn. Work the last 4½ (5, 5½, 6) motifs, fasten off.

SLEEVES

With knitting needles, cast on 50 (50, 54, 54) sts and work 2 in. (5 cm) in 2/2 ribbing. Bind off. With crochet hook, work 52 (52, 57, 57) sc in the bound off row of ribbing. Work in pat st as foll: On row 1 instead of skipping 3 sc for each pat rep, skip 1 sc. Beg with row 2, inc 1 st at each edge by working 1 additional dc in the first and last sts of row. When you have 4 extra sts at each edge, beg a new motif (every 9th row). Work inc every 2nd row until you have 16 (16, 17, 17) motifs. Work even until piece measures 17 in. (43 cm). Fasten off.

FINISHING

Block pieces to indicated measurements.
Sew shoulder seams. Work 1 round of sc around neck. Fasten off. Sew sleeves to armholes, matching center of sleeve with shoulder seams. Sew side and sleeve seams.

PULLOVER

SIZE

Woman's Small (Medium, Large, X Large), bust 30-32 (33-35, 36-38, 39-42) in. - 76-81.5 (84-89, 91.5-97, 99-107) cm. Finished bust measurements: 41 (44, 47) in. - 104 (112, 120) cm, length: 23½ in. (60 cm), sleeve seam: 17¾ in. (45 cm).

MATERIALS

11 (12, 13) skeins cotton linen blend (approx. 150 yds per 50 g skein) color camel.
Crochet hook U.S. size E/4 (U.K. size 9) (Metric size 3.5) or size needed to obtain gauge. Knitting needles U.S. size 3 (U.K. size 10) (Metric size 3).
To save time, take time to check gauge!

GAUGE

5 motifs x 12 rows = 4 in. (10 cm).

STITCHES

Chain (ch),
single crochet (sc),
double crochet (dc),
slip stitch (sl st).
Judith stitch: Multiple of 4 + ch 2.
Row 1: Ch 1 (= 1 border st), 1 sc in the 3rd ch from the hook, sc across. The last sc counts as the border st.

Row 2: Ch 3 (= 1 border st), *skip 1 sc, 1 dc in each of the foll 3 sc, then pass the hook in front of the 3 previous sts, insert hook in back loop of st, yo and draw through loop, yo and draw through 2 loops on hook = 1 group*, rep * to *, end with 1 dc in the last ch (= 1 border st).
Row 3: Ch 1 (= 1 border st), 1 sc in each of the foll sts, end 1 sc in the 3rd ch of the border st. Rep rows 2 and 3.
1/1 ribbing: Row 1: *K1, p1*. Rep * to * across.
Row 2 and all foll rows: Work sts as established in previous row.

BACK

Ch 106 (114, 122) and work in Judith st = 26 (28, 30) groups = 1 border st at each edge. Work until piece measures 20½ in. (52 cm), work 1 row of sc. Fasten off.

FRONT

Work same as back.

SLEEVES

Ch 54 (62, 70) and work in Judith st = 13 (15, 17) groups + 1 border st at each edge. At each edge of every 2nd row (Sc row), work 2 sc in each edge st, 12 times. At each edge of every 4th row (sc row), work 2 sc in each edge st 4 times. Work inc sts in Judith st = 21 (23, 25) groups + 1 border st at each edge. Work until piece measures 15¼ in. (39 cm) from beg with 2½ in. (6 cm) straight at top of sleeve. Fasten off.

FINISHING

Block pieces to indicated measurements. With knitting needles, pick up and knit 108 (116, 124) sts from lower edge of back and work 3¼ in. (8 cm) in 1/1 ribbing. Bind off loosely. Work same ribbing on front. With knitting needles, pick up and knit 54 (58, 62) sts from lower edge of each sleeve and work 2½ in. (6 cm) in 1/1 ribbing. Bind off loosely. Sew shoulder seams over 6½ (7, 7½) in. - 17 (18, 19) cm. Sew sleeves to armholes, matching center of sleeve with shoulder seams. Sew side and sleeve seams.

FRONT-BACK

6¾-7-7½ 7-7⅞-8⅝ · ⁵⁄₈ 6¾-7-7½
(17-18-19)(18-20-22)(17-18-19)

20½ (52)

20½-22-23⅝
(52-56-60)

SLEEVE

16½-18-19¾

15⅜ (39)

10¼-11¾-13⅜
(26-30-34)

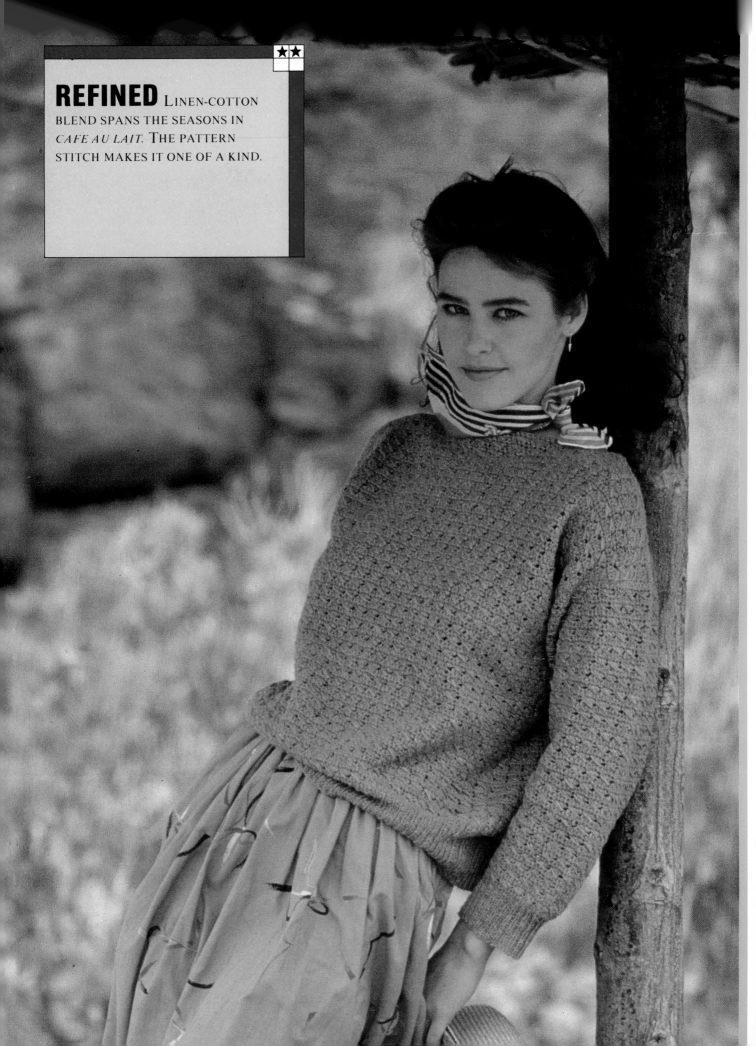

REFINED LINEN-COTTON BLEND SPANS THE SEASONS IN *CAFE AU LAIT*. THE PATTERN STITCH MAKES IT ONE OF A KIND.

REFINED STYLING LENDS THESE JACKETS EXTRA CHIC. THE CROCHETED FABRIC GIVES THEM AN APPEALING, BODY-SKIMMING LOOK.

WHITE JACKET

SIZE

Woman's Small (Medium, Large), bust 33-35 (36-38, 39-42) in. - 84-89 (91.5-97, 99-107) cm. Finished bust measurements: 38½ (42½, 45¾) in. - 98 (108, 116) cm, length: 23¼ (24, 24¾) in. - 59 (61, 63) cm, sleeve seam: 16½ in. (42 cm).

MATERIALS

13 skeins sport weight cotton yarn (approx. 110 yds per 50 g skein) color white.
Crochet hook U.S. size E/4 (U.K. size 9) (Metric size 3.5) or size needed to obtain gauge. **To save time, take time to check gauge!**

GAUGE

19 dc and 16 rows = 4 in. (10 cm).

STITCHES

**Chain (ch),
single crochet (sc),
half double crochet (hdc),
double crochet (dc),
slip stitch (sl st).
Pattern stitch:** Ch an even number of sts + ch 2.
Row 1: wrong side of work row: 1 dc in the 4th ch from the hook, *1 dc in the foll ch*, rep * to *.
Row 2: right side of work row: ch 1, 1 sc in the first dc, *1 sc by inserting hook around the vertical post of the foll dc from right to left, 1 sc in the foll dc*, rep * to *, end with 1 sc in the last dc.
Row 3: Ch 2, *1 dc in the foll sc*, rep * to *.
Rep rows 2 and 3.
Shrimp stitch: Work like sc, but work from left to right instead of right to left.

BACK

Ch 92 (100, 108) + ch 2 to turn. Work in pat st. Work even until piece measures 3½ (4, 4¼) in. - 9 (10, 11) cm from beg, dec 1 st at each edge (sl st over first st, work to last st, turn, leaving last st unworked). Then at each edge of every 3rd row 4 times total = 84 (92, 100) sts and piece measures 7 (7½, 8) in. - 18 (19, 20) cm from beg. Now inc 1 st at each edge of every 4th row 4 times (work 2 st in each edge st on each inc row) = 92 (100, 108) sts and piece measures 15 (15¼, 15¾) in. - 38 (39,

40) cm from beg. Shape armholes: *Sl st over first 3 sts and work to last 3 sts, turn, leaving last 3 sts unworked. Work 1 row even.* Work * to * 3 (4, 4) times. *Sl st over first st, work to last st, turn, leaving last st unworked. Work 1 row even.* Work * to * 1 (1, 2) times = 72 (74, 80) sts until armhole measures 8¼ (8½, 9) in. - 21 (22, 23) cm. Work over the first 28 (29, 31) sts to first marker. Turn. Sl st over first 4 sts, work to end of row, turn. Work to end of row. Turn, sl st over first 3 sts, work to end of row. Work 1 more row and fasten off. Work 2nd shoulder by rev shapings.

RIGHT FRONT

Ch 34 (40, 44) + ch 2 and work in pat st. At right edge of every row, inc 2 sts by working 3 sts in right edge st 3 times, inc 1 st by working 2 sts in right edge st 5 (5, 6) times = 45 (51, 56) sts. Work until piece measures 3½ (4, 4¼) in. - 9 (10, 11) cm.

At left edge, dec 1 st by working to 1 st before end of row, turn, leaving last st unworked. Then at left edge of every 3rd row dec 1 st 4 times total = 41 (47, 52) sts. Work even until piece measures 7 (7½, 8) in. - 18 (19, 20) cm from beg. At left edge inc 1 st, then inc 1 st at left edge of every 4th row 4 times = 45 (51, 56) sts. Work until piece measures 15 (15¼, 15¾) in. - 38 (39, 40) cm, shape armhole. With right side facing, at left edge, work to last 3 sts, turn, sl st over first 3 sts. Work to end of row. Turn and work to last 0 (3, 3) sts, turn. Sl st over first 1 (3, 3) sts, work to end of row. Turn. *With right side facing, work to last st, turn, leaving last st unworked. Work 1 row even.* Rep * to * 2 (0, 1) time total = 35 (39, 42) sts. Work until armhole measures 8¼ (8½, 9) in. - 21 (22, 23) cm from beg. Place marker after 14 (17, 18) sts at right edge, then fasten off all sts.

LEFT FRONT

Work same as right front, rev shapings.

SLEEVES

Ch 46 (50, 52) + ch 2 and work in pat st. Work even for 3¼ in. (8 cm). Then at each edge of every 2nd row, inc 1 st 15 (15, 16) times. (For each inc, work 2 sts in each edge st.) You now have 76 (80, 84) sts. Work until piece measures 18½ in. (47 cm) from beg, then shape sleeve cap. Sl st over 4 sts and work to last 4 sts, turn, leave last 4 sts unworked. Sl st over first 3 sts once, work to last 3 sts, leave last 3 sts unworked, turn. *Sl st over first st, work to last st, turn, leaving last st unworked.* Rep * to * 26 (27, 28) times. Work 1 row over rem 10 (12, 14) sts. Fasten off.

FINISHING

Block pieces to indicated measurements. Sew shoulder seams. Along the right front neck edge, work 16 (19, 22) dc, work 37 (41, 43) dc along back neck and 16 (19, 22) dc along left front neck edge. Continue in pat st. On the first, 3rd, 5th, 6th and 7th row, dec 1 st at each edge and on the 8th row, dec 2 sts at each edge. Fasten off. Gather top of sleeve and set in sleeves. Sew side and sleeve seams. With double strand of yarn, work around edge of jacket as foll: **Round 1:** Beg at side seam, sl st around piece, join round with sl st. **Round 2:** Ch 2, 1 sc in each sl st, join round with sl st in the 2nd ch at beg. **Round 3:** Work in shrimp st, working the first st in the first ch. Join round with sl st in the first ch at the beg. Work same border along the lower edge of the sleeves.

BLACK JACKET

SIZE

Woman's Small (Medium, Large), bust 33-35 (36-38, 39-42) in. - 84-89 (91.5-97, 99-107) cm. Finished bust measurements: 39 (43, 46) in. - 100 (110, 118) cm, length: 23¼ (24, 24¾) in. - 59 (61, 63) cm, sleeve seam: 16½ in. (42 cm).

MATERIALS

13 (14, 16) skeins fingering weight yarn (approx. 247 yds per 50 g skein) color black.
Crochet hooks U.S. sizes B/1 and D/3 (U.K. sizes 12 and 10) (Metric sizes 2.5 and 3.5) or size needed to check gauge. **To save time, take time to check gauge!**

GAUGE

22 sts and 18 rows = 4 in. (10 cm) with larger hook.

STITCHES

**Chain (ch),
single crochet (sc),
double crochet (dc),
slip stitch (sl st).
Pattern stitch:** Worked on an even number + 2 ch sts.
Row 1: Wrong side of work: 1 dc in the 4th ch from the hook, *1 dc in the foll ch*, rep * to * across.
Row 2: Ch 1, 1 sc in the first dc, *1 sc inserting hook from right to left around the post of the foll dc*, rep * to *, end with 1 sc in the last dc.
Row 3: Ch 2, *1 dc in the foll sc*, rep * to * across. Rep rows 2 and 3.
Shrimp stitch: Worked same as sc, but work from left to right instead of right to left.

BACK

With larger hook ch 109 (117, 125) and work in pat st = 107 (115, 123) sts. Work even until piece measures 3½ (4, 4¼) in. - 9 (10, 11) cm from beg, dec 1 st at each edge (sl st over first st, work to last st, turn, leaving last st unworked). Then at each edge of every 4th row, dec 1 st 3 times = 99 (107, 115) sts. When piece measures 7 (7½, 8) in. - 18 (19, 20) cm from beg, inc 1 st at each edge of every 6th row 4 times total (work 2 sts in each edge st on each inc row) = 107 (115, 123) sts. When

BACK

LEFT FRONT

SLEEVE

piece measures 15 (15¼, 15¾) in. - 38 (39, 40) cm from beg, shape armholes: *Sl st over first 2 sts and work to last 2 sts, turn, leaving last 2 sts unworked. Work 1 row even.* Work * to * 3 (4, 5) times. *Sl st over first st, work to last st, turn, leaving last st unworked. Work 1 row even.* Work * to * 6 times = 83 (87, 91) sts until armhole measures 7 (7½, 8) in. - 18 (19, 20) cm. Work over the first 35 (36, 37) sts. Turn and work even in pat st to end of row, turn. Work to last 4 sts, turn. Work 1 row even, turn. Work to last 4 sts, turn. Work 1 row even. Then work to last 2 sts, turn, leaving last 2 sts unworked. Fasten off rem 25 (26, 27) sts. Leave the center 13 (15, 17) sts unworked, then work the last 35 (36, 37) sts by rev shapings.

RIGHT FRONT

With larger hook ch 43 (49, 57) and work in pat st = 41 (47, 55) dc. At right edge of every row, inc 2 sts by working 3 sts in right edge st 3 times. Inc 1 st by working 2 sts in right edge st 8 times. Then at right edge of every 2nd row, inc 1 st by working 2 sts at right edge twice = 57 (63, 71) sts. Work until piece measures 3½ (4, 4¼) in. - 9 (10, 11) cm. At left edge, dec 1 st by working 1 st before end of row, turn. Then at left edge of every 6th row dec 1 st 3 times = 53 (59, 67) sts. Work even until piece measures 7 (7½, 8) in. - 18 (19, 20) cm from beg. At left edge inc 1 st, then inc 1 st at left edge of every 6th row 4 times

total = 57 (63, 71) sts. Work until piece measures 15 (15¼, 15¾) in. - 38 (39, 40) cm, shape armholes. With right side facing, *at left edge, work to last 4 sts, turn, work 1 row even*, work * to * 1 (2, 3) times, **work to last 2 sts, turn, work 1 row even**, work ** to ** 4 (3, 3) times, ***work to last 2 sts, turn, leaving last st unworked, work 1 row even***, work *** to *** 4 times = 41 (45, 49) sts. Work until armhole measures 8¼ (8½, 9) in. - 21 (22, 23) cm from beg, fasten off.

LEFT FRONT

Work same as right front, rev shapings.

SLEEVES

With larger hook ch 55 (59, 63) and work in pat st = 53 (57, 61) sts. Work even for 3¼ in. (8 cm). Then at each edge of every 3rd row, inc 1 st 18 (18, 19) times. (For each inc, work 2 sts in each edge st.) You now have 89 (93, 99) sts. Work until piece measures 18½ in. (47 cm) from beg, then shape sleeve cap. *Sl st over 2 sts and work to last 2 sts, turn*, work * to * 3 times. Then work the foll 25 (26, 28) rows as foll: sl st at beg of work, work to last st, turn, leaving last st unworked. *Sl st over 2 sts, work to last 2 sts, turn, leaving last 2 sts unworked*. Work * to * 4 times total. Work 1 row over rem 11 (13, 15) sts. Fasten off.

FINISHING

Block pieces to indicated measurements. Sew shoulder seams. With larger hook, along the right front neck edge, work 16 (19, 22) dc, work

37 (41, 43) dc along back neck and 16 (19, 22) dc along left front neck edge. Continue in pat st. On the first, 3rd, 5th, 6th and 7th row, dec 1 st at each edge and on the 8th row, dec 2 sts at each edge. Fasten off. Gather top of sleeve and set in sleeves. Sew side and sleeve seams. With smaller hook and double strand of yarn, work around edge of jacket as foll: **Round 1:** Beg at side seam, sl st around piece, join round with sl st. **Round 2:** Ch 2, 1 sc in each sl st, join round with sl st in the 2nd ch at beg. **Round 3:** Work in shrimp st, working the first st in the first ch. Join round with sl st in the first ch at the beg. Fasten off. Work same border along the lower edge of each sleeve. Fasten off.

RIGHT FRONT

SLEEVE

PULLOVER

SIZE

Woman's Medium (Large, X Large), bust 33-35 (36-38, 39-42) in. - 84-89 (91.5-97, 99-107) cm. Finished bust measurements 40 (44, 48) in. - 102 (112, 122) cm, length: 27½ in. (70 cm), sleeve seam: 17¾ in. (45 cm).

MATERIALS

22 (23, 24) skeins "Scheepjeswol Mayflower Helarsgarn" (100% cotton - approx. 88 yds per 50 g skein) color red or white. Crochet hook U.S. size F/5 (U.K. size 8) (Metric size 4) or size needed to obtain gauge. Knitting needles U.S. size 3 (U.K. size 10) (Metric size 3). **To save time, take time to check gauge!**

GAUGE

Approx. 4 fan sts = 4¼ in. (11 cm) and 7 rows = 4 in. (10 cm).

STITCHES

**Chain (ch),
single crochet (sc),
half double crochet (hdc),
slip stitch (sl st).**
Fan stitch: Multiple of 4 + 3. Worked on a ch base.
Row 1: Ch 3 (counts as first dc), 1 dc in the 4th ch from hook, *skip 3 ch, 1 fan st = 1 sc, ch 3, 3 dc in the foll ch*, rep * to *, end by skipping 1 ch, 1 sc in last ch.
Row 2: Ch 3, 1 dc in the last sc of the previous row, 1 fan st in the ch-3 space of the previous fan st, 1 fan st in the last ch-3 space of each fan st across row, end with 1 sc in the last st of the row. Always rep row 2.
1/1 ribbing: Row 1: *K1, p1*. Rep * to * across.
Row 2 and all foll rows: Work sts as established in previous row.

BACK

With smaller size needles, cast on 84 (93, 102) sts

and work 2¾ in. (7 cm) in 1/1 ribbing. Bind off. With crochet hook, continue into bound off sts as foll: 2 dc in the first st, *skip 3 sts, 1 fan st in the foll st, skip 4 sts, 1 fan st in the foll st*, rep * to * 8 (9, 10) times = 18 (20, 22) fan sts, ending by skip 1 st, 1 sc in the last st. Rep 2nd row of fan st until piece measures 27 in. (69 cm), ending with wrong side of work row.
Last row: Ch 3, 2 dc in the last sc of the previous row, *1 sc in the ch-3 sp of the fan st, 3 dc in the foll sc*, rep * to *, end with 1 sc in the last st. Fasten off.

FRONT

Work same as back.

SLEEVES

With smaller size needles, cast on 47 sts and work 2¾ in. (7 cm) in 1/1 ribbing. Bind off. With crochet hook, crochet into bound off sts as foll: 2 dc in the first st, *skip 3 sts, 1 fan st in the foll st, *, rep * to * 10 times = 11 fan sts, ending by skip 1 st, 1 sc in the last st. Rep 2nd row of fan st until piece measures 7 in. (18 cm). At beg of foll 2 rows, inc 1 fan st as foll: ch 3, 1 dc in the last sc of the previous row, 1 fan st in the middle dc of the first fan st, 1 fan st in the last ch-3 sp of the first fan st, 1 fan st in the last ch-3 sp of each of the fan sts across. Work these 2 inc rows when sleeve measures 11 in. (28 cm) and 15 in. (38 cm). Work these 17 fan sts until sleeve measures 19¾ in. (45 cm), ending with last row as on back. Fasten off.

FINISHING

Block pieces to indicated measurements. Sew shoulder seams over 5 (6, 6½) in. - 13 (15, 17) cm from armhole edge. Sew sleeves to side seams, matching center of sleeve with shoulder seam. Sew side and sleeve seams.

BACK

127

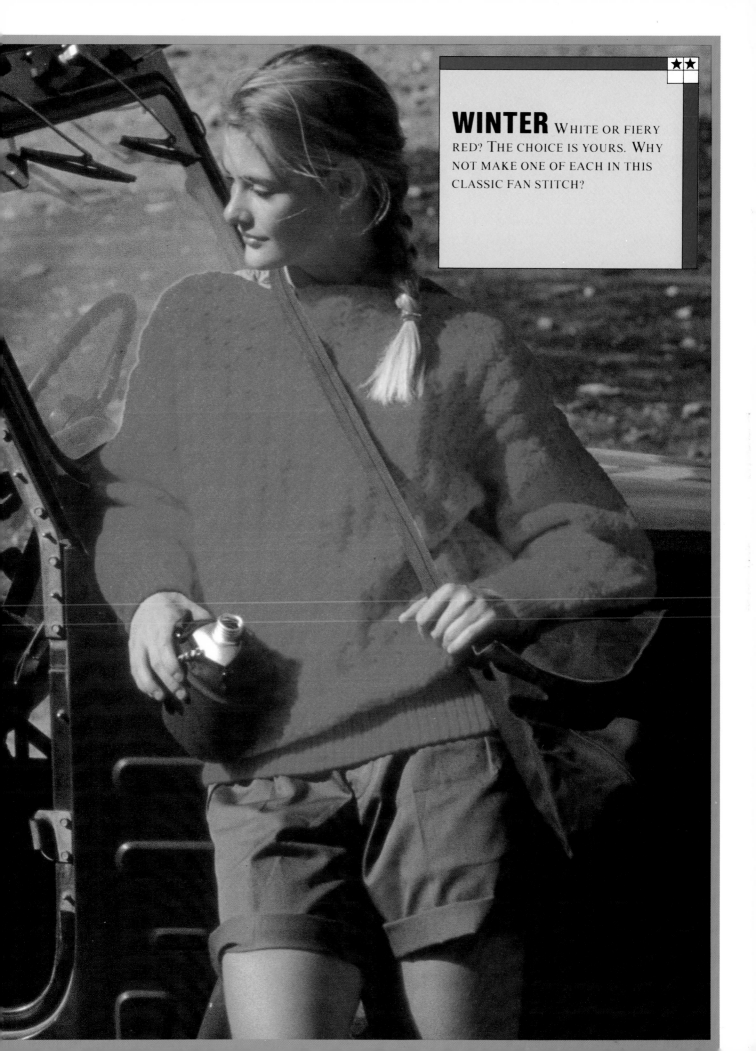

WINTER WHITE OR FIERY RED? THE CHOICE IS YOURS. WHY NOT MAKE ONE OF EACH IN THIS CLASSIC FAN STITCH?

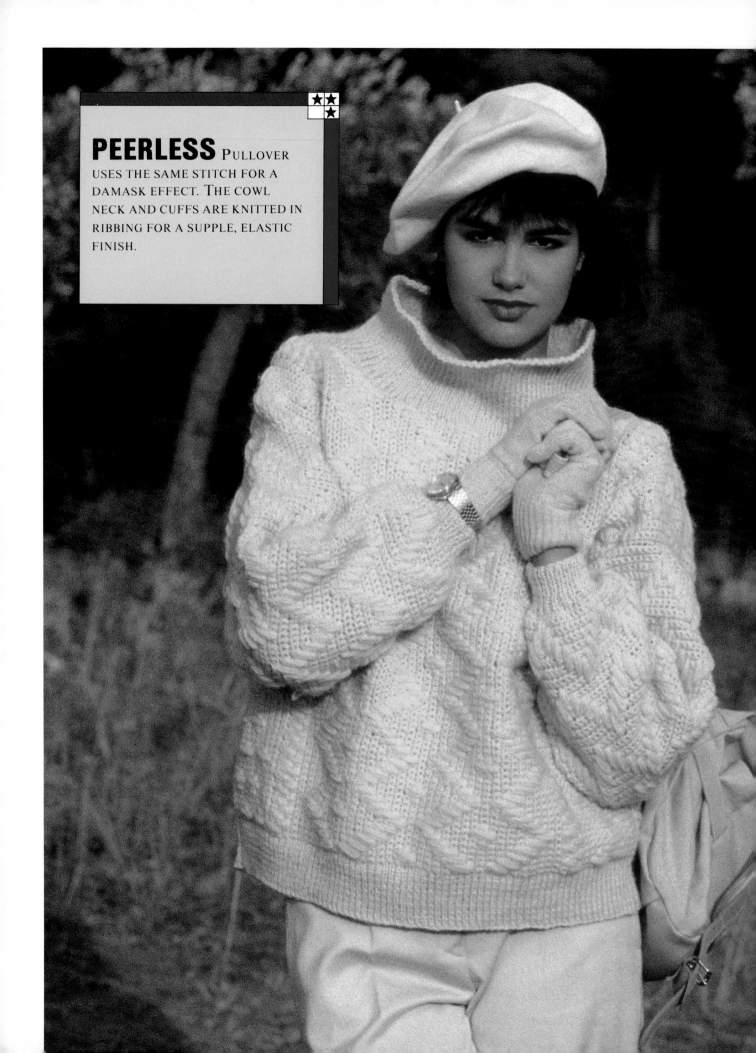

PEERLESS PULLOVER USES THE SAME STITCH FOR A DAMASK EFFECT. THE COWL NECK AND CUFFS ARE KNITTED IN RIBBING FOR A SUPPLE, ELASTIC FINISH.

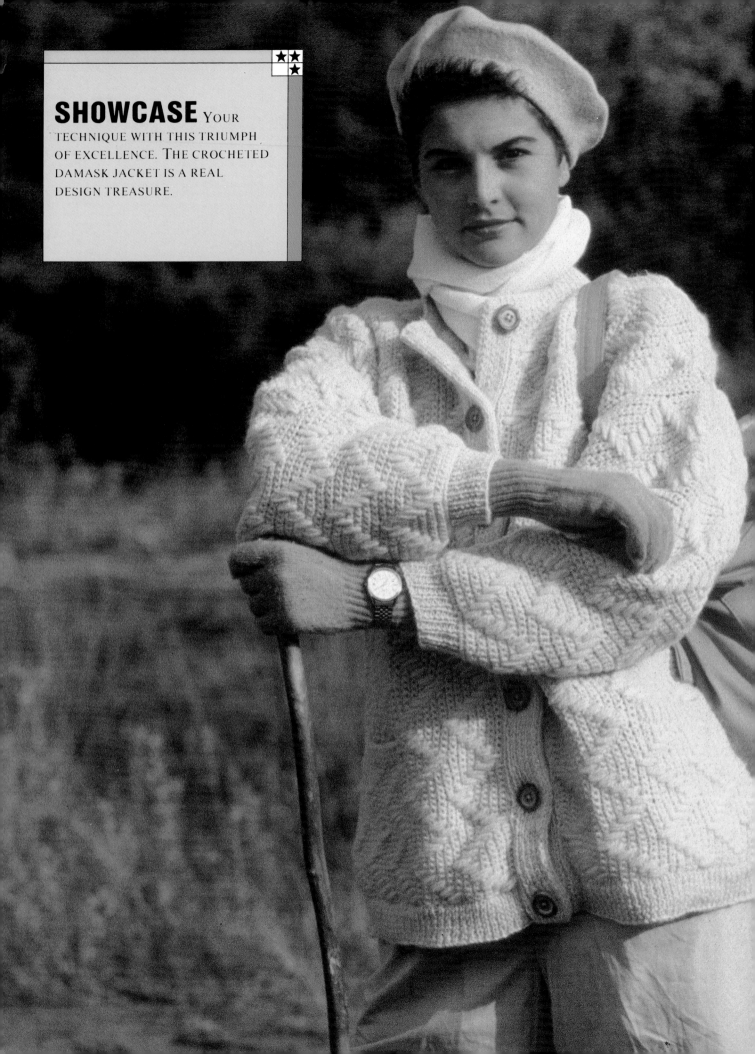

SHOWCASE YOUR
TECHNIQUE WITH THIS TRIUMPH
OF EXCELLENCE. THE CROCHETED
DAMASK JACKET IS A REAL
DESIGN TREASURE.

ZIG-ZAG PULLOVER

SIZE

Woman's Small (Medium, Large), bust 30-32 (33-35, 36-38) in. 76-81.5 (84-89, 91.5-97) cm. Finished bust measurements: 43½ (46½, 49) in. - 111 (118, 125) cm, length: 23¼ (24½, 25¾) in. — 59 (62, 65.5) cm, sleeve seam: 16½ in. (42 cm).

MATERIALS

16 (18, 20) skeins Shetland worsted weight yarn (approx. 140 yds per 50 g skein) color ecru. Crochet hook U.S. size G/6 (U.K. size 7) (Metric size 4.5) or size needed to obtain gauge. Knitting needles U.S. size 4 (U.K. size 9) (Metric size 3.5). Circular or double pointed needles U.S. size 4 (U.K. size 9) (Metric size 3.5) **To save time, take time to check gauge!**

GAUGE

15 sts and 23 rows = 4 in. (10 cm).

STITCHES

**Chain (ch),
single crochet (sc),
slip stitch (sl st).
1/1 ribbing: Row 1:** *K1, p1*. Rep * to * across. **Row 2 and all foll rows:** Work sts as established in previous row.

BACK

Working from side to side, beg at left edge. With crochet hook ch 83 (88, 92) = ch 1 (counts as first st). **Row 1:** 1 sc in the 2nd ch from the hook, 1 sc in each ch = 83 (88, 93) sc. **Row 2 and all foll wrong side of rows:** Ch 1, 1 sc in each sc across. **Row 3:** Ch 1, 1 sc in each sc. **Row 5:** Ch 1, 5 sc, *1 long st in the 3rd row below: insert hook in the st in the 3rd row below

foll sc, yo and draw up loop, yo, insert hook from front to back of the same st of the 3rd row, yo, draw through long loop, yo, insert hook in same st, yo, draw through long loop, yo and draw through 5 loops on hook, yo and draw through last 2 loops, 1 sc, 1 long st in 3rd row below, 7 sc*, rep * to *, end with point 1 (2, 1) on chart, 1 sc in the last sc. **Row 7:** Ch 1, 6 sc, *1 long st in first row, 9 sc*, rep * to *, end with point 1 (2, 1) on chart, 1 sc in last sc. **Row 9:** Ch 1, 1 sc in each of the first 2 sc, *1 long st in the 7th row below, 7 sc, 1 long st in the 7th row below, 1 sc*, rep * to *, end with point 1 (2, 1) on chart, 1 sc in the last sc. **Row 11:**

SLEEVE

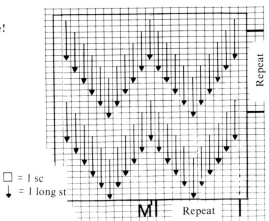

☐ = 1 sc

↓ = 1 long st

FRONT-BACK

SLEEVE

133

Ch 1, 1 sc in the first sc, 1 long st in the 5th row below, 9 sc*, rep * to *, end with point 1 (2, 1) on chart, 1 sc in the last sc. Continue **Row 12** by foll the chart to point 4 (5,6). Then work point 6 to point 7, then from point 9 (8, 7) to point 10. Piece will measure 21¾ (23¼, 24½) in. - 55.5 (59, 62.5) cm from beg, fasten off.

FRONT

Work same as back until piece measures 6 (6½, 7) in. - 15 (16.5, 18) cm from beg, then shape neck. With right side facing, at left edge of every 2nd row, leave 3 sts unworked once, leave 2 sts unworked twice, leave 1 st unworked 3 times. Work wrong side of work rows without decreases. Work over rem 73 (78, 83) sts to center of work (= M on chart). Work the 2nd half by rev shapings (ch the specified number of sts at neck edge and work these sts in pat st). Work to end of chart. Fasten off.

SLEEVES

Ch 45 (47, 49) + ch 1 to turn. Work in pat st by centering chart (= M on chart). Continue in pat st by foll chart. At each edge of every 4th row, inc 1 st 12 times. At each edge of every 6th row, inc 1 st 5 times. (To inc, work 2 sts in each edge st.) Work inc sts in pat st = 79 (81, 83) sts. Work for a total of 6 zigzag motifs, then work the last 4 rows of chart. The sleeve will measure 15 in. (38 cm) from beg. Fasten off.

FINISHING

Block pieces to indicated measurements. Sew shoulder seams. With double pointed knitting needles, pick up and knit 176 (180, 184) sts around neck and work 4 rows in 1/1 ribbing. Bind off loosely. With knitting needles, pick up and knit 140 (148, 156) sts along lower edge of back and work 2 in. (5 cm) in 1/1 ribbing. Bind off loosely. With knitting needles, pick up and knit 40 (42, 44) sts along each sleeve edge and work 1½ in. (4 cm) in 1/1 ribbing. Bind off. Work same ribbing on front. Sew sleeves to side seams, matching center of sleeve with shoulder seam. Sew side and sleeve seams.

ZIG-ZAG CARDIGAN

SIZE

Woman's Small (Medium, Large), bust 30-35 (36-38) in. - 76-89 (91.5-97) cm. Finished bust measurements: 49½ (51¾) in. - 126 (131.5) cm, length: 25½ in. (65 cm), sleeve seam: 18¼ (46.5 cm).

MATERIALS

18 (20) skeins worsted weight Shetland yarn (approx. 140 yds per 50 g skein) color ecru. Crochet hook U.S. size G/6 (U.K. size 7) (Metric size 4.5) or size needed to obtain gauge. Knitting needles U.S. size 4 (U.K. size 9) (Metric size 3.5). 7 buttons. **To save time, take time to check gauge!**

GAUGE

15 sts and 24 rows in pat st = 4 in. (10 cm).

STITCHES

Chain (ch), single crochet (sc), slip stitch (sl st).
Stockinette stitch: *Knit 1 row on right side of work, purl 1 row on wrong side of work*.
1/1 ribbing: Row 1: *K1, p1*. Rep * to * across.
Row 2 and all foll rows: Work sts as established in previous row.

BACK

Working from side to side, beg at left edge. With crochet hook ch 93 + ch 1 to turn. Work in pat st as foll: **Row 1:** 1 Sc in the 2nd ch from the hook, 1 sc in each ch = 93 sc. **Row 2 and all foll wrong side of work rows:** Ch 1, sc across. **Row 3 and 5:** Ch 1, sc across. **Row 7:** Ch 1, 6 sc, *1 long st: insert hook in the st found in the first row below next st, yo and draw up loop, yo, insert hook from front to back of the same st of the first row, yo, draw through long loop, yo, insert hook in same st, yo, draw through long loop, yo and draw through 5 loops on hook, yo and draw through last 2 loops, 9 sc*, rep * to * across, end with 6 sc instead of 9 sc. **Row 9:** Ch 1, 5 sc, *1 long st worked 3 rows below next st, 1 sc, 1 long st worked 3 rows below next st, 7 sc*, rep * to * across, end with 5 sc

instead of 7 sc. **Row 11:** Ch 1, 4 sc, *1 long st worked in the 5th row below next st, ch over the next 3 sc, 1 long st worked in the 5th row below next st, 5 sc*, rep * to * across, end with 4 sc instead of 5 sc. Continue by foll chart. Always rep rows 21 to 34 of chart, making 10 (11) zigzags total. After the last rep work the last 4 rows of chart. Piece will measure 23½ (25¾) in. - 60 (65.5) cm from beg, fasten off.

LEFT FRONT

Ch 93 + ch 1 to turn. Work in pat st by foll chart. After 8 rows, work the first 70 sts, then work the rem 23 sts for 32 rows (pocket front). Fasten off. Ch 23. Fasten off. Work the 70 sts at right edge, join the 23 st ch and work across in pat for 32 rows. Then work 70 sts at right edge and 23 sts from pocket front and work in pat st until piece measures 9 (9¼) in. - 23 (26) cm from beg. With right side facing, sl st over first 3 sts, work to end of row, turn. Work to end of wrong side of work row. On right side of work rows, sl st over 2 sts 3 times, and sl st over 1 st once. Always work wrong side of work rows without dec. Work rem 83 sts until 5 zigzag motifs are complete, then work last 4 rows of chart. Fasten off.

RIGHT FRONT

Work same as left front, but beg at center edge. Ch 83 + ch 1 to turn. Work in pat st by foll chart. At right edge of every right side of work row, inc 1 st once, inc 2 sts 3 times, inc 3 sts once = 93 sts. (For 2 and 3 st incs, ch the specified number of sts at end of wrong side of work row and work in pat over them on right side of work row.) Beg the pocket after row 34, rev placement of left front. When pocket is complete, work 8 rows, then fasten off.

RIGHT SLEEVE

Ch 45 (47) + ch 1 to turn. Work in pat st by centering chart at point M. Inc 1 st at each edge of every 5th row 18 times. (For inc, work 2 sts in each edge st.) Work inc sts in pat st. You now have 81 (83) sts and 7 complete zigzag motifs.

After the 7th rep, work last 4 rows of chart. Sleeve will measure 16¾ in. (42½ cm) from beg. Fasten off.

LEFT SLEEVE

Work same as right sleeve, centering chart at point M1.

FINISHING

Block pieces to indicated measurements. With knitting needles, pick up and knit about 29 sts along top of each pocket and work ¾ in. (2 cm) in 1/1 ribbing. Bind off. Sew pocket lining and borders in place. Sew shoulder seams. With knitting needles, pick up and knit about 40 (42) sts along edge of each sleeve and work 1½ in. (4 cm) in 1/1 ribbing, bind off loosely. Sew sleeves to side seams, matching center of sleeve with shoulder seam. Sew side and sleeve seams. With knitting needles, pick up and knit 287 (299) sts along lower edge of body and work in 1/1 ribbing for 1¾ in. (4.5 cm). Bind off loosely. With smaller size needles, cast on 22 sts and work as foll: **Row 1:** (wrong side facing): P10, p1 in back of st, 11 sts in 1/1 ribbing, beg with k1.

Row 2: 11 sts in 1/1 ribbing, k1 in back of st, k10 (st st). Work until piece fits along left front edge to neck, bind off first st of wrong side of work, place rem 21 sts on holder. Sew to left front. Work same band for right front, beg with 11 sts in 1/1 ribbing, p1 in back of st, p10 (st st). When piece measures ¾ in. (2 cm) from beg, make first buttonhole: right side facing: k1, work 2 sts, bind off 3 sts, work 10 sts, bind off 3 sts, work 3 sts. On foll row, cast on 3 sts over bound off sts. Mark positions for 5 more buttons on left band and work buttonholes on right front band to correspond, allowing for last buttonhole on neckband. Bind off last st of wrong side of work row (on st st section). Place rem 21 sts on holder and sew to right front. With knitting needles, pick up 21 sts from right front holder, pick up and knit 97 (101) sts around neck and 21 sts from left front holder and work ¾ in. (2 cm) in 1/1 ribbing. Then make 1 buttonhole above previous ones. Continue ribbing until band measures 1¼ in. (4 cm), then bind off loosely. Fold the front bands to inside and sl st in place. Reinforce buttonholes and sew on buttons.

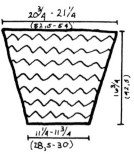

20¾ - 21¼
(52,5-54)

16¾
(42,5)

11¼-11¾
(28,5-30)

SLEEVE

FRONT

BACK

23½-25¾
(60-65,5)

23¾
(60,5)

5½-7¼
(14-11,5)

6-9¼
(23-24)

6
(15)

15¼
(39)

2½
(6,5)

3¼-3¼
(8-1)

9¼-9¼
(23-24)

12¼
(31)

23¾
(60,5)

FRONT-BACK PULLOVER

(chart with grid, marked rows 1, 2, Repeat at bottom; rows 3, 4, 5, 6, 7, 8, 9, 10 marked on right side; M markers)

□ = 1 sc
↓ = 1 long st

FRONT-BACK CARDIGAN

(chart with grid; "Repeat" marked on left side; "Row 8" at bottom left, "Row 7" at bottom right; M markers at bottom)

GOLD PULLOVER

SIZE
Woman's Small (Medium, Large), bust 30-32 (33-35, 36-38) in. - 76-81.5 (84-89, 91.5-97) cm. Finished bust measurements: 41½ (45, 48) in. - 106 (114, 122) cm, length: 23¾ in. (60 cm), sleeve seam: 17 in. (43 cm).

MATERIALS
16 (16, 17) skeins "Scheepjeswol Mayflower Cotton 8" (100% cotton - approx. 180 yds per 50 g skein) color gold. Crochet hook U.S. size B/1 (U.K. size 12) (Metric size 2.5) or size needed to obtain gauge. Knitting needles U.S. size 2 (U.K. size 12) (Metric size 2.5). **To save time, take time to check gauge!**

GAUGE
30 sts and 24 rows in pat st = 4 in. (10 cm).

STITCHES
Chain (ch), single crochet (sc), double crochet (dc), treble crochet (tr), slip stitch (sl st).
Pattern stitch: Multiple of 4 + 2. At beg of row, ch 1 counts as first sc, ch 3 counts as first dc.
Row 1: Sc across by inserting hook under both loops of previous row.
Rows 2 to 6: Sc in the back loop of the sts of the previous row.
Row 7: Wrong side of work: Ch 3 (= border st), working under both loops of previous row: skip 1, *1 dc in the 2nd, 3rd and 4th sts, 1 tr in the first st by working behind the 3 dc*, rep * to * across. End with 1 dc (= 1 border st).
Row 8: Right side of row: Ch 3 (= 1 border st), work under both loops of previous row, skip 1, *1 dc in the 2nd, 3rd and 4th sts, 1 tr in the first st by working in front of the 3 sts*, rep * to * across, end with 1 dc (= 1 border st).
Row 9: Like row 1.
Rows 10 to 14: Like rows 2 to 6.
Row 15: Wrong side of work: Ch 3 (= 1 border st), working under both loops, *skip 3 sts, 1 tr in the 4th st, 1 dc in front of the tr in the skipped first, 2nd and 3rd sts*, rep * to * across, end with 1 dc (= 1 border st).
Rep rows 1 to 16.
1/1 ribbing: Row 1: *K1, p1*. Rep * to * across.
Row 2 and all foll rows: Work sts as established in previous row.

BACK
With crochet hook ch 162 (174, 186) + ch 1. Foundation row: Sc across, beg with 2nd ch from hook = 162 (174, 186) sc. Continue in pat st, beg with 2nd row. Work until piece measures 21¾ in. (55.5 cm), ending with 6 rows of sc. Fasten off.

FRONT
Work same as back until you have 5 rows less than back. Mark center 76 (80, 84) for neck. Work 1 row of sc to last 2 sc before neck marker, sl st first st of next row. Work 1 more row to last sc, turn and work 1 row = 39 (43, 47) sc. Fasten off. Work 2nd half by rev shapings.

SLEEVES
Ch 86 (90, 94) + ch 1 (counts as first sc). Sc across, beg with the 2nd ch from hook = 86 (90, 94) sc. Continue by working in pat st, beg row 2. At each edge of every 3rd row, inc 1 st 8 times. At each edge of every 4th row, inc 1 st 16 times = 134 (138, 142) sts. Work until piece measures 13¾ in. (35.5 cm), then work 6 rows of sc. Fasten off.

FINISHING
Block pieces to indicated measurements. With knitting needles, pick up and knit 110 (118, 126) sts along lower edge of front and back and work 2 in. (5 cm) in 1/1 ribbing. Bind off loosely. With knitting needles, pick up and knit 48 (50, 52) sts along lower edge of each sleeve and work 1¼ in. (4 cm) in 1/1 ribbing. Bind off loosely. Sew shoulder seams. With crochet hook work 1 row of sc around neck, join with sl st, fasten off. Sew sleeves to side seams, matching center of sleeve with shoulder seams. Sew side and sleeve seams.

FRONT-BACK

11-11½-11¾ (28-29-30)   4¾-5½-6¼ (12.5-14-15.5)

21¾ (55.5)

2 (5)

20¾-22½-24 (53-57-61)

17¼-17¾-18¼ (44-45-46.5)

15½ (39.5)

1½ (4)

SLEEVE

11-11½-12 (28-29-30.5)

HIGHLIGHT YOUR SUMMER TAN WITH THESE COTTON PULLOVERS. THE BATWING SILHOUETTE IS A BREEZE TO WEAR AND SIMPLE TO MAKE.

BATWING PULLOVER

SIZE
Woman's Small (Medium, Large), bust 30-32 (33-35, 36-38) in. 76-81.5 (84-89, 91.5-97) cm. Finished bust measurements: 41½ (44, 46½) in. - 105 (111, 118) cm, length: 21¼ (21½, 22) in. 54 (55, 56) cm, sleeve seam: 15¾ (40.5 cm).

MATERIALS
13 (14, 14) skeins "Scheepjeswol Mayflower Cotton 8" (100% cotton - approx. 187 yds per 50 g skein) color teal. Crochet hook U.S. size B/1 (U.K. size 12) (Metric size 2.5) or size needed to obtain gauge. Knitting needles U.S. size 2 (U.K. size 12) (Metric size 2.5). **To save time, take time to check gauge!**

GAUGE
30 sts and 24 rows = 4 in. (10 cm).

STITCHES
**Chain (ch),
single crochet (sc),
double crochet (dc),
treble crochet (tr),
slip stitch (sl st).**
Pattern stitch: Multiple of 8 + 1 border st at each edge. **Row 1:** Ch 1, sc across, working under the 2 strands of the previous row. Turn.
Rows 2 to 6: Ch 1, sc across, working in the back loop of the st of the previous row. Turn.
Row 7: Wrong side of work: Mark center st, ch 3 (= border st), working under both loops of each st, *skip 3 sts, 1 tr in the 4th st, 1 dc in the first, 2nd and 3rd skipped sts by passing hook in front of the 4th st*, rep * to * to the center of the row, then **skip 1 st, 3 dc in 2nd, 3rd, and 4th sts, 1 tr

in skipped st by passing the hook behind the 3 dc**, rep ** to **, rep ** to **, end 1 dc (= border st).
Row 8: right side of work: Mark center st, ch 3 (= border st), working under both loops of each st, *skip 1 st, 3 dc in the 2nd, 3rd and 4th sts, 1 tr in skipped st by passing hook in front of the 3 dc (insert hook from back to front of st)*, rep * to * to center of work, then **skip 3 sts, 1 tr in the 4th st, 1 dc in the first, 2nd and 3rd skipped sts by working behind the tr*, rep * to * across, end 1 dc (= border st). Rep rows 1 to 8.
1/1 ribbing: Row 1: *K1, p1*. Rep * to * across.
Row 2 and all foll rows: Work sts as established in previous row.

WORKED IN 1 PIECE, BEG AT LOWER EDGE OF LEFT SLEEVE with crochet hook ch 86 (90, 94) + ch 1 (counts as first sc). **Row 1:** Work 85 (89, 92) sc, beg in 2nd ch from hook = 86 (90, 94) sc. Continue with the 2nd row of pat st. Inc 1 st at each edge of every 3rd row 28 times. (Work 2 sts in each edge st for each inc.) Work inc sts in pat st. On the 7th row, over the 90 (94, 98) sts, work as foll: ch 3 (= 1 border st), 0 (2, 0) dc, *skip 3 sts, 1 tr in the 4th st, 1 dc in the first, 2nd, 3rd skipped sts by passing the hook in front of the tr*, rep * to * 10 (10, 11) times, then *skip 1 st, 1 dc in the 2nd, 3rd and 4th sts, 1 tr in

1 tr in skipped st by passing hook behind the 3 dc*, rep * to * 10 (10, 11) times. End with 0 (2, 0) dc in 1 dc (= border st). Continue on the 142 (146, 150) sts work until piece measures 14¼ in. (36.5 cm), ending with the 8th row of pat st. Ch 74 (76, 78) + ch 1 and join to right edge, work across 142 (146, 150) sts, then ch 74 (76, 78). Continue in pat st over 290 (298, 306) sts for 5¼ (5½, 6) in. - 13.5 (14, 15) cm, mark center 6 sts. Work first 35 (36, 37) motifs + 1 border st. Work even for 10 (10¾, 11½) in. -25.5 (27.5, 29) cm, then leave sts unworked. Work 2nd half the same, then ch 6 across both halves and work 290 (298, 306) sts in pat st for 5¼ (5½, 6) in. - 13.5 (14, 15) cm, ending with 6th row of pat st. Leave 74 (76, 78) sts unworked at each edge and work 2nd sleeve by rev shapings. (For each dec, sl st over first st on row and leave last st unworked.)

FINISHING
Block pieces to indicated measurements. With knitting needles, pickup and knit 50 (52, 54) sts along lower edge of each sleeve and work 1½ in. (4 cm) in 1/1 ribbing. Bind off loosely. With knitting needles, pick up and knit 118 (126, 134) sts along lower edge of back and work 2½ in. (6 cm) in 1/1 ribbing. Bind off loosely. Work same ribbing on front. Join the side and sleeve seams by holding right sides tog and using crochet hook join with 1 row of sc, working through both thicknesses. Work 1 round of sc around neck by working 1 sc in each row of sc and 2 sc in each row of dc. Join with sl st. Fasten off.

TODDLER'S FLOWER BUD PULLOVER

SIZE
Child's size 1 (2, 3) years, chest 21 (22, 23) in. - 53.5 (56, 58.5) cm. Finished chest measurements: 22½ (24½, 27) in. - 57 (63, 69) cm, length: 11 (13½, 15) in. - 28.5 (34, 38) cm, sleeve seam: 8½ (9½, 10¾) in. - 21.5 (24.5, 27.5) cm.

MATERIALS
4 (5, 6) skeins fingering weight yarn (50 g skein) color ecru. Crochet hook U.S. size C/2 (U.K. size 11) (Metric size 3) or size needed to obtain gauge. Knitting needles U.S. size 2 (U.K. size 12) (Metric size 2.5). 3 buttons. **To save time, take time to check gauge!**

GAUGE
27 sc and 32 rows = 4 in. (10 cm).

STITCHES
**Chain (ch),
single crochet (sc),
double crochet (dc),
slip stitch (sl st).**
Cross stitch: Worked over 2 sts.
Rows 1 and 2: 1 sc in each sc.

Row 3: Insert hook in the first sc (working under both loops), yo and draw through 1 loop, insert hook in the sc of the previous row under same st, yo and draw through a long loop, yo and draw through 2 loops, yo, draw through 2 loops (= 1 long st), 1 long st in the next sc.
Row 4: 1 sc in each sc.
Row 5: 1 long st in each sc, but insert hook in the long of the previous row instead of the sc. Always rep rows 4 and 5.
Flower stitch: Worked over 15 (17, 19) st.
Rows 1 to 4: 1 sc in each st = 15 (17, 19) sc.
Row 5: 7 (8, 9) sc, ch 8, 1 sc, ch 8 and 1 sc all in the foll sc, ch 8, 7 (8, 9) sc.
Row 6: 7 (8, 9) sc, ch 1, skip ch 8 of previous row, 1 sc, ch 8, 1 sc, ch 8 of the previous row, 7 (8, 9) sc.
Rows 7 and 8: 1 sc in each st.
Row 9: 4 (5, 6) sc, insert hook through the ch-8 sp and in the foll sc, work 1 sc, 5 sc, insert hook through the 3rd ch-8 sp and in the foll sc, work 1 sc, 4 (5, 6) sc.
Row 10: 6 (7, 8) sc, ch 3, sk 3 sts, 1 sc in each of the foll 6 (7, 8) sc.
Row 11: 6 (7, 8) sc, 7 dc in the ch-3 sp of the previous row and around the center ch-8 sp of the 5th row, 6 (7, 8) sc.
Row 12: 6 (7, 8) sc, ch 3, skip the fan st of the foll row, 6 (7, 8) sc.

SLEEVE

FRONT-BACK

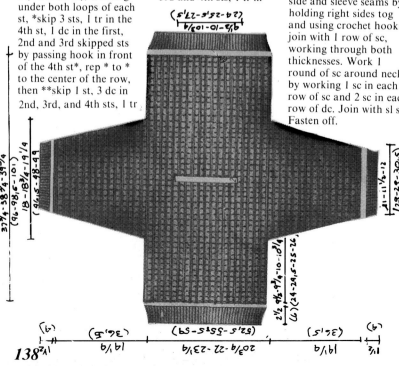

Rep rows 1 to 12.

Half patent stitch: wrong side of work on an odd number of sts:

Row 1: right side of work: 1 border st, p1, *k1, p1*, rep * to *, end with 1 border st.

Row 2: 1 border st, k1, *sl the foll st purlwise, yo (wrap the yarn from front to back around needle), k1* rep * to *, 1 border st.

Row 3: 1 border st, p1, *knit the foll st, dropping the yo, p1*, rep * to *, end with 1 border st. Always rep rows 2 and 3.

BACK

With crochet hook ch 80 (88, 96) + ch 1 to beg first row. Work 1 sc in the 2nd ch from hook and sc in each ch across = 80 (88, 96) sc. Work as foll: 5 sc, 2 long sts, *15 (17, 19) sts in flower st, beg with the 2nd row, 2 long sts*, work * to * 4 times total, 5 sc. Work until piece measures 10¼ (12¾, 14¼) in. - 26.5 (32, 36) cm, fasten off.

FRONT

Work same as back until piece measures 9 (11½, 13) in. - 23.5 (29, 33) cm from beg. Mark the center 18 (20, 24) sts. Work left shoulder as foll: work to first marker, turn, leave rem sts unworked. Sl st over the first 5 sts once. Work to end of row, turn. Work to end of row, turn. Sl st over first 2 sts and continue on rem 24 (27, 29) sts until piece measures 9½ (12, 13½) in. - 26.5 (32, 36) cm from beg. Fasten off. Work left shoulder by rev shapings, but work until piece measures 10¼ (12¾, 14¼) in. - 24.5 (30, 34) cm. Fasten off.

SLEEVES

Ch 49 (53, 57) + ch 1. Work 1 sc in the 2nd ch from hook and work 1 sc in each of the foll ch = 49 (53, 57) sc. Work as foll: 15 (16, 17) sc [the 15 (16, 17) sts of flower st], 2 long sts, 15 (17, 19) sts of flower st, 2 long sts, 15 (16, 17) sc [the first 15 (16, 17) sts of flower st]. Inc 1 st at each edge of every 4th row 10 (5, 1) time. Inc 1 st at each edge of every 6th row 3 (8, 12) times = 75 (79, 83) sts. (For each inc, work 2 sts in each edge st.) Work new sts in pattern st. When piece measures 7¾

(8¾, 10) in. - 19.5 (22.5, 25.5) cm, fasten off.

FINISHING

Block pieces to indicated measurements. With knitting needles, pick up and knit 27 (29, 33) sts along the right shoulder of front and work in half patent st. When piece measures 1/3 in. (1 cm), make 2 buttonholes as foll: right side facing: work 7 (8, 9) sts in half patent st, bind off 3 sts, work 7 (7, 9) sts, bind off 3 sts, work 7 (8, 9) sts. On foll row, cast on 3 sts over bound off sts. Continue in half patent st until border measures 3/4 in. (2 cm). Bind off loosely. Work same on back shoulder omitting buttonholes. With knitting needles, pick up and knit 79 (83, 87) sts around neck and work in half patent st for 1/3 in. (1 cm). 3 sts from the right edge, bind off 3 sts. On foll row, cast on 3 sts over bound off sts. Continue until border measures 3/4 in. (2 cm). Bind off. With knitting needles, pick up and knit 77 (81, 87) sts and along lower edge of back and work in half patent st for 3/4 in. (2 cm). Bind off loosely. Make same border on front. With knitting needles, pick up and knit 43 (47, 51) sts along each sleeve edge and work in half patent st for 3/4 in. (2 cm). Bind off loosely. Lap front shoulder border over back and sew in place. Sew sleeves to side seams, matching center of sleeve with shoulder seam. Sew side and sleeve seam. Sew on buttons.

BABY CABLE PULLOVER

SIZE

Child's size 1 (2, 3) years, chest 21 (22, 23) in. - 53.5 (56, 58.5) cm. Finished chest measurements: 23 (24½, 26½) in. - 57 (63, 69) cm, length: 11 (13½, 15) in. - 28.5 (34, 38) cm, sleeve seam: 8½ (9½, 10¾) in. - 21.5 (24.5, 27.5) cm.

MATERIALS

4 (5, 6) skeins fingering weight yarn (50 g skein) color ecru.
Crochet hook U.S. size C/2 (U.K. size 11) (Metric size 3) or size

needed to obtain gauge. Knitting needles U.S. size 2 (U.K. size 12) (Metric size 2.5). 3 buttons. **To save time, take time to check gauge!**

GAUGE

27 sc and 32 rows = 4 in. (10 cm). 11 sts of cable pat = 1½ in. (4 cm).

STITCHES

Chain (ch), single crochet (sc), slip stitch (sl st).

Pattern stitch: Alternately work vertical bands and cable bands. Beg each row with ch 1 to turn. Work 1 sc in the last st of the previous row. Insert hook in the back loop in each st of the previous row.

Cable pattern: Worked over 11 sts.

Row 1: Right side of work: 11 sc, work through the back loop, ch 1, turn.

Row 2: 4 sc, ch 3, skip 3, 4 sc, ch 1, turn.

Row 3: Insert hook in the foll st (work through both loops), yo and draw through 1 loop, then insert hook in the sc of the first row, yo and draw up a long loop, yo, draw through 2 loops, yo, draw through 2 loops (= 1 long st), 1 long st in the foll st, 2 sc, ch 3, skip 3, 2 sc, 1 long sc in foll 2 sc.

Rows 4, 6, 8, 10: 4 sc, ch 3, skip 3, 4 sc.

Row 5: 2 long sts, working both in the long st of the previous row, 2 sc, 1 bobble (insert hook in the first row in the ch-3 sp of the 2nd, 3rd and 4th row, yo, draw through a long loop), *yo, insert hook in the same sc and draw up a long loop*, work * to * twice, yo and draw through 6 loops, ch 1, make another bobble in the same sc, 1 sc in each of the foll 2 sc, 1 long st in each of the foll sc.

Row 7: 1 long st around each of the long sts of the previous row, 2 sc, ch 3, skip 3, 2 sc, 1 long st around each of the long sts of the previous row.

Row 9: 1 long st around each of the long sts of the previous row, 2 sc, 1 long st in the ch-3 sp by working around the ch between the bobble of the 5th row, 1 bobble, ch 1 and 1 bobble, 2 sc, 1 long st in each of the foll 2 long sts.
Always rep rows 7 to 10.

Half patent stitch: wrong

side of work on an odd number of sts:

Row 1: right side of work: 1 border st, p1, *k1, p1*, rep * to *, end with 1 border st.

Row 2: 1 border st, k1, *sl the foll st purlwise, yo (wrap the yarn from front to back around needle), k1*, rep * to *, 1 border st.

Row 3: 1 border st, p1, *knit the foll st, dropping the yo, p1*, rep * to *, end with 1 border st. Always rep rows 2 and 3.

BACK

With crochet hook ch 79 (85, 93) + ch 1 to beg first row. Work 1 sc in the 2nd ch from hook and sc in each ch across = 79 (85, 93) sc. Work in pat st as foll: 8 (9, 11) sc, 11 sts in cable pat (beg with 2nd row), 15 (17, 19) sc, 11 sts of cable pat, 15 (17, 19) sc, 11 sts of cable pat, 8 (9, 11) sc. Work until piece measures 10¼ (12¾, 14¼) in. - 26.5 (32, 36) cm, fasten off.

FRONT

Work same as back until piece measures 9 (11½, 13) in. - 23.5 (29, 33) cm from beg. Mark the center 17 (19, 21) sts. Work left shoulder as foll: work to first marker, turn, leave rem sts unworked. Sl st over the first 5 sts once. Work to end of row, turn. Work to end of row, turn. Sl st over first 3 sts and continue on rem 23 (25, 28) sts until piece measures 9½ (12, 13½) in. - 26.5 (32, 36) cm from beg, fasten off. Work right shoulder by rev shapings, but work until piece measures 10¼ (12¾, 14¼) in. - 24.5 (30, 34) cm. Fasten off.

SLEEVES

Ch 51 (55, 59) + ch 1. Work 1 sc in the 2nd ch from hook and work 1 sc in each of the foll ch = 51 (55, 59) sc. Work in pat st as foll: 7 (8, 9) sc, 11 sts in cable pat, 15 (17, 19) sc, 11 sts in cable pat, 7 (8, 9) sc. Inc 1 st at each edge of every 4th row 10 (5, 1) time. Inc 1 st at each edge of every 6th row 3 (8, 12) times = 77 (81, 85) sts. (For each inc, work 2 sts in each edge st.) Work new sts in pat sts. When piece measures 7¾ (8¾, 10) in. - 19.5 (22.5, 25.5) cm, fasten off.

FINISHING

Block pieces to indicated

measurements. With knitting needles, pick up and knit 27 (29, 33) sts along the right shoulder of front and work in half patent st. When piece measures 1/3 in. (1 cm), make 2 buttonholes as foll: right side facing: work 7 (8, 9) sts in half patent st, bind off 3 sts, work 7 (7, 9) sts, bind off 3 sts, work 7 (8, 9) sts. On foll row, cast on 3 sts over bound off sts. Continue in half patent st until border measures 3/4 in. (2 cm). Bind off loosely. Work same on back shoulder omitting buttonholes. With knitting needles, pick up and knit 79 (83, 87) sts around neck and work in half patent st for 1/3 in. (1 cm). 3 sts from the right edge, bind off 3 sts. On foll row, cast on 3 sts over bound off sts. Continue until border measures 3/4 in. (2 cm). Bind off. With knitting needles, pick up and knit 77 (81, 87) sts and along lower edges of back and work in half patent st for 3/4 in. (2 cm). Bind off loosely. Make same border on front. With knitting needles, pick up and knit 43 (47, 51) sts from each sleeve edge and work in half patent st for 3/4 in. (2 cm). Bind off loosely. Lap front shoulder border over back and sew in place. Sew sleeves to side seams, matching center of sleeve with shoulder seam. Sew side and sleeve seams. Sew on buttons.

11¼ - 11¾ - 12½
(28,5 - 30 - 32)

7¼ - 8¼ - 10
(18,5 - 22,5 - 25,5)

7¼ - 8 - 8½
(18,5 - 20 - 21,5)

SLEEVE

4¾ - 5 - 5¼
(12 - 13 - 13,5)

9 - 11¼ - 13
(23,5 - 29 - 33)

FRONT-BACK

11½ - 12¼ - 13¼
(29 - 31 - 34)

EMBELLISH A
PULLOVER WITH BABY CABLES OR
FLOWER BUDS FOR CHARMING
RESULTS. SHOULDER BUTTONS
MAKE DRESSING SIMPLE — A
MAJOR CONSIDERATION WITH
TODDLERS.

BEGUILING TOP WITH

SPAGHETTI STRAPS IS CERTAIN TO
BEAT THOSE SUMMERTIME BLUES.
PAIR IT WITH CARDIGAN COVER-
UP IN MATCHING PATTERN
STITCH.

CARDIGAN AND TOP

SIZE

Woman's Small (Medium, Large), bust 30-32 (33-35, 36-38) in. - 76-81.5 (84-89, 91.5-97) cm. Cardigan: Finished bust measurements: 42½ (45, 47) in. -108 (114, 120) cm, length: 22½ in. (57 cm), sleeve seam: 18 in. (46 cm). Top: 33¾ (37, 40) in. - 86 (94, 102) cm. length 13¾ in. (35 cm).

MATERIALS

Cardigan: 12 (13, 13) skeins "Scheepjeswol Mayflower Cotton 8" (100% cotton - approx. 180 yds per 50 g skein) color blue. Top: 4 (5, 5) skeins color blue. 5 buttons.
Crochet hook U.S. size B/1 (U.K. size 12) (Metric size 2.5) or size needed to obtain gauge. Knitting needles U.S. size 2 (U.K. size 12) (Metric size 2.5). **To save time, take time to check gauge!**

GAUGE

13 groups (= 2 crossed dc) x 12 rows = 4 in. (10 cm).

STITCHES

Chain (ch), single crochet (sc), double crochet (dc), slip stitch (sl st).
1 group tog: Work 1 dc in the 2nd st, until you have 2 loops on the hook, work 1 dc in the first st, until you have 3 loops on the hook, yo and draw through 3 loops on the hook.
Pattern stitch: Multiple of 2 + ch 3. Ch 1 at each edge of row.
Row 1: (right side of work): 1 dc in the 6th ch from the hook, 1 dc by passing the hook behind the 5th ch from the hook,

skip 1 ch, 1 dc in the foll dc, 1 dc in the skipped st by passing the hook behind the work = 1 group, rep * to *, end 1 dc for the border st.
Row 2: (wrong side of work): Ch 3 (= border st), *1 dc in the 2nd st, 1 dc in the first st by passing the hook in front of the 2nd st, working from back to front of st*, rep * to *, end with 1 dc in the 3rd ch (= 1 border st).
Row 3: Ch 3 (= 1 border st), *1 dc in the 2nd st, 1 dc in the first st by passing the hook behind the 2nd st*, rep * to * across, end 1 dc (= 1 border st).
Rep rows 2 and 3.
Shrimp stitch: Worked like sc, but worked left to right instead of right to left.
1/1 ribbing: Row 1: *K1, p1*. Rep * to * across.
Row 2 and all foll rows: Work sts as established in previous row.

CARDIGAN: BACK

With crochet hook ch 142 (150, 158) + ch 3 to turn (counts as first st). Work in pat st = 70 (74, 78) groups + 2 border sts. Work until piece measures 20 in. (51 cm) from beg. Mark the center 24 (26, 28) groups. Work to first marker. Fasten off. Beg after 2nd marker and work rem groups = 23 (24, 25) groups + 1 border st on each shoulder. Fasten off. The total height is 20½ in. (52 cm) from beg.

RIGHT FRONT

Ch 70 (74, 78) + ch 3 (counts as first st). Work in pat st = 34 (36, 38) groups + 2 border sts. Work until piece meaures 9¼ in. (24 cm) from beg. End with right side of work row. Shape neck:
Row 1: (wrong side of work): work to last group of sts on row, work 1 group tog, 1 border st.
Row 2: Ch 3, 1 group tog, work to end of row. Rep rows 1 and 2, 10 (11, 12) times. Work over rem 23 (24, 25) groups + 2 border sts until piece measures 20½ in. (52 cm) from beg. Fasten off.

LEFT FRONT

Work same as right front until piece measures 9¼ in. (24 cm) from beg. End with right side of work row. Shape neck: **Row 1:** (right side of work) Ch 3, work 1 group tog, work to end of row. **Row 2:** Work to last group of sts on row, work 1 group tog, 1 border st. Rep rows 1 and 2, 10 (11, 12) times. Work over rem 23 (24, 25) groups + 2 border sts until piece measures 20½ in. (52 cm) from beg. Fasten off.

SLEEVES

Ch 80 (82, 84) + ch 3 (= border st). Work in pat st = 39 (40, 41) groups + 2 border sts. On every 2nd row, work 2 dc in the st at each edge 20 (22, 24) times = 59 (62, 65) groups. After every 2nd inc, work these dc in pat st. When piece measures 16 in. (41 cm), fasten off.

FINISHING

Block pieces to indicated measurements. With knitting needles, pick up and knit 107 (113, 119) sts along lower edge of back and work 2 in. (5 cm) in 1/1 ribbing. Bind off loosely. With knitting needles, pick up and knit 51 (53, 55) sts along lower edge of each front and work 2 in. (5 cm) in 1/1 ribbing. Bind off loosely. With knitting needles, pick up and knit 46 (48, 50) sts along lower edge of each sleeve and work 2 in. (5 cm) in 1/1 ribbing. Bind off loosely. Sew shoulder seams. Along the front and back neck edges, work as foll: **Row 1:** (right side of work): Beg at lower edge of right front: With crochet hook work 1 sc in every 2 rows of the knitted border, then 2 sc in every row along the edges of front, (2 sc in the first neck dec), 1 sc in every st of the back neck, 2 sc in every row along edges of left front (2 sc in first neck dec). **Row 2:** Along the straight edge of the right front, make 5 buttonholes spaced as foll: 10¼, 8, 5½, 3¼, 3/4 in. (26, 20, 14, 8, 2 cm) from lower

edge. For each button-hole: ch 3, skip 3 sc. **Row 3:** 1 sc in each sc, 3 sc in each ch-3 sp over the buttonholes. **Row 4:** Work in shrimp st. Fasten off. Reinforce buttonholes. Sew on buttons. Sew sleeves to side seams, matching center of sleeve with shoulder seams. Sew side and sleeve seams.

TOP: BACK

With crochet hook ch 114 (124, 134) + ch 3 to turn (= 1 border st). Work in pat st = 56 (61, 66) groups + 2 border sts. Work until piece measures 11¾ in. (30 cm). Fasten off.

FRONT

Work same as back. Block piece to indicated measurements. With knitting needles, pick up and knit 104 (110, 116) sts along lower edge of each piece and work 2 in. (5 cm) in 1/1 ribbing. Bind off loosely. Sew side seams. Along the top edge, join yarn and with crochet hook ch 1 in first st at 1 side seam. Work 1 round in sc, then sl st to join and work 1 round of shrimp st. Fasten off. Straps: Make 2 chains about 15¾ in. (40 cm) long. Work 1 sc in the 3rd ch from hook, then work 1 sc in each ch across. Fasten off. Sew chain straps to top of front about 7½ (8, 8¼) in. - 19 (20, 21) cm from side seams of front and 9 (9¼, 9¾) in. - 23 (24, 25) cm from side seams of back.

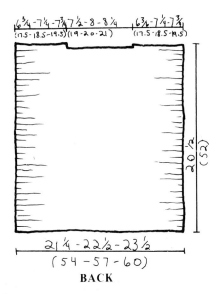

6¾ - 7¼ - 7¾ 7½ - 8 - 8¼
(17.5 -18.5 -19.5) (19 -20 -21)

20½
(52)

21¼ - 22½ - 23½
(54 - 57 - 60)

BACK

6¾ -7¼ -7¾
(17.5 -18.5 -19.5)

11
(28)

9¾
(24)

10¼ -10¾ -11½
(26 -27.5 -29)

1/2 FRONT

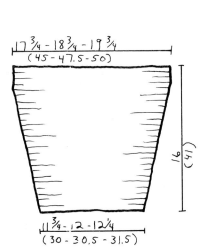

6¾ -7¼ -7¾
(17.5 -18.5 -19.5)

17¾ - 18¾ - 19¾
(45 - 47.5 - 50)

16
(41)

11¾ - 12 - 12¼
(30 - 30.5 - 31.5)

SLEEVE

INDEX

A

Acrylic Yarn 38, 39, 85, 101
Afghan Stitch 10
Alpaca Yarn 51, 79

B

Back Relief dc 12
Back Relief sc 11
Backstitch 14
Bag 22
Bibliography 16
Blocking and Pressing 14
Boatneck Sweaters 34, 39, 56, 81, 85,
                86, 101, 106, 107, 112, 120, 129,
                                    136, 137
Border Stitches 12
Buttonholes 14

C

Cardigan Sweaters 26, 35, 44, 45, 53,
                62, 70, 71, 89, 94, 96, 105,
                               125, 132, 143
Chain Stitch (ch) 8
Children's Sweaters 22, 31, 32, 38, 44,
                45, 56, 57, 66, 67, 86, 106,
                              114, 115, 140, 141
Coats and Jackets 18, 29, 35, 51, 60,
                70, 89, 94, 96, 132
Cotton Yarn 22, 23, 34, 56, 57,
                81, 82, 86, 103, 106, 107, 119,
                121, 124, 125, 128, 129, 136, 137,
                                    143
Cowl Neck 130

D

Decreasing 13
Double Crochet (dc) 9

F

Filet Crochet 34
Filet Stitch 11
Front Relief dc 11
Front Relief sc 11

G

Gauge 13

H

Half-Double Crochet (hdc) 9, 15
Hooks 15

I

Increasing 13
Invisible Weaving 14

J

Jacquard Crochet 35, 38, 39, 43, 45,
                62, 63, 66, 67, 70, 71
Joining Methods 14

M

Mohair Yarn 19, 21, 35, 43, 44,
                45, 58, 52, 53, 62, 63, 70,
                                 71, 89, 111, 112

P

Plaids 46, 52, 53
Pullovers 19, 21, 22, 31, 32,
                38, 39, 43, 52, 56, 57, 63,
                66, 67, 79, 81, 82, 85, 86,
         90, 101, 103, 107, 111, 112, 114,
    115, 119, 120, 121, 124, 128, 129,
                130, 136, 137, 140, 141

R

Relief Stitches 11, 82, 82, 85, 86,
                89, 90, 94, 96, 101, 103, 106,
                               107, 111, 112
Reversing Shapings 13

S

Shrimp Stitch 8
Single Crochet (sc) 8, 15
Slip Knot 7
Slip Stitch (sl st) 8, 14
Substitutions 14
Sweater Sew 143

T

Treble Crochet (tr) 10

W

Wool Yarn 17, 26, 29, 31, 32,
                60, 66, 67, 90, 94, 96, 103, 114,
                115, 120, 125, 130, 132, 140, 141
Woven Look 51, 79

Y

Yarn Over (yo) 8
Yarns 14, 15